ENDORSEMENTS

"It is good to see a New Testament scholar who wants to put the whole Bible together for us. I like it. You will be richer for reading *Christian Faith in the Old Testament*."

Dennis F. Kinlaw
Founder of The Francis Asbury Society.

"Steeped in decades of close attention to the Book of Hebrews, Gary Cockerill approaches the Old Testament as the promise leading to fulfillment in Christ. For all of us who believe that the Old Testament should be read the way Jesus and the apostles interpreted it, *Christian Faith in the Old Testament* is a gold mine."

Michael Horton
J. G. Machen Professor of Systematic Theology and Apologetics,
Westminster Seminary California
Author, *The Christian Faith: A Systematic Theology for Pilgrims on the Way*

"As a pastor, *Christian Faith in the Old Testament: the Bible of the Apostles* really connects with me. I will use this well-written and informative book often in my reading, preaching, and teaching. In addition, I will encourage my congregation to read it! Dr. Cockerill helps everyone to grasp the wholeness of Scripture and provides aids to help us live an obedient life that reflects the full-scope of the Bible's teaching."

Steve Schellin
Senior Pastor, Southland Community Church
Greenwood, Indiana

"Modern critical scholarship often questions the coherence and authority of the Old Testament, and many sincere believers are often confused and baffled by it. Just what does the Old Testament have to do with the Christian gospel? In this excellent and very edifying book, Gary Cockerill shows how—and why—the Old Testament is important. *Christian Faith in the Old Testament* offers insight for theologians (after a decade of teaching, I have learned from it) as well as much-needed and very accessible help for ordinary Christian readers of the Bible. This is a wonderful book—one to which I shall return often."

Dr. Thomas H. McCall
Associate Professor of Biblical and Systematic Theology,
Trinity Evangelical Divinity School;
Director, Carl F. H. Henry Center for Theological Understanding

CHRISTIAN FAITH

in the

OLD TESTAMENT

The Bible of the Apostles

GARETH LEE COCKERILL

Gareth Lee Cockerill

Hebrews 13:8

THOMAS NELSON
Since 1798

NASHVILLE   DALLAS   MEXICO CITY   RIO DE JANEIRO

Published in Nashville, Tennessee, by Thomas Nelson. Thomas Nelson is a registered trademark of HarperCollins Christian Publishing, Inc.

Thomas Nelson, Inc., titles may be purchased in bulk for educational, business, fundraising, or sales promotional use. For information, please e-mail SpecialMarkets@ThomasNelson.com.

Page design and layout: Crosslin Creative
Images: istock.com, VectorStock.com

Unless otherwise noted, Scripture quotations are taken from THE NEW KING JAMES VERSION. © 1982 by Thomas Nelson, Inc. Used by permission. All rights reserved.

Those marked ESV are from THE ENGLISH STANDARD VERSION. © 2001 by Crossway Bibles, a division of Good News Publishers.

Those marked KJV are from the KING JAMES VERSION.

Those marked NCV are from the New Century Version®. © 2005 by Thomas Nelson, Inc. Used by permission. All rights reserved.

Those marked NIV are from the HOLY BIBLE: NEW INTERNATIONAL VERSION®. © 1973, 1978, 1984 by International Bible Society. Used by permission of Zondervan Publishing House. All rights reserved.

Those marked NRSV are from the NEW REVISED STANDARD VERSION of the Bible. © 1989 by the Division of Christian Education of the National Council of the Churches of Christ in the U.S.A. All rights reserved.

Those marked MSG are from *The Message* by Eugene H. Peterson. © 1993, 1994, 1995, 1996, 2000. Used by permission of NavPress Publishing Group. All rights reserved.

Those marked PHILLIPS are from J. B. Phillips: THE NEW TESTAMENT IN MODERN ENGLISH, Revised Edition. © J. B. Phillips 1958, 1960, 1972. Used by permission of Macmillan Publishing Co., Inc.

Those marked The Voice are from *The Voice*™. © 2012 Ecclesia Bible Society. Used by permission. All rights reserved.

Library of Congress Cataloging-in-Publication Data

Cockerill, Gareth Lee, 1944

Christian faith in the Old Testament

1.—. I..

9781401677350

Printed in the United States of America

14 15 16 17 18 RRD 6 5 4 3 2 1

To my wife, Rosa.

CONTENTS

AUTHOR'S PREFACE

Christian Faith in the Old Testament: The Bible of the Apostles is the result of more than thirty years of study, meditation, and prayer. God has given me the opportunity to preach and teach this material in a variety of contexts. Almost everything that I have done has contributed to this volume. My study of the book of Hebrews has fueled my interest in the continuing relevance of the Old Testament.[1] Teaching biblical theology and the principles of biblical interpretation has forced me to think deeply about the way the Bible fits together as a whole. Service to the church in Sierra Leone, West Africa, afforded me the opportunity to grasp the message of the Bible in a fresh way. Several series of Bible studies that I have done in camps and conferences have found their way into this book. I offer what insight has been given me out of a sense of vocation, with deep thanksgiving to God, and with the hope that it will glorify God by enriching ordinary people in their understanding of, and obedience to, his word.

I owe a debt of gratitude to a multitude of people. More scholars have contributed to my understanding of scripture than I can name or remember. Those familiar with Christopher J. H. Wright will easily note my debt to him and to his work on Old Testament ethics. I am very thankful to Alee Anderson, Study Resources Editor at Thomas Nelson, for her enthusiasm, support, and editorial guidance. Frank Couch, Vice President of Thomas Nelson for Study Resources and Translation Development, has also been a great encouragement. I am also thankful to Heather McMurray, who helped kick-start the publishing process for this book. Pastor Steve Schellin graciously read the entire manuscript and provided feedback, as did my good friend Dave Steveline and my father, W. Lee Cockerill. My son-in-law, Dr. Carey Vinzant, helped me with chapter 2 in particular and also with other parts of the book. I am grateful to Dr. John Neihof, President of Wesley Biblical Seminary, for his encouragement. I'm

---

1. Gareth Lee Cockerill, *Hebrews*, New International Commentary on the New Testament, (Grand Rapids: Eerdmans, 2012).

also grateful to the former and current directors of Reformed Theological Seminary library, Dr. Kenneth Elliott and John Crabb, for providing me with a research room. Dr. John McCarty, Circulation Director, has also been a great help. My thanks to all who have provided an endorsement for this book.

I am especially grateful to my wife, Rosa, who has encouraged me at every step, given me feedback on the manuscript, and provided me with the resources and leisure necessary to complete this project. Sometimes she has even cut the grass so that I could write. It is to her that I lovingly dedicate this book.

INTRODUCTION

An Invitation to Embrace the Old Testament

© Gareth Lee Cockerill

The inscription high above the door of the old Roman Catholic cathedral in St. Louis caught my attention. After the construction of the new cathedral, the pope designated this historic church as the Basilica of St. Louis, King of France. This inscription was not only in the expected Latin, but also in Hebrew. At the top were clear, gold Hebrew letters that formed the Old Testament covenant name of God: YHWH. This was the name by which God revealed himself to Moses in Exodus 3: *Jehovah* or, more accurately, *Yahweh* ("I Am.")[2] Below this Hebrew word

---

2. The casual English reader might not realize how often this name occurs in the Old Testament because most of our English Bibles translate it as LORD (with small caps).

was a Latin inscription, still in letters of gold: *"Deo Uni et Trino"* ("to God One and Three.")[3]

Before I saw the Latin I thought I was looking at a synagogue. Then I recognized the appropriateness of joining these two inscriptions. Christians have always affirmed that the God they know as Triune through the coming of the Lord Jesus Christ is a fuller revelation of the God of the Old Testament. Their God was the Creator who made covenant with Abraham, Isaac, and Jacob and delivered their descendants from slavery in Egypt. In controversy with the Gnostics, Irenaeus and other early Christian writers resolutely affirmed that the Father of our Lord Jesus Christ was the Creator/covenant-making God of the Old Testament. He had revealed himself in his co-eternal Son and was at work in the world through the equally co-eternal Holy Spirit. This truth is affirmed by the Apostles' Creed:

"I believe in God, the Father Almighty, maker of heaven and earth; and in Jesus Christ his only begotten Son. . . . I believe in the Holy Spirit . . . ."

In fact, continuity with the Old Testament is the bedrock of the New Testament, stated or assumed on every page. Jesus "beginning at Moses and all the Prophets . . . expounded to them in all the Scriptures the things concerning Himself" (Luke 24:27; cf. 24:44–49). God, who "at various times and in various ways spoke to our forefathers through the prophets, has now spoken to us in one who is Son" (Heb. 1:1–2, my own translation). Paul "reasoned with them from the Scriptures, explaining and demonstrating that the Christ had to suffer and rise again from the dead, and saying, 'This Jesus whom I preach to you is the Christ'" (Acts 17:2–3).

Paul and the other New Testament writers clearly recognized the Christian faith in the Old Testament. The Old Testament was indeed the Bible of the Apostles. The first Christians were thoroughly convinced that God had revealed the salvation now provided by Christ in the Old

---

3. These words over the entrance are part of a larger inscription affirming the dedication of the cathedral "to God one and triune" in 1834.

Testament. Christ was God's intended fulfillment of its story, promises, prophecies, and types. They understood the fullness of the Old Testament through Christ. They grasped Christ's identity and significance for the world through the Old Testament. The Gospel writers believed that this perspective had its origin in Jesus.

Modern Christians, on the other hand, are often ignorant of the Old Testament and its significance. For some it is, at best, historical background for the New Testament. For others, it is a collection of primitive stories, now superseded in Christ. Some avoid it because it is hard to understand or because some parts of it seem incredible or morally problematic. We read Psalms for comfort and Proverbs for wisdom (after all, we can get these two books bound at the back of our New Testaments), teach (some of) the stories of Abraham and Moses in Sunday school, and read Isaiah at Christmastime. We have lost the Bible of the Apostles, and in so doing we have lost much. We end up with an anemic view of Christ, a superficial understanding of the atonement, and an individualistic view of the church. Our God shrinks because we no longer see the majesty of his creation, the grandeur of his work in history, or the glory of his salvation in Christ. We have little basis for social ethics. We live in rootless isolation because we no longer see ourselves as children of Abraham and part of the people of God, stretched out across history and on its way to glory. If we do not have the Bible of the Apostles, we will not have the true apostolic faith.

This book is dedicated to helping ordinary, intelligent, modern Christians reestablish their apostolic roots in the Old Testament, the Bible of the Apostles.[4] First, the pages that follow are designed to help the reader understand how each major part of the Old Testament fits into the total scope of biblical revelation. Second, this study gives needed guidance concerning the way in which each part of the Old Testament applies to

---

4. This is not a book about Old Testament problems. No one would deny that the Old Testament presents some interpretive challenges. Occasionally we may touch on some of these, but they are not the topic under discussion. Our purpose is to help the reader get the big picture. We don't want anyone to miss the forest by stumbling over the stumps.

contemporary believers. How do the various sections of the Old Testament, given before Christ, function as Scripture for people who live after Christ's coming?

Thus, our approach will not be thematic, nor will we divide the Old Testament material by historical period. We will consider each part of the Old Testament in the order familiar from our English Bibles. We begin with a chapter on Genesis 1–11, followed by a chapter on Genesis 12–50, and two chapters on Exodus through Joshua. These chapters will introduce three guidelines that are helpful in grasping the Old Testament's continuing relevance as Scripture: the example guideline, the picture (or typological) guideline, and the pattern guideline. Next come chapters on Judges through 2 Kings, 1 Chronicles through Esther, Job through the Song of Songs (Song of Solomon NKJV), and Isaiah through Malachi. We will conclude with a brief chapter on fulfillment in the New Testament. We will suggest reasons for making the above divisions in the respective chapters that follow rather than cluttering this introduction with argument. Appendix 1 argues for the integrity of our Old Testament as the Bible used by Jesus and the apostles. The chart in Appendix 2 provides a graphic overview of Scripture's unity. Each part of this chart also occurs in the chapter of the book to which it belongs.

The choice to follow this approach is motivated by practical, literary, and theological concerns. The practical advantages are obvious. This is the order in which modern readers encounter their Bibles. We want to know how this Bible fits together and how it applies to us. From the literary point of view, it is clear that different parts of the Old Testament play different roles. The Prophets,[5] for instance, call God's people back to the covenant established in the first five books of the Bible that we call the Pentateuch or the books of Moses.[6] The Psalms give God's people words to express their prayer and praise.

---

5. Isaiah, Jeremiah, Lamentations, Ezekiel, Daniel, Hosea, Joel, Amos, Obadiah, Jonah, Micah, Nahum, Habakkuk, Zephaniah, Haggai, Zechariah, Malachi.

6. Genesis, Exodus, Leviticus, Numbers, Deuteronomy.

However, foundational to this approach is the theological perspective and interpretive practice of the New Testament. Over the centuries the books of the Old Testament have gradually assumed the order in which they now appear in our Bibles. This order reflects the New Testament conviction that all of God's previous revelation is fulfilled in Christ. Fulfillment in Christ shifted the focus of the Old Testament from the Pentateuch to the Psalms, and especially to the Prophets. The Prophets did more than call God's people back to the foundational covenant established in the first five books of the Old Testament. Both Psalms and the Prophets pointed forward to the grand and glorious fulfillment of that covenant in Christ. Thus, it was most appropriate that the Old Testament end with the Prophets who looked forward to the coming of Christ rather than with Chronicles, the final book of the Jewish Bible, that looked forward only to the return of Israel from exile. In Malachi, the last book of our Old Testament, God declares, "Behold, I send My messenger, and he will prepare the way before Me. And the Lord, whom you seek, will suddenly come to His temple" (Mal. 3:1).

The book that you have begun to read—*Christian Faith in the Old Testament: The Bible of the Apostles*—is the result of more than thirty-five years of meditation and study.[7] I have taught this material in both popular and academic contexts. I offer it here with the prayer that it will help its readers be true "Berean" Christians. When Paul left Thessalonica, he went to Berea. Acts 17:11 tells us that the Bereans were more fairminded than the Thessalonians because they received God's word readily and searched the Old Testament scriptures daily to see whether the things Paul taught them were true. This book is written to help modern Christians faithfully and fruitfully search those same Old Testament scriptures, the Bible of the Apostles.

---

7. Thus I have profited from many who have written on the Old Testament using other approaches.

CHAPTER 1

GOD'S DESIGN ESTABLISHED *and* LOST

Genesis 1–11

INTRODUCTION

Richard Dawkins betrays the weakness of his atheism by admitting that the world appears to be the product of design.[8] When we open the pages of Scripture we find a world carefully crafted to carry out the divine purpose. We do not live in a self-produced universe. We are not dealing with a blind "Mother Nature." We are confronted with a creation: a world designed by and dependent upon God. We come face to face with this Creator God: "In the beginning God created the heavens and the earth" (Gen. 1:1). God's role as universal Creator is the foundation of all biblical teaching (Heb. 11:3). It determines the way in which we understand the world, our place in it as human beings, and our destiny.

This shapes our worldview

---

8. "Biology is the study of complicated things that give the appearance of having been designed for a purpose" *The Blind Watchmaker: Why the Evidence of Evolution Reveals a Universe without Design* (City: Norton, 1996), 1; "Animals give the appearance of having been designed by a theoretically sophisticated and practically ingenious physicist or engineer . . ." Ibid., 36.

Genesis 1–2 sets the stage for the biblical drama by affirming God as Creator, the world as his creation, and humanity as made in the divine image. If we add human disobedience/divine grace to these three, we have the setting for the biblical story that follows. We can think of these four—God as Creator, the world as creation, humanity in God's image, sin/grace—as the four sides of a picture frame that appropriately highlights God's gracious design for humanity to live in joyful community as his people in the world he created to be their home (see **Figure 1**). This world is the result not of blind chance but of divinely planned opportunity for human fulfillment. If it is the setting for The Greatest Show on Earth, it is a show produced and directed by the gracious Creator and Redeemer of mankind.[9]

Figure 1

A SOVEREIGN, PURPOSEFUL CREATOR
WHO BLESSES AND JUDGES

	CREATOR	
LIMITED,	**God's Plan for the World**	MADE
BUT	1. Obedient fellowship with God.	IN
MEANINGFUL,	2. Harmonious fellowship among God's people.	THE
GOOD,		IMAGE
AND	3. Responsible enjoyment of God's world.	OF
PURPOSEFUL		GOD
	SIN / GRACE	

(left side: CREATION; right side: HUMANITY)

---

9. Not, as Richard Dawkins imagines in *The Greatest Show on Earth: The Evidence for Evolution* (New York City: Free Press, 2010), by blind chance.

I. GOD'S PLAN ESTABLISHED: THE PICTURE FRAME AND THE PICTURE (GENESIS 1-2)

A. The Creator

The top of the frame appropriate for the picture of God's plan can be nothing other than the Creator himself (see **Figure 1**). Many features of Genesis 1–2 show us that God is the sovereign, purposeful Creator who blesses and judges. His sovereignty is immediately evident. All he has to do is say, "Let there be . . . ," and what he speaks becomes reality. Note the things that God names. On the first day of creation he calls the light "Day" and the darkness "Night" (Gen. 1:5). On the second, he designates the expanse as "Heaven" (or "Sky"; Gen. 1:8). On the third, he names the dry land "Earth" and the gathered waters "Seas" (Gen. 1:10). In the biblical world, to name something is to have authority over it. The visible world consists of sky, earth or dry land, and bodies of water or seas. Time is governed by day and night. Thus, by God's naming these things, he proclaims himself the sovereign Lord of space and time.

Many commentators have noted how the first three days of creation lay a foundation for the second three: On day one God created day and night, and on day four he established the greater and lesser lights to rule the day and night; on day two he created the sky and separated the waters above from those below, and on day five he created the birds of the sky and sea creatures for the water; on day three he separated the earth from the seas and had the earth produce vegetation, and on day six he created land animals and humanity. Days one through three established and ordered a world; days four through six populated that world. This ordered cadence of days underscores divine sovereignty. Such order also demonstrates that God acts purposefully. His revealed purpose climaxes in his creation of humanity on day six.

Beginning with day three (Gen. 1:9–13) Genesis says, "And God saw that it was good." In fact, this statement occurs twice on each of the two climactic days, days three (Gen. 1:10, 12) and six (Gen. 1:25, 31). The whole concludes with, "God saw *everything that He had made, and indeed* it was *very* good" (italics added). Everything conformed to God's gracious purpose. The Creator God alone is the one who has the right to evaluate his creation. He determines what is good and is the judge of his creation's conformity to that good. He is the judge of the human beings with which it climaxes.

> The Creator God alone is the one who has the right to evaluate his creation. He determines what is good and is the judge of his creation's conformity to that good.

This panoramic account of creation assumes the goodness of the God who so lavishly prepares a world and gives it to human beings as their home and for their enjoyment. This goodness comes to clear expression with the blessings of day five (Gen. 1:22) and day six (Gen. 1:28–30). Creation concludes with this second bountiful blessing for humanity, given to the first human beings God created. He is not only the Judge to whom humans are accountable, he is also the Blesser who gives them all to enjoy.

B. Creation

The left side of our picture frame (**Figure 1**) is the creation derived from this Creator-God. If God is the "Sovereign, Purposeful Creator who Judges and Blesses," then his creation is "Limited, but Meaningful, Good, and Purposeful." The features of this creation account that affirm the sovereignty of God assert the limited nature of his creation. It is finite, derived from, dependent upon, and determined by him. Its ordered structure and evident design affirm its meaningfulness and the purpose for which he made it. By declaring the creation to be good, Genesis lays the foundation for human accountability before God.

C. Humanity in God's Image

Creator and creation establish the context for the right-hand side of the picture frame (**Figure 1**): humanity, created in God's image. Human beings, like other animals, are part of God's creation. They, too, are from "the Earth" (Gen. 1:24, 2:7). And yet human beings are a unique part of God's creation, made in the "image" and "likeness" of God. God affirms the creation of humanity in his image as his intention (Gen. 1:26). Genesis 1:27 confirms that God carried out his intention. The description of God's forming Adam from the dust but uniquely breathing into him the breath of life gives this reality concrete shape (Gen. 2:7).

Theologians continue to debate the full significance of the divine image. Several aspects of this reality, however, are evident from Genesis. The image of God distinguishes humanity from other animals. No animal could be a suitable companion for Adam (Gen. 2:18–20). Only the woman God made from Adam's side whom he called "bone of my bones" and "flesh of my flesh" (Gen. 2:23) could be a helper comparable to him, one who also shared in the divine image. Thus the divine image includes the ability to live in companionship with other persons and to fulfill God's plan for a harmonious human community. Because human beings

> Only the woman God made from Adam's side whom he called "bone of my bones" and "flesh of my flesh" (Gen. 2:23) could be a helper comparable to him.

are made in God's image, they are able to live in fellowship with God, the source of all true community. The divine image includes the ability to love and to be accountable.

The dominion over creation given to humanity by God was also closely associated with the divine likeness (Gen. 1:26, 29). God established humanity as his vice-regent over creation, which was to be humanity's home. The first humans were privileged to enjoy creation's blessing, charged with caring for it, and accountable to God for performance of this charge. Adam and Eve were given the abundance of the Garden of Eden for their enjoyment, but were also responsible to "tend and keep it" (Gen. 2:15). They were accountable to obey God's command.

D. Sin and Grace

The first three sides of this picture frame bring God's plan or design for humanity into clear focus (**Figure 1**). First, God created human beings for obedient fellowship with himself. They were made in his image and were his vice-regents over creation. Fellowship with him was the source of their blessing. It was the foundation of the other aspects of his design. Second, they were given the gift of harmonious fellowship with one another. Eve was God's gracious gift to Adam so that he would not be "alone." The innocence of their nakedness exemplified the uncluttered and noncompetitive nature of the free companionship they enjoyed (Gen. 2:25). Third, they were given responsible enjoyment of the Garden and the world God had created. It was to be their home, the blessed place of their fellowship with God and with one another, the context and sustainer of the fruitfulness with which the Creator had blessed them.[10] This indeed was the God-intended blessedness enjoyed by the first humans in the Garden. We have not, however, looked at the bottom of the frame—Sin and Grace. The whole of Scripture that follows is the story of both human destruction and divine restoration of this divine order.

---

10. I am grateful to Christopher J. H. Wright, *Old Testament Ethics for the People of God* (Downers Grove: InterVarsity, 2004), 17–99, especially 17–20, whose "ethical triangle" has helped me to see the threefold nature of God's plan. It is gratifying to see this threefold nature confirmed by the work of others, such as Sandy Richter, *The Epic of Eden: A Christian Entry into the Old Testament* (Downers Grove: IVPAcademic, 2008), who thus describes Adam and Eve in the Garden of Eden : "This was God's perfect plan: the *people* of God in the *place* of God dwelling in the *presence* of God" (104, italics original).

II. GOD'S PLAN LOST: THE NEED FOR RESTORATION (GENESIS 3–11)

A. Living Contrary to God's Plan: Through Sin

In contrast to Genesis 1, which begins with "In the beginning God," Genesis 3 begins with, "Now the serpent." We know nothing about the serpent but that he "was more cunning than any beast of the field which the LORD God had made" (Gen. 3:1). We know that he was part of the creation and subject to the Creator. We are warned about his craftiness. The writer provides no other information about the origin of this tempter or his relationship to the devil. Genesis acknowledges that temptation comes from outside the original human pair. Yet Genesis refuses to lessen their accountability by attributing the responsibility for their sin to another. They are not the source of temptation. They are, however, as far as humanity is concerned, the source of disobedience. **Figure 2** shows what we learn about the nature of sin and its effects from Adam and Eve, Cain, the people before the flood, and those who built the tower of Babel. We find these accounts in Genesis 3–11.

Figure 2

ADAM AND EVE	CAIN	PEOPLE BEFORE THE FLOOD	PEOPLE AT BABEL
Sin is:	Sin is:	Sin is:	Sin is:
1. distrust of God's goodness. 2. deliberate disobedience of God's command. 3. disavowal of God's personal lordship.	a power that controls us.	universal and pervasive.	corporate; it dominates society.

Adam and Eve. In Genesis 3:1–7 we have a clear color photograph of the sin that separates humanity from God. The serpent's opening line calls God's goodness into question: "Did God actually say, 'You shall not eat of any tree in the garden'?" (Gen. 3:1 ESV). The woman is sucked into the conversation in defense of God. In verse 4 the serpent's insinuation becomes a direct assault on the character of God: God is holding out on you; he knows that if you disobey his command and eat the fruit he has forbidden, you will become like him. Eve's sin begins by distrusting God's goodness. She will not trust God to know and do what is good for her. Direct disobedience follows: she took and ate, and even "gave to her

> Here is sin in a nutshell: distrust of God's goodness, deliberate disobedience of his command, disavowal of his . . . lordship.

husband with her, and he ate." Adam's silence and easy accommodation only emphasize his culpability. He is the one who had received God's prohibition on eating from the Tree of Life. Thus, Adam and Eve's distrust and deliberate disobedience led to the displacement of God as the center of their lives. They disavowed his lordship. They would no longer depend on God to determine what was good for them. They would determine for themselves what was in their best interest. If God would not look out for them, they would look out for themselves. Here is sin in a nutshell: distrust of God's goodness, deliberate disobedience of his command, disavowal of his personal lordship in life.

Cain. A look at the account of Cain and Abel in Genesis 4 shows the awful power that sin, upon entering the human race, had gained over that race's members. God warned Cain, "Sin is crouching at the door. Its desire is for you, but you must rule over it" (Gen. 4:7 ESV). The power of sin within humanity, here in the form of jealousy, is depicted as a beast anticipating its prey. Lamech (Gen. 4:19–24), Cain's descendant, demonstrates the way in which the power of sin hardens and brutalizes. The fact that he is the first to have two wives suggests his lustfulness. His declaration to his wives, however, is the key to what sin has done in his life: "I have killed a man for wounding me, a young man for striking me. If Cain's revenge is sevenfold, then Lamech's is seventy-sevenfold" (Gen.

4:23–24 ESV). To paraphrase, "Don't mess with me: you step on me, I'll kill you!"

The Flood. The account of the flood in Genesis 6–9 is the story of sin's thorough and pervasive penetration of the human race. "Every intent" of the human heart was "only evil continually" (Gen. 6:5). "The earth also was corrupt before God, and the earth was filled with violence" (Gen. 6:11, like Lamech's violence).

The Tower of Babel. Few Old Testament accounts are more relevant than the story of the Tower of Babel in Genesis 11:1–9. Sin becomes corporate; it penetrates and shapes society. Notice first that there is no communication between God and humanity in this account. Human beings say, "Come, let us . . ." (Gen. 11:3, 4). God says, "Come, let us . . ." (Gen. 11:7). This is a "secular" society—one that excludes God. While the individual may be weak, together they think they can be self-sufficient. Together they will determine their own destiny, decide what is right for them, and thus be their own god. Adam and Eve put the self in God's place. Here society as a whole, the collective, has displaced him. Notice, they plan to build not only a city but "a tower whose top is in the heavens" (Gen. 11:4). When they say that they will make a "name" for themselves, they mean that they will determine their own destiny. After all, they can use technology: "let us make bricks and bake them thoroughly." Here we can see the authority claimed by modern states and the widespread expecta-

> **Few Old Testament accounts are more relevant than the story of the Tower of Babel in Genesis 11:1–9.**

tion that the state can and will supply all of our needs. Loyalty due God alone is given to a political or social entity of our own making. The rest of the Bible will show that such a deified human society is hostile to the people of God, demanding that they conform to its values (Rev. 18:1–24, esp. verse 24). Babel is the exact opposite of the city of God where his people will truly be at home.

Figure 2 diagrams what we have been saying about the nature of sin. The account of Adam and Eve shows us that it is distrust of God's goodness, deliberate disobedience of his command, and disavowal of his personal lordship in life. Cain and his descendants show the power of sin to control and harden, to take us where we never intended to go. The flood reveals the pervasive and destructive nature of sin within the human heart. Finally, the Tower of Babel shows the corporate or societal nature of sin: recognizing their own impotency, human beings put their hope in the collective as their god.

Genesis makes it clear that the sin we have been describing has terrible consequences for human life. To those consequences we now turn.

B. Living Outside God's Plan: Under the Curse (Gen. 3–11)

Several years ago my wife, Rosa, and I took our grandson through the Creation Museum near Cincinnati, Ohio. We walked from the first part of the museum, which depicted the beauty of human life after creation, into the area that depicted the chaos that resulted from sin. The pictures of violence, misery, and suffering brought home as nothing else could the dire, awful consequences of disobedience. The world is not suffering from a minor maladjustment. It is suffering from the rupture of God's plan.

Genesis shows how sin ruptured each part of God's original, gracious plan for humanity: obedient fellowship with God; harmonious fellowship among the people of God; and responsible enjoyment of the world, the environment given by God as the venue for enjoying his blessings. Sin alienated human beings from the "home" God had prepared for them. This disruption is both the immediate effect of sin and the result of God's judgment on sin. **Figure 3** continues the theme of **Figure 2** by showing how each aspect of God's plan was marred in relation to Adam and Eve, Cain and his family, the people before the flood, and the people at the tower of Babel.

Figure 3

GOD'S PLAN FRACTURED BY SIN	ADAM AND EVE Gen. 3:1–24	CAIN AND HIS FAMILY Gen. 4:1–26	PEOPLE BEFORE THE FLOOD Gen. 6:1–9:29	PEOPLE AT BABEL Gen. 11:1–9
1. Obedient fellowship with God—worship	Naked, hid (3:10); skins (3:21)	Hidden from God's face (4:14)	God sorry he made humanity (6:6–7)	God totally ignored (11:1–9)
2. Harmonious fellowship with God's people—family	Blame (3:12); pain in birth, desire for husband (3:16)	Fugitive and a wanderer (4:12)	The earth was filled with violence (6:11)	Languages confused (11:7–9)
3. Responsible enjoyment of the world—home	Ground cursed (3:17); out of garden (3:23)	Cursed from the ground (4:11)	He will blot them out from the earth (6:7)	People scattered from Babel (11:7–8)

Adam and Eve. Let's return to Genesis 3. Adam and Eve hid themselves from God (Gen. 3:8). They no longer lived in obedient fellowship with him. God's judgment exiling them from the Garden, their home and the place of his direct presence, further underscored the rupture of divine fellowship. Their realization of their nakedness (Gen. 3:7) put an end to the free, harmonious fellowship they had once known. Adam's blaming Eve (Gen. 3:12) further demonstrates their loss of community. Whatever the exact meaning of Genesis 15:16b, "Your desire shall be for your husband, and he shall rule over you," God announces the demise of the noncompetitive companionship they once enjoyed. Adam's leadership has become abusive and self-serving, while Eve's support has become manipulative. Their family has become strained and dysfunctional. God's blessing of fruitfulness (Gen. 1:28) is now marred by the pain and danger of childbirth. What was once responsible enjoyment of the blessings of creation (Gen. 1:29) has become painful toil, the struggle to make a living. Not only have they been exiled from their home in Eden, but the entire creation has become an alien place. Without God they have no home.

The God who blessed with fruitfulness and abundance at creation now curses. Because of sin, humanity now lives under God's curse.

Cain. Disobedience begets disobedience. Brokenness begets brokenness. The loss of home and disintegration of family begun by Adam and Eve reaches a new low when brother (Cain) kills brother (Abel). Cain receives an intensification of the same curse from God. According to Genesis 4:11–14, he is banned from God's face (obedient fellowship with God); he is a fugitive on the earth (harmonious fellowship with God's people); and the ground he works will be cursed (responsible enjoyment of the world). He is without home or resting place.

The People before the Flood. The people of Noah's generation have long ago lost fellowship with God. Their violence has destroyed the harmonious community of God's people. Their wickedness has become so extreme that God wipes them off the land/world given as humanity's home and for humanity's enjoyment (Gen. 6:5–7). (In the flood, God literally undoes his action separating the land from the waters in Genesis 1.)

The Tower of Babel. The judgment of God falls on the people of Babel (Gen. 11:1–9). Genesis ridicules their pride and their pitiful attempts to put their collective in God's place. For all their technological bravado, they have only "brick for stone, and slime . . . for mortar" (Gen. 11:3 KJV). They plan to build a tower whose top reaches the heavens. Their efforts are so puny, however, that God is described as going "down" so that he can see what they are doing. They have totally cut communication with God, so there is no fellowship with him. His judgment brings an end to their attempts at community and fellowship with one another, destroying their collective exploitation of the world he had given for human enjoyment. Apart from God, human beings cannot make a home for themselves in this world.

These chapters show us that sin by its very nature ruptures God's plan for abundant human life. Once obedient fellowship with God is gone, harmonious fellowship among God's people and responsible enjoyment of the world inevitably go with it. Apart from God, human beings are homeless in an alien world. God's judgment confirms this rupture, but his judgment is also a mercy that restrains sin (Gen. 3:22–24; 11:6). Judgment is not the last word. God will restore his broken plan for humanity. **Figure 4** shows how each episode of Genesis 1–11 ends on a note of hope with God's promise of restoration to come.

C. Living in Anticipation of God's Plan: By Grace (Gen. 3–11)

Figure 4

	ADAM AND EVE Gen. 3:1–24	CAIN AND HIS FAMILY Gen. 4:1–26	PEOPLE BEFORE THE FLOOD Gen. 6:1–9:29	PEOPLE AT BABEL Gen. 11:1–9
GOD'S PROMISE	Eve's seed will crush the serpent's head (3:15)	God has appointed another child (4:25)	God will restrain his judgment (9:11)	God will bless the world through Abram (12:1–3)

Adam and Eve. If disobedience were the last word, there would be no Bible. God, however, will restore his plan for the human race. As soon as sin invades the world, the promise of God proclaims its demise—subtly at first, but with ever-increasing clarity. After each sinful episode, Genesis returns to the promise of God (see **Figure 4**). In his curse on the serpent, God promises deliverance even before he has pronounced punishment on Adam and Eve. The "seed" or "offspring" of the woman will "bruise" the serpent's head, though the serpent will "bruise" his heel (Gen. 3:15). Mel Gibson's *The Passion of the Christ* opens with the agony of Christ in the Garden of Gethsemane. When Christ submits to the will of the Father, embracing the cross, his foot crushes the head of the tempter in the form of a serpent. The promise of Genesis 3:15 finds fulfillment in the saving death of the Son of God.

Cain. But that time of deliverance is far in the future. In the meantime Eve suffers the murder of one son by another (Gen. 4:1–16). Where is the seed or offspring described in the promise? God answers this question when Eve has another son, Seth, and can say, "God has appointed another seed for me instead of Abel, whom Cain killed" (Gen. 4:25). Never was Carl Sandburg's declaration more appropriate: "A baby is God's opinion that the world should go on."[11] This baby is the source and promise of the future offspring who will more than restore all that has been lost by sin. God will restore the broken human family through the family line.

The Flood. The account of the flood depicts both the pervasive wickedness of humanity and the terrible judgment of God. Yet God finds one man, faithful Noah, and his family, through whom he will carry out his plan of restoration. God begins again by renewing the blessing of fruitfulness given at the creation (Gen. 8:1–6; 9:1–2, albeit with reservations), by providing for the restraining of violence (Gen. 9:4–7), and making a promise/covenant of his grace (Gen. 9:1–17).

The Tower of Babel. But alas, what about Babel? People have completely cut God out of their reckoning. They refuse to communicate with him. He has scattered them across the world. In order to redeem the scattered nations of the world, God turns to one man, Abram, whose name he will change to Abraham, and to his family. God promises that Abraham

> In order to redeem the scattered nations of the world, God turns to one man, Abram, whose name he will change to Abraham, and to his family.

and his descendants will be the vehicle through whom God will restore the divine plan (Gen. 12:1–9), fractured by disobedience, and offer this restoration to the scattered nations of the world. It is to that promise that we turn in chapter 2.

These early chapters of Genesis describe God's plan for the world (**Figure 1**), the nature of sin (**Figure 2**), the terrible consequences of sin brought by the rupture of that plan through disobedience (**Figure 3**), and God's promise of restoration (**Figure 4**). These facts are as true

11. Carl Sandburg, *Remembrance Rock* (New York: Harcourt Brace, 1948), 7.

today as they have ever been. They are also fundamental to the biblical drama that follows. **Figure 5** is a graphic depiction of these truths. We will add to this figure in the following chapters as we show how Genesis 1–11 serves as the basis for the rest of the Bible. You will find the complete chart in Appendix 2.

Figure 5

GOD'S PLAN FOR THE WORLD

CHAPTER 2

GOD'S PROMISE *of* RESTORATION

The Example Principle

Genesis 12–50

On June 4, 1940, Winston Churchill rose to address the British Parliament. The British Expeditionary Force and its French allies had been forced to retreat to Dunkirk on the coast of France, where they had been surrounded and cut off from support. Using every available boat, British naval and civilian personnel had braved the channel to rescue this beleaguered army. Over three hundred thousand men had been courageously transported to safety. In the wake of this heroic defeat, the prospect of invasion threatened Great Britain. Churchill's words brought courage to a despairing nation: "[W]e shall fight on the beaches, we shall fight on the landing grounds, we shall fight in the fields and in the streets, we shall fight in the hills; we shall never surrender."[12]

The description of sin and its terrible consequences in Genesis 1–11 might lead us to despair. Sin has left human beings helplessly estranged from God, alienated from one another, and exiles in the world God

---

12. Winston S. Churchill, *Their Finest Hour*, vol. 2 of *The Second World War* (New York: Bantam Books, 1962), 103.

created to be their home. We, however, have something that is even more trustworthy than Churchill's courageous words: we have the promise of God! This divine promise was anticipated by God's curse on the serpent in Genesis 3:15, by the birth of Seth (Gen. 4:25–26), and by the salvation of Noah and his family. Genesis 10 recounts the genealogy of the nations of the world that have, according to Genesis 11:1–9, been scattered through rebellion. Then Genesis 11:10–32 focuses our attention on the genealogy of the man who, with his family, will be the bearer of God's promise: Abraham. In Genesis 12:1–9 God promises Abraham that he will restore his original plan for humanity through Abraham and his descendants; through Abraham God will bless the scattered and estranged nations of the world. The rest of the Bible is the fulfillment of this promise. Genesis 11:30 introduces the immediate problem that Abraham must overcome by trusting God's promise: Sarah, his wife, was barren; "she had no child."

It is crucial to note that God's restoration begins with a promise. Sin began, as we saw in chapter 1, when Adam and Eve doubted God's goodness and refused to trust him. Abraham and all God's people must begin by learning to trust God—to live in the assurance that he will fulfill his promise. God teaches them faith by demonstrating his faithfulness to them.

I. THE GOD OF THE PROMISE: COMPLETE ASSURANCE

A promise is only as good as the one who makes it. Thus the character of God is the foundation of our hope. As we have seen, God revealed his purposefulness, goodness, power, and sovereignty in creation. However, distrust and the alienation resulting from human disobedience have distorted this revelation. God will teach Abraham and his descendants that he cares for human beings, that his power is sufficient to bring restoration, and, most of all, that he is absolutely dependable.

A. God's Incomprehensible Dependability

God's interaction with Abraham and his children shows that he is always faithful. He always acts consistently with the holy, loving character that he revealed in creation. He is consistent in his antipathy to sin because it cuts human beings off from the source of life and leads to their destruction. Above all, he is absolutely faithful to his promise of restoration.

By contrast, the pagan deities of the ancient world were notoriously capricious and undependable. With only minor changes, the character of these gods was the same whether Egyptian, Babylonian, Greek, or Roman. They often personified human characteristics or experiences. They were depicted as governing the various areas of human life such as love, sexuality, war, death, the home, or even trickery. Many of the gods described in various mythologies seem so similar that the primary difference was their names. Furthermore, these gods were no more faithful than the sinful humans who invented them. They were simply bigger, more powerful, immortal human beings. Thus they could be bribed and manipulated. They engage in petty jealousy, lechery, conspiracy, and vindictive reprisals. They were as understandable and undependable as the human beings who created them.

The God of Abraham, on the other hand, does not partake of human fickleness or caprice. He is not the invention of the human mind. He is not a bigger, better human being. God told his people, "For My thoughts are not your thoughts, nor are your ways My ways" (Isa. 55:8). He is not defined in relation to us; we are defined in relation to him. We can never comprehend this sovereign God because we did not make him in our image. We can, however, come to know and trust him because he made us in his image.

Thus the Old Testament's view of God's otherness is the foundation of its confident assertion that God is trustworthy. God, precisely because he is not like humanity, can be trusted not to share in the failures that are inevitable in human beings' interactions with one another. Yet his otherness is also the challenge of faith: we are called to trust him even when his ways seem inscrutable. Right relation to the God of Abraham consists in trusting his faithfulness even when we cannot understand what he is doing.

This is the kind of faith that Abraham demonstrated. From the human point of view it made no sense when God told Abraham to leave everything he had ever known and go "to a land that I will show you" (Gen. 12:1–9). Why in the world did God make Abraham wait twenty-five years from the time he promised him a son until that son's birth (Gen. 21:1–8)? And what conceivable reason could God have had for commanding Abraham to offer this promised son as a sacrifice (Gen. 22:1–19)? And yet, when Abraham trusted and obeyed, he always found God faithful.

B. God's Amazing Love

God's inexplicable love is closely bound to his faithfulness. We have already seen that God freely created the world as an act of overflowing love, a bursting forth of divine generosity. In the world God has made we see his passion for beauty and his masterful artistry in calling it forth from nothing: "The heavens declare the glory of God" (Ps. 19:1). It is within this masterpiece of God's own art that he situated humanity, giving us the task of being its caretakers. In so doing, God gave us the gifts of presence, people, and place:[13] Adam and Eve enjoyed the presence of the living God. They were a family, the nucleus of a people who were to live in loving fellowship with one another. They were given creation, and especially the Garden of Eden, as the place that would be their home. Home is where we are not strangers but are loved and affirmed as those who belong. For those made in God's image, home is where God is. It is the place of fellowship with God and with the people of God. Thus when God gave them *home* he gave them what they needed most.

Creation was an illustrious disclosure of God's love. Restoration, however, is the amazing demonstration of its unfathomable greatness.

---

13. Sandy Richter, *The Epic of Eden: A Christian Entry into the Old Testament* (Downers Grove: IVPAcademic, 2008), 104.

Through human disobedience we have lost our place in the Garden. The flaming sword God placed at the Garden's entrance to keep human beings out reminds us that, by our own choice, Paradise is no longer our home (Gen. 3:24). As those who have chosen our own way, we no longer belong. Nevertheless, God's love for us continues even though we have rejected him. He does not abandon us to die alone. Instead, God shows his care for us through his promise to save us from sin and death. God's promise of restoration, anticipated by Genesis 3:15, takes concrete shape with Abraham. Through him God will bless all nations by restoring presence, people, and place. This promise, of course, finds fulfillment in the cross, which shows how God loved his own "to the end" (John 13:1). It includes the gift of the Holy Spirit (Gal. 3:14). It will find ultimate fulfillment at Christ's return in the new heaven and earth (Rev. 21:3). God's people will once again be at home with family.

God's promises show us his love and his holiness together in human history. Because God loves us, he does not leave us to die alone. At the same time, because he is holy, he does not deny or minimize the reality that we are sinners and that sin kills us. In God's promises he shows us that he is both fully aware that we need saving and fully committed to saving us. Thus his faithfulness is the result of both his love and his holiness.

C. God's All-Sufficient Power

God's promises are trustworthy not only because he is loving and holy but also because his power is all-sufficient. In contrast to the pagan deities, the God of Abraham is never tricked or thwarted, and his hands are never tied. Not only can we trust that God wants to save us and is committed to do so, but we can also trust that no obstacle will ever arise that can stand in the way of his saving purpose. This is why God can say chidingly to his people, "Has the LORD's arm been shortened?" (Num. 11:23). The same God who spoke the "Let there be . . ." of Genesis 1, who called everything forth from nothing, also promises salvation to his people. This is the power that will overcome sin and death by raising Jesus from the dead. As God said to Abraham, "Is anything too hard for the Lord?" (Gen. 18:14). Not only does God want to save his people, but he can, and this is the basis of our confidence that he will. This trust in God's promises gives us security even as we live in a fallen world. Although evil is real and pervasive, the loving, holy, and all-powerful God is for us. No greater assurance could be given, and this assurance bears the fruit of hope in our lives as people who have trusted God's saving promises.

By trusting God's promise Abraham experienced God's power as well as his faithfulness and love. Because he obeyed God's call to leave earthly home and family, he became a stranger and alien in the land that God promised to his descendants (Gen. 23:4). He had no rights and was at the mercy of the citizens of that land. Yet God protected him and provided abundantly for him. Most important of all, God demonstrated his power by giving him Isaac, the son of promise, through ninety-year-old barren Sarah (Gen. 17:17). By trusting God's promises, we, like Abraham, come to experience his faithfulness, his love, and his power at work in our own lives. This experience of God changes how we see everything. Hope is the product of looking at the world through the eyes of faith.

II. THE CONTENT OF THE PROMISE: FULL RESTORATION

It is time to take a good look at what God promised Abraham. God promised Abraham that through him and his descendants redemption would be provided for all the peoples of the world. In Genesis 11:1–9 the judgment of God left the nations scattered, homeless, and alienated from God. In Genesis 12:1–9 God's promise asserts that he will bless these nations through Abraham and his descendants. God's rescue strategy is comprehensive. His blessing will reach "far as the curse is found." He promises that his redemption will heal and restore everything that was broken by disobedience. God will offer restoration to all of the human family who will turn to him with the faith of Abraham.

God assures us of his promise by reaffirming it to Abraham's son Isaac and to his grandson Jacob. In fact, as descendants of Abraham, Isaac and Jacob are part of the promise's fulfillment. **Figure 1** shows that God's promise provides restoration for all three of the fundamental relationships marred by disobedience: to God, to one another, and to the world.

Figure 1

	ABRAHAM Gen. 12:1–9;13:15; 15:5	ISAAC Gen. 26:3–4	JACOB Gen. 28:13–14
G O D	Genesis 12:7 The LORD appeared to Abram . . .	Genesis 26:3 I will be with you and bless you.	Genesis 28:15 I am with you and will keep you wherever you go . . .
P E O P L E	Genesis 12:2 I will make you a **great nation**. Genesis 15:5 Look now toward heaven, and count the stars . . . So shall your **descendants** be.	Genesis 26:4 I will make your **descendants** multiply as the stars of heaven . . .	Genesis 28:14 And your **descendants** shall be as the dust of the earth; you shall spread abroad to the west and to the east, to the north and to the south . . .
L A N D	Genesis 12:1 Go to a **land** I will show you. Genesis 13:15 All the **land** which you see I give to you and your descendants forever.	Genesis 26:3 For to you and your descendants I will give all these **lands**, and I will perform the oath which I swore to Abraham your father.	Genesis 28:13 I am the LORD God of Abraham your father and the God of Isaac; the **land** on which you lie I will give to you and your descendants.
P R O M I S E	Genesis 12:3 And in you **all families of the earth shall be blessed**.	Genesis 26:4 . . . And in your seed **all nations of the earth shall be blessed**.	Genesis 28:14 . . . and in you and in your seed **all the families of the earth shall be blessed**.

A. Obedient Fellowship with God

The top row of **Figure 1** refers to our relationship with God. We saw clearly in chapter 1 that distrust and disobedience marred this relationship. In fact, the first human beings displaced God as the Lord of their lives by putting themselves in that place. They would decide what was

> **Without God, human community is at best dysfunctional.**

good for them. Thus Adam and Eve hid from God. This loss is fundamental. As God's image-bearers they were made to live in obedient fellowship with him. All joy and all other blessings flowed from this primary relationship. Without God, human community is at best dysfunctional. Restoration begins when God appears to Abraham. He promises Isaac and Jacob that he will be with them. This part of the promise is so fundamental that God becomes known throughout Scripture as the "God of Abraham, Isaac, and Jacob."

B. Harmonious Fellowship Among God's People

Sin has also universally marred relationships between human beings, so that Adam and Eve play the blame game and Cain murders Abel. Humanity falls into a deepening cycle of disunity and distrust. Even in the Garden, it was "not good" for the man to be alone (Gen. 2:18), but that is exactly what sin does to human beings: it fractures the human family and alienates human beings from each other. In the end, sin always leaves human beings "alone."

In the second row of **Figure 1** we see that God addresses this problem by promising a multitude of descendants to Abraham, Isaac, and Jacob. God's solution to this part of the problem is a family, a people of God, a new humanity living in harmony because it lives in obedient fellowship with God. God is not just referring to biological progeny; this family/ people will include all who, like Abraham, live by faith in God and his promise. This family will be a place for his blessing to happen and a means by which it happens. In the Garden, God instituted the family as the primary framework within which people were to learn through experience what it means to love and be loved, to give and receive, and to serve and be served. He intends for that kind of joyful, harmonious relationship to become a reality in the restored people/family promised to Abraham.

C. Responsible Enjoyment of the World

Sin has also marred the way in which humanity relates to the created world, so that the ground brings forth thorns and thistles, and humanity

> Humanity is now set adrift to wander in the world, the same world God made with the intention that humanity would . . . enjoy its benefits.

eats its fruit only by hard labor. Of course, the final graphic statement of this problem is humanity's being driven from the Garden and separated from its blessings by the flaming sword (Gen. 3:24). Humanity is now set adrift to wander in the world, the same world God made with the intention that humanity would rule it, care for it, and enjoy its benefits.

The third row of **Figure 1** shows us how God addresses this problem by promising Abraham, Isaac, and Jacob their own place: the promised land, a new Eden. The promises in Genesis about the land imply a place of belonging, responsibility, and service. They also imply that the land is the context within which humanity, as the biological creatures we are, is to live in relationship with God and manifest his peace in our life together. This promise is not just about property in the usual sense; it is closer to the idea of *home*. Hebrews 11 tells us that Abraham, Isaac, and Jacob were looking forward to something more than the land of Canaan; they were on their way to a permanent "homeland" (Heb. 11:13–16).

The Greek word translated "homeland" can also be used for one's native or home city; it describes the place where one belongs. God's promise of restoration means not only that the world will be made right, but that a restored humanity will come again into its proper place in the new, restored world. This promise finds ultimate fulfillment in the new heaven and earth at Christ's return (Rev. 21:1–22:5). The Garden of Eden will become the eternal city of God.

By meeting Abraham, Isaac, and Jacob and making specific promises to be their God, to give them descendants, and to give them the land, God speaks to the whole problem. He specifically promises to remedy the problem of sin in each of the key relationships it has broken: humanity to God, human to human, and humanity to the created world. The bottom row of **Figure 1** is climactic. It shows not only that God addresses the whole problem, but that he offers this solution to the whole world. Abraham and his descendants are not merely the recipients of this promise but the agents through which God will make these blessings available to the

> Abraham and his descendents are not merely the recipients of this promise but the agents through which God will make these blessings available to the . . . nations.

scattered nations of the earth. He is no local deity but the God who created all and will restore all. By promising to bless all people, God makes it clear that he does not intend a minimal repair but rather a grand renovation. **Figure 2** enables us to see how God's promise of restoration in Genesis 12–33 corresponds to what was lost by sin according to Genesis 1–11. This figure extends **Figure 5** in chapter 1 and is included in the chart found in Appendix 2.

Figure 2

GOD'S PLAN FOR THE WORLD

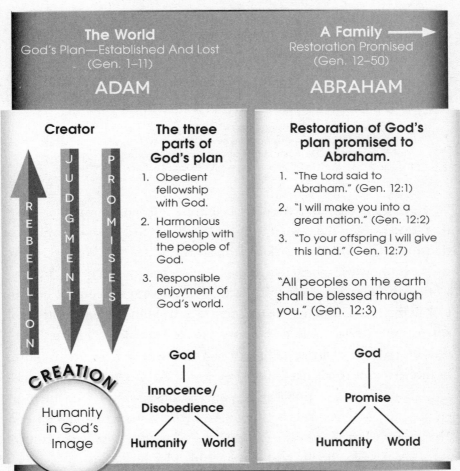

The World
God's Plan—Established And Lost
(Gen. 1–11)

ADAM

A Family ⟶
Restoration Promised
(Gen. 12–50)

ABRAHAM

Creator

REBELLION

JUDGMENT

PROMISES

CREATION

Humanity in God's Image

The three parts of God's plan

1. Obedient fellowship with God.

2. Harmonious fellowship with the people of God.

3. Responsible enjoyment of God's world.

God
|
Innocence/
Disobedience
/ \
Humanity   World

Restoration of God's plan promised to Abraham.

1. "The Lord said to Abraham." (Gen. 12:1)

2. "I will make you into a great nation." (Gen. 12:2)

3. "To your offspring I will give this land." (Gen. 12:7)

"All peoples on the earth shall be blessed through you." (Gen. 12:3)

God
|
Promise
/ \
Humanity   World

III. THE RECIPIENTS OF THE PROMISE: EXAMPLES TO FOLLOW

As we look at God's redemptive promise in Genesis, we have to look not only at the promise and the one who made it but also at those to whom God made the promise. The life stories recorded for us in Genesis are not mere narrative; on the contrary, they are presented to us so that we can learn from them. "The Example Principle" given in **Figure 3** summarizes the relevance of their lives. It is the first of three guidelines that help us grasp the significance of the Old Testament. The second and third guidelines will be given in chapters 3 and 4.

Figure 3

 1st GUIDELINE—THE EXAMPLE PRINCIPLE

We also are heirs of God's promise to Abraham. Thus we come to understand God by seeing how he revealed himself to Abraham, Isaac, Jacob, and other Old Testament people. We follow their examples of trust and obedience and avoid the pitfalls exposed by their failures.

In other words, the lives described in Genesis are depicted for us so that we can see in them what to do and what not to do as we live in relationship with God. When we look at the way God deals with these people, we see how he leads them to a deeper dependence upon him and how he works to bring redemption, transformation, and reconciliation. When we look at their responses to God, we come to understand the implications of entrusting ourselves to God's promise. We see examples of both faith and unbelief. We see that responding to God's promise in faith and walking in the resultant obedience brings blessing. We also see that responding to God's promise with unbelief, flippancy, complacency, or the intent to pursue our own agenda brings not blessing but destruction and misery. The lives in Genesis are case studies that spell out the outcomes of different ways of responding to God's promise in different situations.

This principle is useful in studying all of the people in the Old Testament. It is particularly appropriate, however, when studying the narrative of Genesis 12–50. Abraham, Isaac, Jacob, Jacob's sons (especially Joseph), Sarah, Rebecca, Leah, and Rachel are the beginning, the fathers and mothers of the people of God. The way in which God deals with them discloses the pattern for his dealing with their children.

A. Abraham: The Person Who Pursues God's Blessing by Faith

Abraham is the Old Testament's example par excellence of faith in God's promises. The life of Abraham demonstrates a faith that steps out for God (Gen. 12:1–9), a faith that waits patiently for God to fulfill his word (Gen. 13–21), and a faith that surrenders all to God by resting in him alone (Gen. 22). See **Figure 4**. Each of these types of faith has something to teach us. Together they show how God deepened Abraham's trust. Abraham had to step out in obedience to God's command and find God faithful before he could be asked to wait for God to fulfill the promise of a son. The fulfillment of that promise further strengthened his faith. Then the time was ripe for God to call him to a complete surrender of his own agenda by asking him to sacrifice that son of promise.

Figure 4

ABRAHAM'S JOURNEY OF FAITH

A. Faith that steps out on the divine promise—obedience to the command of God. (Gen. 12:1–9)

B. Faith that waits for the divine fulfillment—patience with the plan of God. (Gen. 15:1–17:22)

C. Faith that rests in the divine character—surrender to the will of God. (Gen. 22:1–19)

Yet Abraham is a person with whom we can identify. He also had his failures and struggles on this journey of faith. His first failure comes right after the account in Genesis 12:1–9 of his stepping out in faith. When Abraham went down to Egypt he lied about Sarah's being his wife because he didn't trust God to take care of him (Gen. 12:10–20). When Pharaoh took Sarah into his harem, God's promise of a son, through whom the blessing would be passed on, was at risk. Later, when Sarah remained barren, Abraham's faith wavered again. He tried to fulfill God's promise in his own way by taking Hagar as his wife (Genesis 16–17). From the first of these failures we learn that God is faithful to his promise even when we fail. Abraham doubted, but God protected him and kept

Sarah from sleeping with Pharaoh. From the second, we learn to trust God rather than to take things into our own hands. Now let's have a look at how Abraham embodies the life of faith.

Figure 5

ABRAHAM AND THE FAITH THAT STEPS OUT ON GOD'S PROMISE. (GEN 12:1-9)

1. Faith takes hold of God's promise. "I will bless you." (Gen. 12:2)

2. Faith lets go of the past. "Get out of your country . . ." And Abraham departed. (Gen. 12:1, 4)

3. Faith receives God's confirmation. "Then the Lord appeared . . . (so) he built an altar." (Gen. 12:7)

4. Faith looks toward God's future. "And the Canaanites were in the land . . . . So Abram journeyed . . ." (Gen. 12:6, 9)

Faith That Steps Out. First, Abraham is an example of faith that steps out (**Figure 5**). Genesis 12:1–9 tells how God calls Abraham to a life of covenant relationship with himself. This passage also tells how Abraham has to leave behind the security of the familiar in order to pursue God's blessing by faith. This process begins with the act of taking hold of God's promise. God says, "I will bless you" (12:2). Abraham treats God's promise as a present reality; he takes God's promise seriously enough to act on it without hesitation. He gets up and goes to the land God would show him. Second, faith means making a definitive commitment despite the risk. As Genesis 12:1, 4 makes clear, such a commitment entails a decisive letting go of the past with its security. His father's house was familiar. It was home. Yet Abraham considered the reality of God's promise to be more important and valuable than the security and familiarity of family, neighbors, and homeland. He left all that provided safety and material security to become an alien in a strange land without root, connection, or resource—except God! Third, see how God validates Abraham's faith in Genesis 12:7: God appears to Abraham in the land of Canaan assuring him that this is the land he will give him. So Abraham builds an altar.

God's confirmation results in Abraham's worship. Trust leads to deeper personal relationship with God and to adoration. Finally, this faith that steps out offers one other lesson: according to Genesis 12:6, 9 this faith looks toward God's future. Abraham is proactive; rather than waiting passively, he moves toward the realization of God's promise, fully expecting that it will be there to meet him. Abraham models a faith that obeys God without hesitation and that is undeterred by the loss of worldly security. He acts in this way because he trusts God to fulfill his promise of restoration. Our life with God usually begins with the faith that steps out. Sometimes God also calls us to such acts of faith after we have begun to follow him. God called the great missionary Adoniram Judson to leave his country and preach the gospel in Burma. He abandoned the prestige and security that could have been his as the pastor of a respected Boston church for harsh suffering and bitter bereavement.

> Sometimes God calls us to trust him through stepping out in a specific act of obedience. Sometimes he calls us to trust him by waiting for him to act.

Faith That Waits. Genesis 15:1–17:22 shows us Abraham as an example of faith that waits (**Figure 6**). Sometimes God calls us to trust him through stepping out in a specific act of obedience. Sometimes he calls us to trust him by waiting for him to act. Both are expressions of living in sync with God's timetable. The same faith that earlier required Abraham to step toward God's future now requires him to trust that the realization of God's promise will come when God knows it is best, not when it might seem best to Abraham.

Figure 6

ABRAHAM AND *THE FAITH THAT WAITS* ON THE FULFILLMENT OF GOD'S PROMISE

1. An inexplicable delay—Abraham has no heir. (Gen. 15:1–6)
   ". . . the heir of my house is Eliezer . . ." (Gen .15:2)

2. A human solution—take Hagar in my place. (Gen. 16:1–16)
   "O that Ishmael might live before you!" (Gen. 17:18)

3. The divine fulfillment—barren Sarah shall bear a son.
   (Gen. 17:1–22.)
   "Sarah your wife will bear you a son, and you shall call his name Isaac; I will establish my covenant with him for an everlasting covenant, and with his descendants after him." (Gen. 17:19)

God's promise to Abraham is dependent on Abraham's having a son. How can God make him a great nation, give him the promised land, and bless the world through him if he has no son? We are introduced to the problem even before we are told of God's promise: Genesis 11:30 tells us that Sarah, Abraham's wife is barren; Abraham has no son and thus no heir. Thus, when we read of God's promise in Genesis 12:1–9, we are already thinking, "But Abraham has no son."

The more time that passes, the more Sarah and Abraham age, the more acute this problem becomes. Initially, Abraham may have thought that Lot, his nephew, whom he brought with him, would be heir to the promise of God. Sarah was barren (Gen. 11:30), so Lot was the back-up plan (Gen. 12:5). Genesis 13:1–14:24, however, makes it clear that Lot is more interested in the wealth and pleasure to be had by associating with the people of Sodom. Finally, in Genesis 15:1–6, when the Lord reiterates his commitment to Abraham, Abraham brings this problem to God.

To paraphrase, God says to Abraham, "I am your shield, your very great reward" (Gen. 15:1). Abraham responds, "Yes, Lord, but I don't have any heir. One who has been 'born in my house,' Eliezer of Damascus, is my heir. Since Lot my nephew is gone, my servant and steward will be my heir." This second human solution was in full accord with the custom of the time. Abraham, however, isn't very happy with this plan. Although Eliezer was "born in his house," he was of foreign origin and was not born from Abraham's body. Sometimes, as we wait for God to act in answer to our prayers, we envision various human solutions or possibilities. But God acts in his own way. God uses this opportunity to reassure Abraham by reinforcing his promise and to make one thing clear: the promised son and heir will be Abraham's physical child—from Abraham's "body" (Gen. 15:4, literally *loins*), not just born in his "house" (Gen. 15:3)! The events of Genesis 15:7–22 are God's reinforcement of his promise. In Abraham's time two people would make a covenant by cutting an animal in two and then by passing between the two parts. By this act they invoked death upon themselves if they were faithless to the covenant. The "smoking oven" or "pot" and "burning torch" (Gen. 15:17) that pass between the parts of these dead animals represent God. By using this custom God affirms his faithfulness to Abraham in the strongest possible way. See Abraham's deepening relationship with God. After Abraham obeyed God's initial invitation, God appeared to him (Gen. 12:1–9). Now, after a definitive act of trust in God's promise (Gen. 15:6), God makes this covenant with him.

God has repeated his promise, he has clarified it and reinforced it, but he has not yet fulfilled his promise. Time goes on. Abraham and Sarah have been in the promised land for ten years (Gen. 16:3). Finally, Abraham, at Sarah's suggestion, mistakenly tries to fix the problem. He will help God fulfill his promise. It is difficult for us to imagine the pressure that was on Sarah. Barrenness in general was such a disgrace, but she could not give birth to the promised son. So we should not be surprised when she offered her maid to Abraham as a substitute (Gen. 16:1–3). Such an arrangement was a common contemporary custom if a wife could not bear children. At least to some degree, the children of her maid were to be thought of as her own. This was a common-sense solution, "keeping the business in the family."

So Abraham fathers Ishmael by Sarah's maid Hagar. This plan was logical. God had said that Abraham's son and heir would be from his body (Gen. 15:4), but did this son need to come from Sarah's body as well? Ishmael's birth, however, aggravates Sarah's problem rather than fixing it. Sarah is now childless, while her servant Hagar has borne a son. Hagar now looks with disdain upon Sarah, leaving her in a worse situation than before (Gen. 16:4–16). God allowed Abraham and Sarah to live with their unsatisfactory solution to this problem for thirteen years. Abraham was eighty-six when he fathered Ishmael (Gen. 16:16). He is ninety-nine when God appears to him and corrects him (Gen. 17:1).

We, like Abraham, must learn the faith that waits on God. We may not have as specific a promise as Abraham did. However, God has promised to care for his own. He invites us to come to him with our needs. We often speculate about how God will answer—through nephew Lot or servant Eliezer? Then we try to take matters in our own hands and "fix it" Hagar-Ishmael style. Faith that waits means not trying to do God's job for him. God not only has an end in mind, he also has means in mind to accomplish his end. God would teach us, as he did Abraham, to have the faith that waits on him to fulfill his promise in his way. Sometimes he lets us live with our own solutions for a while, as he did Abraham and Sarah.

It is important to note that when God does come to Abraham in Genesis 17:1–27, he does not begin by reprimanding Abraham for trying to fix this problem. He repeats and expands his promise as he did in Genesis 15:1–6, the last time he spoke with Abraham. As we saw in the last part of that chapter God reinforced his promise by making a covenant with Abraham. Now he asks Abraham to institute circumcision as a sign of his loyalty to that covenant. That sign will be in the part of Abraham's body through which God will give him the promised son. Then, instead of reprimanding Abraham, God simply affirms that the promised son will be through Sarah; just as Abraham will be the father of many peoples, so Sarah will be their mother (Gen. 17:15–19). God's covenant is with her as well as with Abraham. God emphasizes the importance of this covenant by giving this couple, known to this point as Abram and Sarai, the new names by which we know them best: Abraham and Sarah. God's promise to Abraham and Sarah (whom he has claimed as his own in the act of naming them) is that Sarah—always barren and now well beyond menopause—will bear Abraham's son, and that God's promises will come to fruition through this promised child. There will be no mistake: this is the work of God. Abraham commits himself to wait for God's fulfillment by circumcising himself; God recognizes that Abraham is now fully committed and calls the faith that is willing to do things God's way "righteous."

After God affirms that the promised son will come through Sarah, Abraham mentions Ishmael: "Oh that Ishmael might live before you" (Gen. 17:18). Only then does God address the issue of Abraham's own attempt to fulfill the promise. Note how gently he does so: he promises to bless Ishmael too, but reaffirms that his promise will be through barren Sarah's son, Isaac. God need not rebuke them. They themselves experience the difficulties they have caused for themselves by trying to fulfill God's promise on their own. God leads them on, teaching them the faith that waits. In Genesis 18 God comes to Abraham and Sarah in person with the definite promise that Sarah will bear Isaac within the next year! In chapter 21 Isaac is born. God can lead us, too, beyond our attempts to fulfill his promise for him. He can bring us to a deeper trust in him.

It is interesting to note that in Genesis 20, just before the birth of Isaac, God has to rescue his promise once more from Abraham's lack of trust. As Abraham lied about Sarah to Pharaoh in chapter 13 at the beginning of his walk with God, so he now lies about her to Abimelech, king of Gerar. Once again, God saves Sarah from being violated. We might understand how Abraham's faith failed at the beginning, but shouldn't he have known better by now? As soon as we ask this question, we remember our own faithlessness.

The faith that steps out requires immediate action; the faith that waits requires the opposite response: patience in dependence on God. The first is required when there is a clear act of obedience before us, the second when we are waiting for God to do his work. We need wisdom to know which kind of faith is required in a particular situation. That wisdom comes from walking closely with our God.

Faith That Rests. When Abraham stepped out in faith, God took care of him. When Abraham learned the faith that waits on God to fulfill his promise, he was not disappointed. His experience of God has strengthened his faith. Now he is ready for God's great test of faith. Genesis 22:1–19 shows Abraham as an example of faith that rests completely in God. In his willingness to offer Isaac at Mount Moriah, Abraham demonstrates a trust in God that sees God's promise as so real and sure that nothing can shake it. Abraham is able to rest in the trustworthiness of God's character even when God's command is inscrutable and apparently self-contradictory. See **Figure 7**.

Figure 7

ABRAHAM AND *THE FAITH THAT RESTS* IN THE CHARACTER OF GOD'S PROMISE

A. A command without a promise. (Gen. 22:1–2)

　1. A familiar voice. *God . . . said to him, ". . . . go."*

　2. A specific request. *". . . your son, your only son, Isaac, whom you love!"*

　3. An absurd demand. *". . . offer him there as a burnt offering . . ."*

B. An obedience without explanation. (Gen. 22:3–10)

　1. Abraham obeyed promptly. (Gen. 22:3–5)
　　"I and the boy will . . . worship and come again to you."(ESV)

　2. Abraham obeyed persistently. (Gen. 22:6–8)
　　"My son, God will provide for himself the lamb for a burnt offering."

　3. Abraham obeyed completely. (Gen. 22:9–10)
　　Abraham stretched out his hand and took the knife . . .

C. A provision without limitation. (Gen. 22:11–19)

　1. An immediate provision. *And Abraham looked up and . . . saw a ram.* (NIV)

　2. An eternal provider. *"The–Lord–Will–Provide."*

　3. A universal promise. *". . . and through your offspring all nations on earth will be blessed, because you have obeyed me."* (NIV)

Genesis 22:1–2 describes God's command to Abraham. The command is specific and pointed: Abraham is to offer his beloved son, Isaac, the one whom God miraculously gave through Sarah, as a burnt offering. It seems perverse, murderous, even pagan, to sacrifice the miraculous fulfillment of God's promise and the source of Abraham's future descendants, but one thing is sure: Abraham knows the voice that has commanded him. The fact that it is God's voice means that no explanation is needed. Abraham promptly goes (Gen. 22:3–10) and prepares for the journey. Even in the face of Isaac's innocent query about the sacrifice, Abraham follows through, probably saying as much to himself as to Isaac that "God will provide for Himself the lamb" (Gen. 22:8). Even when Isaac rests bound upon the altar, Abraham continues in complete obedience; he does not wait for a way out but takes the knife in hand. At this moment God intervenes (Gen. 22:11–19). He shows Abraham that, indeed, he has already provided: the ram is waiting. That ram is no accident, but is the work of God's own providence, his commitment to give his people what they need when they need it—always. Out of Abraham's faith, God will bring a family and then a nation through which "all the nations of the earth will be blessed" (Gen. 22:18). This is possible because Abraham finally sees the whole of his world through the eyes of faith. Abraham has come to such a place that he is able to trust God

> As we walk with God . . . he brings us to the place where we are willing . . . to obey implicitly trusting his character even when we do not understand his purposes.

simply because he is God. Once he hears God's voice, he knows nothing else needs to be said. As we walk with God, stepping out and waiting in faith, he brings us to the place where we are willing to rest in him, to obey implicitly trusting his character even when we do not understand his purposes. This type of faith is available only to those who have come to know their God through long walking with him. If the immature attempt to replicate this type of faith, they will likely follow the wrong voice and end up in folly.

B. Lot: The Person Who Toys with God's Blessing

Lot provides a useful second illustration of the example principle because he stands in sharp contrast to Abraham. Abraham abandons human security and lives as a stranger in this world while he waits for the promise of God. Lot, on the other hand, professes faith but clings to the security and benefits this world can give. Lot shows us the worldly, compromised life and its consequences. In Lot we see a tragic pattern of double-mindedness. Lot repeatedly tries to live out his relationship with God on the basis of what he perceives to be the bare minimum God will tolerate. Lot is not a true pagan. He is a more miserable figure: the one who fears God but still craves and pursues the comfort and pleasure that pagans worship. Lot is the archetype of the person who calls upon the name of the Lord but still lives an idolatrous life. He is a warning lest we who are Christians try to live as close to the sinful world as possible (Gen. 13:1–18). His story shows us the dire consequences of such a life (Gen. 14, 18–19; see **Figure 8** for an outline of his life).

Figure 8

LOT: THE PERSON WHO TOYS WITH GOD'S BLESSING

I. The wrong choice. (Gen. 13:1–18)

II. A second chance. (Gen. 14:1–24)

III. The inevitable consequences. (Gen. 18:1–19:38)

The Wrong Choice. The tragedy that is Lot's life begins with a fateful decision, described in Genesis 13:1–18 (**Figure 9**). Lot chooses to go his own way. Abraham left his earthly home in pursuit of the promise of God. Lot leaves Abraham for a prosperous, but wicked, earthly home. Lot chooses material wealth over godly company, and this leads to him choosing to live near Sodom—and then in Sodom. Having walked away from his own godly family, keeping company with the people of Sodom and their wickedness is the next step. When the fellowship of God's people is no longer a priority, the next step is moral compromise. This becomes even clearer in light of the contrast between Abraham and Lot: Lot goes down to Sodom, while Abraham goes in the other direction and builds an altar to God. One road leads to bad company, the other to fellowship with God.

Figure 9

LOT: THE PERSON WHO TOYS WITH GOD'S BLESSING

I. The wrong choice. (Gen 13:1–18)
If we choose to play with the values of the world we will lose God's blessing.

  A. Embracing a godly heritage. (Gen. 13:1–4)

    1. Lot had witnessed God's faithfulness.

    2. Lot had enjoyed God's blessings.

  B. Recognizing the moment of decision. (Gen. 13:5–9)

  C. Avoiding Lot's choice. (Gen. 13:10–18)

    1. Lot played with the things of the world. (Gen. 13:10–13)

    2. Abraham followed the way of faith. (Gen. 13:14–18)

A Second Chance. Lot's entanglement with the people of Sodom also causes him to be entangled in their problems (Gen. 14:1–24). When Sodom goes to war and loses, Lot and his household are carried away as captives. Lot is a classic example of the person who, because of his own unwise choices, is at exactly the wrong place at the worst possible time. He and his household are caught in the middle of a war they care nothing about simply because Lot considered the land near Sodom to be a good location and chose to live there.

In spite of his prior bad choices, Lot receives another chance: Abraham and his soldiers go after Lot and his household and rescue them from captivity (**Figure 10**). In spite of Lot's faithlessness, Abraham stands by him and works on his behalf. Not only does Abraham do right by Lot, he also shows Lot how to do the right thing. He models godly decision making for Lot. After rescuing Lot, Abraham is greeted by both

Melchizedek, the king of Salem, and Bera, the king of Sodom. Abraham accepts the blessing of Melchizedek and shares bread with him, but pointedly rebuffs the king of Sodom. The message is clear: Abraham wants none of the company that has caused Lot so much grief.

Figure 10

LOT: THE PERSON WHO TOYS WITH GOD'S BLESSING

II. A second chance. (Gen. 14:1–24)
   If we play with the world, we get caught in the world's troubles.

   A. Judgment—Lot was carried off with the people of the world. (Gen. 14:1–12)

   B. Mercy—Lot was delivered by faithful Abraham. (Gen. 14:13–16)

   C. A Second chance—Lot had the example of faithful Abraham. (Gen. 14:17–24)

   1. Melchizedek, king of Salem—choose faith.

   2. King of Sodom—choose the world.

Although Abraham steers clear of those associations that have done Lot such harm, he never stops caring for Lot or interceding on his behalf. The last part of Genesis 18 is the famous conversation in which Abraham pleads with God to show mercy toward Sodom for the sake of the few righteous there. It seems clear that Abraham had no confidence that Lot would leave Sodom; he had already been carried off as a prisoner of war and, when rescued by Abraham, gone back to live in Sodom, the very situation out of which his earlier troubles had come. All Abraham can do is to plead with God to show mercy, but in the end Lot's choices have necessary and unavoidable consequences.

Figure 11

LOT: THE PERSON WHO TOYS
WITH GOD'S BLESSING

III. The inevitable consequences. (Gen. 18:1–19:38)

    A. The one who chooses to be near God. (Gen. 18:1–33)

        1. A joyous visit from God. (Gen. 18:1–8)

        2. The promise of a son. (Gen. 18:9–15)

        3. The privilege of being God's friend. (Gen. 18:16–33)

    B. The one who chooses to be near the world. (Gen. 19:1–38)

        1. A terrifying visit. (Gen. 19:1–11)

        2. A threat to the family. (Gen. 19:6–8, 12–14)

        3. The terror of being an abandoned fugitive. (Gen. 19:15–29)

        4. A pitiful end. (Gen. 19:30–38)

The Inevitable Consequences. Genesis 18:1–19:38 describes the consequences of Lot's choice. The contrast between Abraham and Lot is instructive: while Genesis holds up Abraham as an example of drawing near to God, Lot exemplifies double-mindedness and the misery that compromise brings (**Figure 11**). Genesis shows that the one who professes to worship God but seeks security and comfort somewhere else finds only sorrow. Genesis 19:1–38, while a compelling story in its own right, speaks all the more forcefully when we recognize that it stands in direct contrast to the events described in Genesis 18:1–15. While God's visit to Abraham is a joyous one, this is not so for Lot (Gen. 19:1–29). God's angels come to Sodom to bring the message that Lot's chosen home is about to be destroyed. He can either leave his home or be destroyed with it. Further, while God's visit to Abraham concerns his promise to provide Abraham with family, the angels come to Lot with the message that his own family is in grave danger. Finally, while Abraham is described as God's friend, Lot is presented as a fugitive (Gen. 19:30–38). Lot, although he has tried to make his home in worldly company by worldly means, ends up having no home at all. He clings to his life at Sodom until the last possible moment.

Lot even loses his wife in the course of fleeing because she will not let go of her longing for Sodom. Nor is Lot the only one who loses a spouse; his sons-in-law are destroyed along with everything else in Sodom because they will not come away. Lot and his daughters are all widowed in one fell swoop. All of this comes to a thoroughly tragic end. The one who left the hill country to seek wealth in Sodom returns to the hills in poverty and disgrace. Having lost the home he tried to make for himself at Sodom (and the wife he apparently got for himself there), he now lives in the hills as a widower with his two daughters. Lot's daughters have no husbands to give them children, so they handle things with a worldly pragmatism they learned from their father in Sodom. Knowing that Lot will not consent to father their children, they make sure to get him drunk so that he cannot object. The children they bear father the Moabites and the Ammonites, peoples who war with Abraham's descendants for generations thereafter. Lot's double-mindedness ends in ruin for himself and his wife. It produces children who follow his poor moral example, and their actions become a source of ongoing hardship for God's people.

C. Jacob: The Person Who Tries to Misappropriate God's Blessing

Jacob is our example of the life transformed by grace. He begins as the "supplanter," the manipulator, the thief. The difference between Jacob and Lot lies not in how they begin but in how they finish. The contrast between the two is striking, especially in the portrayal of Jacob as one who wrestles with God. Jacob may actually be the more selfish and destructive of the two, but he is also the one whom God breaks in order to transform. Jacob is an example of how God can transform a self-centered, self-seeking deceiver and manipulator into a godly person (Gen. 25, 27–33). The Scripture shows us how God, by making Jacob face himself, leads him to repentance, surrender, restitution, and reconciliation with both his brother and God. The story of God's dealing with him falls into three periods and two crises (see **Figure 12**). The first period (Gen. 25:19–34; 27:1–28:9) narrates the story of Jacob the self-seeking manipulator and ends with Jacob running away from himself. In the second period (Gen.

29:1–31:55), Jacob is the one manipulated by Laban and thus made to face himself. In period three (Gen. 32:1–21; 33:1–35:29), Jacob is forced to face his brother and his past. This confrontation leads to reconciliation with his brother and with God. These periods are divided by the two crises in which God confronts Jacob. In the first crisis (Gen. 28:10–22), when Jacob is fleeing from his brother, God comes to him at Bethel and promises to be with Jacob and take care of him. Jacob accepts the deal. In the second crisis (Gen. 32:22–32) at Peniel, Jacob faces God. God requires Jacob's surrender and effects his transformation. He discovers that it is God who has been at work throughout his life. He has been struggling with God. Facing himself and his brother are part of his coming face to face with God.

Figure 12

JACOB'S LIFE AT A GLANCE
Three Periods and Two Crises

	Scripture Reference	Location	Main Event	Main Theme
FIRST PERIOD	Genesis 25:19–34 27:1–28:9	Beersheba in the land of Canaan	Jacob cheats Esau	Jacob shows his deceitful character
GOD speaks to Jacob at Bethel (Gen. 28:10–22) Jacob commits himself to God.				
SECOND PERIOD	Genesis 29:1–31:55	Haran in Padan Aram	Laban cheats Jacob	Jacob faces his deceitful character
God wrestles with Jacob at Peniel (Gen. 32:22–32) Jacob surrenders himself to God.				
THIRD PERIOD	Genesis 32:1–21 33:1–35:29	The land of Canaan	Jacob is reconciled to Esau	Jacob lives a new life

Running from Himself: Jacob the Manipulator (First Period). The first period of Jacob's life is described in Genesis 25:19–34; 27:1–28:9. Genesis 25:19–28 sets the stage for the rest of the story by describing the dysfunctional family through which God will carry out his purposes. Such dysfunction is characteristic of humanity alienated from God. Esau and Jacob are twins, born to Isaac and Rebecca as the result of Isaac's intercession. God intends for the elder of the twins (Esau) to serve the younger (Jacob). God will pass the promise of blessing given to Abraham

Facing himself and his brother are part of his coming face to face with God.

and Isaac on through the younger, Jacob. Esau is a macho, hairy outdoorsman. Jacob is a homebody whose name shows that he is a supplanter, a deceptive manipulator. Isaac loved Esau best because he liked the meat he hunted, but Rebecca loved the homebody Jacob. This is the stage upon which the following conflict will unfold.

God has already indicated that he is going to pass his promise on through Jacob. Yet Jacob, the twin born seconds after his brother Esau, is determined to get the rights of the firstborn for himself. He first manages to get his brother's birthright (Gen. 25:29–34), then to steal the blessing of the firstborn (Gen. 27:1–40). These two incidents reveal the self-centered, deceptive character of this "supplanter." Jacob should have gladly shared food with his hungry brother. However, he takes advantage of his brother's slavery to bodily desires (Esau certainly exaggerates in Genesis 25:32 when he says, "I am about to die"). Unless Esau swears—nothing less will do—to give Jacob his right as firstborn, Jacob will give him no food. Esau showed so little concern for his birthright that he sold it to Jacob for a bowl of beans.

The story of Jacob's stealing the blessing of the firstborn from Esau is more involved (Gen. 27:1–40). Their mother, Rebecca, instigates the deception. Isaac, like his son Esau, is given to his bodily desires. He tells Esau to hunt and prepare wild meat for him to eat. Then he will bless him. Rebecca and Jacob show disdain for Isaac. Isaac cannot distinguish the domestic meat Rebecca prepares from the supposedly favorite wild game of Esau. He cannot tell Jacob, wearing Esau's clothes with arms covered by sheepskin, from Esau. And so he blesses Jacob with the blessing of the firstborn, making him lord over Esau. If Esau gets his attachment to bodily desires from Isaac, Jacob inherits his deceitfulness from his mother. The immediate result, however, is that Jacob must flee the murderous anger of Esau (Gen. 27:41–28:9); he must flee from himself, from the duplicity of the life he has lived. Deception has already begun to pay painful dividends. His mother tells him that, when Esau's anger has cooled, she will bring him home (Gen. 27:45). She, however, will never see him again.

God Speaks to Jacob at Bethel (First Crisis). Genesis 28:10–22 describes God's first direct encounter with Jacob. Jacob is expecting nothing. He is fleeing. He comes to a nondescript "certain place" and takes one of the stones "of that place" for a pillow. However, the God of Abraham and Isaac comes to him in a dream. The ladder with the ascending and descending angels shows that God is at work in the world. God himself reiterates the promise of Abraham—descendents and land—to Jacob. Most important of all, God promises to be with Jacob: he will take care of him, bring him back to his homeland, and accomplish his purposes in Jacob. Jacob is overawed. What he thought was an ordinary place is nothing short of "God's House" (Bethel). What grace and divine humility: God comes to the "deceiver" with this offer. Jacob, always after a good deal, accepts: "If you will do what you have said, God, you will be my God." How often God is gracious to us when we are going our own way and suffering the consequences of our own disobedience.

Facing Himself: Jacob the Manipulated (Second Period). Genesis 29:1–31:55 describes the second period of Jacob's life. Jacob arrives at his uncle Laban's home in Haran. Laban is his mother's brother, and he is equal to both his sister and Jacob as a deceiver. Jacob makes a big show at his arrival by removing the well cover and watering the sheep for Rachel, Laban's beautiful daughter. He, however, is at Laban's mercy. He has nothing to give, so he readily offers to work seven years if Laban will give him Rachel, his younger daughter, as wife. When Laban deceives him by giving him Leah, the older sister, instead of Rachel, he has no recourse. He is a foreigner without influence or connection—except Laban. He showed contempt for his father; Laban showed contempt for him. He gave Jacob the wrong woman and, in the dark of night, Jacob didn't even know. He who used bodily desire to manipulate his father and brother has now been manipulated by desire. After requiring Jacob to work another seven years for Rachel, Laban keeps him an additional ten by paying him with flocks. During this time Laban often cheats him by changing his wages. **Figure 13** shows how Laban's treatment of Jacob is the mirror image of Jacob's treatment of his brother. In Laban, God forces Jacob to face himself.

Jacob is beginning to realize that he has prospered, despite Laban, only because God has blessed him. Indeed, it is only God's gracious intervention (Gen. 31:29, 42) that saves Jacob from Laban's wrath when Jacob flees in order to return home.

Figure 13

JACOB TRICKS ESAU	LABAN TRICKS JACOB
The younger brother takes the blessing of the elder.	The elder sister takes the marriage bed of the younger.
The right of the elder brother is taken.	The right of the elder sister is maintained.
Jacob takes Esau's birthright in a business deal.	Laban cheats Jacob of his wages in a business deal.
Jacob and Esau's mother substitutes the younger son for the elder by deceit.	Rachel and Leah's father substitutes the elder for the younger by deceit.

God Wrestles with Jacob at Peniel (Second Crisis). God's second encounter with Jacob is described in Genesis 32:22–32. Jacob's fleeing from Esau was the first occasion for God to encounter him. His returning home to face Esau is the second. He cannot go back to Laban. Esau is coming to meet him with four hundred men. He has faced his deceitful self during his time with Laban. He must face Esau and his past when he returns. Here, however, alone, in the dark of night, on the bank of the brook

Jabbok, he must face God. Suddenly and terrifyingly, in the impenetrable gloom, a "man" is wrestling with Jacob. Throughout his life Jacob has not been wrestling merely with Esau or Laban; he has been wrestling with God. Now that contest is revealed for what it is. God intends to bless Jacob with the blessing of Abraham. Jacob, however, has been trying to force God to do things his way. Finally, grudgingly, he yields to the God who came at Bethel and offered him everything. The surrender is marked by his giving God his name—the name Jacob, "deceiver." God changes his name—and his character. Jacob, however, struggles to the end. How hard it is for us to yield all to God. He wants to know God's name—to have a claim on God equal to God's claim on him. God, of course, refuses, and maims Jacob by touching his thigh. The disjoined thigh is God's way of reminding stubborn Jacob to keep depending on him. When Jacob meets Esau he will not be able to fight or to run. Only God can sustain him. After facing God, humbled Jacob is ready to face his brother.

Facing His Past: Jacob Reconciled with Esau (Third Period). Genesis 32:1–21 and 33:1–11 describe the third period of Jacob's life. Even before wrestling with God, Jacob began to face his past by sending messengers to Esau. The return of those messengers brought terror: Esau was coming with four hundred men (Gen. 32:1–8). After seeking God's mercy and protection (Gen. 32:9–12), Jacob prepares to make restitution for the past by preparing lavish gifts and sending them to Esau (Gen. 32:13–21). By wrestling with Jacob, God brings permanent good out of these preparations.

Observe Jacob's self-disclosure, vulnerability, and humility in Genesis 33:1–7. He presents all of his family to Esau. He bows down a complete seven times as he approaches Esau, denoting his complete subservience. He makes restitution to Esau by the flocks and herds that he gives him. He returns the blessing that he stole: "Please, take my *blessing* that is brought to you because God has dealt graciously with me" (Gen. 33:11, emphasis added). The one who has wrestled with God is reconciled to his brother through humility, confession, and restitution. Jacob now knows: he does not need the primacy or the blessing that he stole from Esau—

because God has blessed him. Thus we see how God has transformed the born deceiver and manipulator, Jacob, and has brought him to this place of reconciliation with his estranged brother. God has done this both through circumstances and through confronting Jacob at crucial points in his life. We are born self-centered deceivers and manipulators, as was

> **The one who has wrestled with God is reconciled to his brother through humility, confession, and restitution.**

Jacob. We, too, live in dysfunctional families and environments as he did. But we have the same God working in our lives to transform us and to reconcile us to one another.

D. Joseph and His Brothers: Character, Godly Sorrow, and Domestic Reconciliation

The story of Joseph (see **Figure 14**) begins in Genesis 37:1–36 with a doting father and jealous brothers who sell their younger half-brother Joseph into Egyptian slavery. It ends with reconciliation and with penitent brothers who receive forgiveness from a gracious Joseph (Gen. 50:15–21). Joseph provides a positive example by living in faithful dependence on the God of the promise despite unjust suffering, deferred hope, and unexpected power. Through his faithfulness God brings reconciliation to his family and blesses the nations by providing food during famine. The brothers' jealousy shows us the ugly results of such behavior. Yet the way in which God brings them to repentance invites us to turn from sin and follow the path of reconciliation.

Figure 14

JOSEPH AND HIS BROTHERS—CHARACTER, GODLY SORROW, AND DOMESTIC RECONCILIATION

I. Joseph in Potiphar's house—the test of character. (Gen. 38:1–39:23)

   A. Joseph did not use circumstances as an excuse. (Gen. 39:6–7)

   B. Joseph was loyal to those who trusted him. (Gen. 39:8–9)

   C. Joseph decisively rejected temptation. (Gen. 39:8)

   D. Joseph put character before reputation. (Gen. 39:12)

II. Joseph in prison—the test of patience and courage. (Gen. 40:1–41:57)

   A. Joseph did not get bitter at hope deferred. (Gen. 40:1–23)

   B. Joseph waited on God's timing. (Gen. 41:1–13)

   C. Joseph bore witness to God's power. (Gen. 41:14–36)

   D. Joseph was the man God could use to bless his family and the world. (Gen. 41:37–57)

III. Joseph in Pharaoh's court—the test of power. (Gen. 42:1–50:26)

   A. Joseph held his brothers accountable. (Gen. 42:6–17; 44:1–17)

   B. Joseph was gracious to his brothers. (Gen. 42:18–20; 43:16–34)

   C. Joseph freely forgave his brothers. (Gen. 45:1–8; 50:15–21)

IV. Joseph's brothers—an example of godly sorrow. (Gen. 42:1–50:26)

   A. Joseph's brothers acknowledged their guilt. (Gen. 42:20–22)

   B. Joseph's brothers accepted responsibility for their sin. (Gen. 43:8–10)

   C. Joseph's brothers made restitution for their sin. (Gen. 44:18–34)

Judah is often the representative of Joseph's brothers. He is the one who suggests selling Joseph into slavery (Gen. 37:26–27). He is also the one who expresses the brothers' repentance and offers to stay in Egypt so that his brother Benjamin can return to his father (Gen. 44:18–34). The example of Joseph is enhanced by comparison and contrast with Judah.

Joseph in Potiphar's House: the Test of Character (Gen. 38:1–39:23). The merchants who bought Joseph from his brothers took him to Egypt and sold him to Potiphar, "an officer of Pharaoh, captain of the guard, an

> He did not rationalize his actions by giving adultery a pretty name. He called it what it was, 'this great wickedness.' (Gen. 39:9)

Egyptian" (Gen. 39:1). Genesis 39:1–23 tells the story of Joseph in Potiphar's house. Because God was with Joseph, all that he did prospered. Thus Potiphar put Joseph over his entire household. Soon Potiphar's wife tried to seduce Joseph. Joseph's refusal demonstrates his character and shows us how to deal with temptation. First, he did not use circumstances as an excuse. He could have said, "I have been unjustly sold as a slave. I am far from home. I have no chance to get a wife. God has failed me. Potiphar shouldn't have left me here in the house alone. No one should blame me." But he did not say any of these things. Instead, he decisively and repeatedly rejected her offers. Second, he was loyal to the one who trusted him. He refused to dishonor his master Potiphar. Third, he decisively rejected this temptation. He did not rationalize his actions by giving adultery a pretty name. He called it what it was: "this great wickedness" (Gen. 39:9). This sin was not just against Potiphar, or against Potiphar's wife, or even against himself, but "against God" (Gen. 39:9).

Finally, Joseph put his integrity and his character before his reputation. When Potiphar's wife grabbed his clothes, he left them in her hand and ran out of the house, even though she could and did use them as evidence against him (Gen. 39:11–18). He would rather be thought guilty though innocent than thought innocent though guilty. He knew that the approval of God was more important than the approval of human beings.

Judah's behavior in Genesis 38:1–30 sets Joseph's behavior in bold relief by being its exact opposite. Joseph was forcefully separated from his people; Judah chose to go and find a wife among the Canaanites. Joseph refused to use his circumstances as an excuse; Judah is only too ready to employ a prostitute after the death of his wife (Gen. 38:12–16). By his purity Joseph was loyal to the God of the promise; by his refusal to give his son to Tamar and thus raise up heirs, Judah ignored God's promise (Gen. 38:6–11). Joseph was concerned about his character; Judah was jealous for his reputation (Gen. 38:20–23).

Thus Joseph shows us how to face temptation, even under adversity. God used these circumstances not merely to test, but to develop and confirm his character. God calls us to be people of character, not people of convenience. It is people of character whom he can use to bring reconciliation.

> God calls us to be people of character, not people of convenience.

Joseph in Prison: the Test of Patience and Courage (Gen. 40:1–41:57). Joseph was sent to prison because of the false accusation made by Potiphar's wife. Genesis 40:1–23 tells about his life there. It is a story of deferred hope. Again, because God was with him, the head of the prison put Joseph over all the prisoners. Two of those prisoners had been Pharaoh's chief butler and chief baker. Each of them had a dream, which God enabled Joseph to interpret. Since the chief butler's dream meant that he would be restored to his post, Joseph requested the butler to ask Pharaoh for his release. However, the restored butler forgot all about Joseph. Joseph had to spend another two years in prison. He learned the patience of waiting for God's time, which came when Pharaoh had two dreams that no one could interpret (Gen. 41:1–13). Only then did the butler remember Joseph and tell Pharaoh that Joseph could explain the dreams for him.

In Genesis 41:14–36 Joseph bears fearless witness to the power of God before Pharaoh: "It is not in me; God will give Pharaoh an answer of peace" (Gen. 41:16). He insists that God has shown Pharaoh what will happen (Gen. 41:25, 28). Furthermore, Joseph asserted that God had given Pharaoh two dreams to show that God had truly determined to bring seven years of plenty and seven of famine upon the land and that God would do it soon (Gen. 41:32). Joseph demonstrated both the patience to wait on God's time and the courage to bear witness for God when that time came.

> Joseph demonstrated both the patience to wait on God's time and the courage to bear witness for God when that time came.

Joseph in Pharaoh's Court: the Test of Power (Gen. 42:1–45:28; 50:15–21). Through these experiences God had prepared Joseph to assume authority over all Egypt under Pharaoh. Pharaoh had entrusted Joseph with the job of storing grain during the seven years of plenty so that there would be food during the seven years of famine. God could now use Joseph to bless Egypt and the surrounding nations by providing food for them, and to bless his own family. Now, however, Joseph had to face the greatest test of all: the test of power.

Joseph recognized his brothers the first time they came with the crowds to buy food in Egypt (Gen. 42:6–38)—but they did not recognize him. His childhood dreams of their bowing before him (Gen. 37:5–11) had come true. He had the power to do anything with them that he desired. Joseph exacted no vengeance. He was a model of tough love that held his brothers accountable while being gracious to them. Thus, although he kept Simeon as surety of their return with his younger brother Benjamin, he returned their money by putting it in the top of their sacks before he sent them home. On their second visit (Gen. 43:1–44:17) he treated them graciously by entertaining them in his house, but then put his cup in Benjamin's sack so that he could arrest Benjamin. It was this threatened loss of Benjamin that brought the brothers to full repentance over what they had done to Benjamin's older brother Joseph. At this repentance Joseph fully and freely forgave them (Gen. 45: 1–8). He told them to bring his father and all their family to Egypt where he would provide for them (Gen. 45:9–28). Genesis 50:15–21 reveals the extent of Joseph's forgiveness and the depth of his faith in the God of the promise. By the time of this passage the restraining presence of Jacob had been removed by death. The brothers were afraid that Joseph would now punish them. Joseph assured them that he had forgiven them. They may have meant evil toward him, but "God meant it for good, in order . . . to save many people alive" (Gen. 50:20). This was the secret of Joseph's life. He had suffered for resisting temptation, waited patiently for God's deliverance from prison, testified to God before Pharaoh, and forgiven his brothers—all because he was confident that God was at work in all things. He was certain that the God of the promise was taking care of him. Since Adam and Eve, sinful human beings had been trying to make themselves God. Despite his great power, Joseph knew that he was not "in the place of God" (Gen. 50:19). Let's look more closely at his brothers.

Joseph's Brothers: an Example of Godly Sorrow (Gen. 42:20–22; 43:8–10; 44:18–34). Joseph's brothers began to acknowledge their guilt on their first trip to Egypt. When Joseph insisted that they could not return to Egypt for more food unless they brought their youngest brother, Benjamin, they admitted to one another, "We are truly guilty concerning our brother, for we saw the anguish of his soul when he pleaded with us, and we would not hear; therefore this distress has come upon us" (Gen. 42:21). The threat against Benjamin reminded them of their sin against Benjamin's older brother Joseph, the only two sons Rachel bore to Jacob. If Joseph's loss had caused their father grief, what would be the result of Benjamin's loss?

When hunger forced them to make a second trip to Egypt, they knew they could not go without Benjamin. Judah, the one who had suggested selling Joseph into slavery, stepped forward and took responsibility before his father for bringing Benjamin safely home (Gen. 43:8–10). Out of godly sorrow they began to make restitution for their sin.

When Joseph determined to keep Benjamin in Egypt, Judah acted on the promise to his father (Gen. 44:18–34). He humbly explained to

> Godly sorrow had led to accepting responsibility for sin, to repentance, and to doing what could be done to make up for past wrong doing.

Joseph what Benjamin's loss would do to his father and offered himself as a slave in Benjamin's place. The one who once cared only about getting rid of his brother now had great concern for his father. He was ready to make amends for what he had done to Joseph by offering himself in place of Benjamin. Godly sorrow had led to accepting responsibility for sin, to repentance, and to doing what could be done to make up for past wrongdoing. When Joseph saw this repentance, his heart overflowed in forgiveness (Gen. 45:1–8). God had used Joseph's tough love to bring reconciliation within his family.

CONCLUSION

These accounts of God's dealing with Abraham, Lot, Jacob, Joseph, and Joseph's brothers amply illustrate the example principle. Their stories help us understand how God deals with his people. Their responses to God are, then, examples for us. Sometimes they are examples to avoid—when they show us how we should not respond to God. At other times they model the faithful obedience that we should imitate. The secondary characteristics of their lives are irrelevant to their exemplary value; we, for instance, are not called to ride camels because Abraham did. Nor do Abraham's lie and Jacob's multiple wives justify deception or polygamy.

Abraham's lie, as we have seen, was an example of failure to trust God. Jacob's marrying multiple wives was no act of faithful obedience.

As noted above, the example principle is applicable to other Old Testament people who encounter God—to lesser characters as well as to people like Moses and David. Genesis 12:1–50:25, however, invites us to give special attention to this principle. God's dealings with the fathers and mothers of his people set the pattern. We have spent time here illustrating this principle so that you will understand it and be able to apply it elsewhere.

CHAPTER 3

RESTORATION INAUGURATED *at* SINAI, *Part A*

The Picture (or Typology) Principle

Exodus to Joshua

INTRODUCTION: WHERE WE HAVE BEEN

Genesis begins with the sad story of human rebellion. God's plan for blessing humanity has been shattered. Human beings no longer live in obedient fellowship with God. Their lives are characterized by strife with one another rather than by the harmonious fellowship God intended. Their relationship with the world God made for them to enjoy has become struggle. What should have been their home has become a place of alienation. Rebellion has warped every aspect of their lives and left them incapable of returning to their former blessing.

Genesis, however, ends with anticipation. God's promise to Abraham assures us that he will restore his gracious plan for humanity. Divine sufficiency will overcome human faithlessness and impotence. The rest of the Bible is the story of God's faithfulness to his promise. The fulfillment of this promise will encompass many steps, it will penetrate every area of human life, and it will be complete. It will go beyond the imagination of those who originally heard God's voice. God intends something more wonderful than what was lost by disobedience in Eden. This fulfillment, however, begins with the human descendants of Abraham. God will inaugurate the rest of his plan by establishing them as his people, by multiplying them and making them a great nation that reflects his character, and by giving them a land as a place of blessing and fellowship with him. They are to be both a testimony and an invitation to the nations. They will also foreshadow God's greater fulfillment to come.

I. RESTORATION INAUGURATED: THE STORY

We find the story of God's delivering Abraham's descendants from slavery in Egypt and his making covenant with them in Exodus through Deuteronomy (see **Figure 1**). Exodus begins by describing God's mighty deliverance from the abject slavery into which they had fallen (Ex. 1:1–15:21). Those who were once oppressed slaves of Pharaoh have become grateful servants of the living God. After a period of testing in the wilderness (Ex. 15:22–18:27) God comes to them on Mount Sinai and establishes his covenant with them (Ex. 19:1–24:18). The narrative continues by describing the construction of the tabernacle that would be the dwelling place of God in the center of their camp and the place of worship under this covenant (Ex. 25:1–40:38). An account of the people's faithlessness interrupts this description of God's provision for them to live in his presence. They violate God's covenant at its most basic level by making an idol, the golden calf (Ex. 32:1–35). Leviticus continues the description of the institutions of this covenant by describing the sacrificial system, the priesthood, and the laws that distinguish between what is clean and unclean. These are the provisions by which God's people must live if this gracious but holy God is to dwell among them.

Figure 1

From Moses' birth (Ex. 2:1–10) to his death (Deut. 34:1–12)

AN OVERVIEW OF EXODUS–DEUTERONOMY

OUT OF EGYPT
OUR GOD
"I am the Lord your God . . ." (Ex. 20:1)

Ex. 1:1–15:21	Delivered from Egypt
Ex. 15:22–18:27	Tested in the wilderness

AT SINAI
MY PRESENCE AMONG MY PEOPLE
". . . you shall be a special treasure to Me . . ." (Ex. 19:5)

Ex. 19:1–24:18	God's covenant with his people
Ex. 25:1–40:38	God's dwelling place among his people
Lev. 1:1–27:34	God's provisions for life in his presence

TOWARD THE PROMISED LAND
MY LAND
"So I have come . . . to bring them . . . to a good and large land . . . flowing with milk and honey . . ." (Ex. 3:8)

Num. 1:1–10:36	God's people organized for the journey
Num. 11:1–25:18	Failure to enter the land— the rebellious exodus generation
Num. 26:1–36:13	Preparation for entering the land— the obedient second generation
Deut. 1:1–34:12	Anticipation of entering the land— moses' warning to all generations

Numbers turns our attention from Sinai toward the promised land. This holy God, who revealed himself on Sinai, now dwells in their midst in the tabernacle. In the first ten chapters God prepares his people to leave Sinai and face the godless nations. He organizes them around his presence as the holy army of the Lord. Chapters 11–25 describe their rebellious journey from Sinai to the boundary of the promised land on the plains of Moab east of the Jordan. God first brought them to Kadesh Barnea on the southern border of that Land. There the generation delivered from Egypt forfeited its inheritance by rebelling against God and refusing to enter the land promised to them (Num. 14:1–45). The rest of this section is the sad story of their forty years of wandering in the desert. It concludes with their idolatrous worshiping of the Baal of Peor on the plains of Moab and their final destruction (Num. 25:1–18). In the final section of Numbers (chaps. 26–36) Moses prepares the next generation to enter the land by warning them against following the example of their elders. Here on the plains of Moab east of the Jordan they defeat two kings and get ready to enter the promised land proper, west of the Jordan.

Deuteronomy records Moses' final speech to them before they enter the land. He reiterates the history of God's goodness to them, reviews again the covenant with its stipulations, and urges them to be faithful. This instruction to the "second" generation calls every following generation to faithfulness. Thus the Pentateuch, the five books of Moses, ends with anticipation. God has delivered them from Egypt, he has made covenant with them and dwells in their midst, and he is about to take them into the promised land. The book of Joshua will confirm this third and final aspect of God's inaugurated restoration by describing both the conquest (Josh. 1:1–12:24) and settlement (Josh. 13:1–21:45) of the land. Joshua ends appropriately with the unity of God's people and a reaffirmation of the covenant (Josh. 22:1–24:33).

II. RESTORATION INAUGURATED: A PICTURE OF FULFILLMENT TO COME

In this chapter we will focus on the way in which God's deliverance of Abraham's descendants from Egyptian slavery foreshadows the—from the Old Testament vantage point—yet-to-come ultimate deliverance of humanity through Christ. Christ will accomplish this deliverance through both his first and second comings.

A. A Bondage That Was Spiritual as well as Physical.

First, we must pay attention to the plight of Abraham's descendants in Egypt. Their situation was a fitting picture of the impotence and misery of human beings enslaved to sin (Ex. 1:8–22). They were living in cruel bondage as slaves of Pharaoh, king of Egypt, condemned to the back-breaking task of building cities that magnified his sovereignty. Where was the promise of God? Yes, God had kept his promise to multiply them, but for what? For this life of dreary servitude? Thus they continually cried unto the Lord for his deliverance (Ex. 2:23).

We must not insert a false dichotomy between physical and spiritual bondage. Their bondage was physical, but it was more. They could not live in obedient fellowship with God because Pharaoh was their master. He, not God, directed their lives. For the same reason, they could not order their common life in a way that reflected God's character. They could not live in harmonious fellowship under God's sovereign direction. And, of course, they had no land to enjoy, no place for their common life in fellowship with God. Their situation aptly pictured the impotent bondage of sinful humanity alienated from God, from each other, and from the world. But God "heard their cry" (Ex. 2:23–25; 3:7–8).

B. A Restoration That Was Genuine but Inadequate.

If the Egyptian slavery of God's people depicts humanity's bondage to sin, then their deliverance must foreshadow Christ's provision of salvation. There are two things to remember if we would understand how this initial restoration of God's plan pictures or typifies the greater restoration to come. First, God's mighty deliverance of Abraham's descendants was a *genuine* restoration. God truly delivered them from physical and spiritual bondage in order to reestablish their relationship with him and constitute them as his people. It is not superficial details but the substance and nature of the deliverance that make it a type or picture of the work of Christ. Second, this restoration, though real, was *inadequate* in both depth and extent. Both of these characteristics are important for understanding the typological function of the deliverance from Egypt and all that was associated with it.

The genuineness of this Old Testament restoration establishes the character of God. It points to the kinds of things that Christ will achieve and the way he will achieve them. At the same time, its inadequacy underscores the need for his coming and highlights his full effectiveness. Together the genuineness and inadequacy of the old lay the foundation for final deliverance in Christ. They provide a picture or a sketch of God's ultimate solution. They furnish an outline and show us the contours that God's full restoration will take. They prepare the people of God to understand and grasp the ultimate fulfillment of his promise to Abraham. That is why we have called this chapter "restoration inaugurated"—not restoration completed.

In chapter 2 we introduced our first guideline for understanding the Old Testament, "The Example Principle." It focused on the way in which people responded to God. We are now ready to introduce our second guideline, "The Picture (Typological) Principle." This principle directs our attention to the way in which God's mighty acts of deliverance, the agents whom he uses, and the gracious institutions he establishes foreshadow the greater and final restoration to come. See **Figure 2**. In the next chapter we will examine how the Sinai covenant reflected God's character and thus how its stipulations continue to direct us to God and to provide moral guidance.

Figure 2

✓ 2nd GUIDELINE—THE PICTURE (TYPOLOGICAL) PRINCIPLE: WHAT GOD HAS DONE.

God's redemption of his people in the Old Testament is a sketch, picture, or type of the deeper redemption provided for his people through Christ's first and second comings. Thus God's Old Testament acts of deliverance look forward to Christ's work. Those God uses to redeem his people foreshadow Christ. The institutions of the old Covenant anticipate the salvation and benefits that Christ provides for the people of God.

III. RESTORATION INAUGURATED AND THE THREE PARTS OF GOD'S PLAN

There are three distinct phases to God's restoration for these initial recipients of the promise. First, by delivering them from Egypt God establishes himself as their God. "I am the Lord your God, who brought you out of land of Egypt, out of the house of bondage" (Ex. 20:1). He restores them to obedient fellowship with himself. Second, by making covenant with them at Sinai he comes to dwell with them and thus constitutes them the family/people of God—"I will take you as My people" (Ex. 6:7). The covenant shows them how to live in his presence and to reflect his character by their common life. Obedience to the Covenant produces harmonious fellowship. Finally, he brings them into the promised land—"For the Lord your God is bringing you into a good land" (Deut 8:7). This land is to be the place where they are free to live in obedient fellowship with God and harmonious fellowship with each other as the people of God. It will also be the place where they can enjoy a restored relationship with creation. Here God intends for them to be *at home.*

Thus, through delivering from Egypt, making covenant, and bringing his people into the promised land, God inaugurates the restoration promised to Abraham. He begins to restore the three relationships that are fundamental to his original plan for humanity and that were lost by sin. **Figures 3 and 4** show the correspondence between God's Original Plan, the Restoration Promised to Abraham, and the Restoration Inaugurated through Exodus, Covenant, and Land. In **Figure 3** we have added the next section to **Figure 2** of chapter 2. You will find the complete chart that includes these figures in Appendix 2. Let us look at the three phases or parts of this inaugurated restoration.

Figure 3

GOD'S PLAN FOR THE WORLD		THE OLD COVENANT
The World God's plan—established and lost (Gen. 1–11)	**A Family** → Restoration promised (Gen. 12–15)	**A Nation** → Restoration inaugurated (Ex.–Josh.)
ADAM	ABRAHAM	MOSES

Creator

The three parts of God's plan

1. Obedient fellowship with God.
2. Harmonious fellowship with the people of God.
3. Responsible enjoyment of God's world.

JUDGMENT · REBELLION · PROMISES

CREATION

Humanity in God's image

God
|
Innocence/Disobedience
/ \
Humanity   World

Restoration of God's plan promised to Abraham.

1. "The Lord said to Abraham" (Gen. 12:1)
2. "I will make you into a great nation." (Gen. 12:2)
3. "To your offspring I will give this land." (Gen. 12:7)

"All peoples on the earth shall be blessed through you." (Gen. 12:3)

God
|
Promise
/ \
Humanity   World

Exodus through Deuteronomy

1. Our God—the exodus. "I am the Lord your God who brought you out of Egypt out of the land of slavery." (Ex. 10:1)
2. My people—Mount Sinai. "I will take you as my own people, and I will be your God" (Ex. 6:7)

Joshua

3. My land—Canaan. "For the Lord your God is bringing you into a good land. (Deut. 8:7)

They forsook the Lord God of their fathers . . . (so) he sold them to their enemies all around." (Judg. 2:12)

God
|
My Law
/ \
Humanity   World

Figure 4

God's Plan Established & Lost *Genesis 1–11*	**Restoration Promised** *Genesis 12–50*	**Restoration Inaugurated** *Exodus–Joshua*
1. Obedient fellowship with God.	→ 1. "I will be with you and bless you . . ." (Gen. 26:3)	→ 1. Our God—the exodus: "I am the Lord your God . . ." (Ex. 20:1)
2. Harmonious fellowship among God's people.	→ 2. "I will make you a great nation . . ." (Gen. 12:2)	→ 2. My people—the Sinai covenant: "I will take you as my people . . ." (Ex. 6:7)
3. Responsible enjoyment of the world.	→ 3. "To your descendants I will give this land." (Gen. 12:7)	→ 3. My land—the place of blessing: "For the Lord your God is bringing you into a good land . . ." (Deut. 8:7)

A. Part One, the Exodus: "Our God"

A Genuine Deliverance. First, God established a true relationship with the descendants of Abraham by delivering them from Egypt. Because he had brought them out of Egypt, they could call him "our God." This deliverance demonstrated both his merciful faithfulness and his power. By delivering them he "remembered" his promise to Abraham. He "heard" their cry (Ex. 2:23–24; 3:7–8). He is indeed their great benefactor. He has done for them what no other could do and what they could not do for themselves. His faithful character is expressed by his covenant name, *Yahweh*, often translated "Lord" in our English Bibles: "I am *Yahweh* your God who brought you out of the land of Egypt, out of the house of bondage" (Ex. 20:2, author translation).

This deliverance demonstrates his mighty power. He is a great king, a mighty warrior. He delivered them with a "mighty hand" and an "outstretched arm" (Deut. 26:8). When Moses goes to Pharaoh the conflict is over who is the sovereign God. Is Pharaoh God, or is the Lord God? Pharaoh was considered the incarnation of the sun god. He claimed to maintain the balance of nature upon which Egyptian life depended. Thus he assumed divine sovereignty over God's people whom he considered his slaves. God demonstrated that he, and he alone, "is the Lord." This demonstration begins with the sign of the serpent the first time Moses confronts Pharaoh (Ex. 7:8–13). God substantiates his identity by the ten plagues (Ex. 7:14–11:10; 12:29–36), by bringing his people through the Red Sea,[14] and by destroying Pharaoh and his army in that sea (Ex. 6:7; 7:5, 17; 8:10, 22; 9:14, 29; 10:2; 11:7; 14:4, 18). By these mighty acts of deliverance God invites Pharaoh and all the people to acknowledge him as the true God and to submit to his sovereignty.

The female cobra was part of Pharaoh's crown and a symbol of Egypt. When Aaron, at Moses' command, threw down his rod and it became a serpent before Pharaoh, he was challenging Pharaoh's authority (Ex. 7:8–13). The magicians of Egypt did the same. When, however, the

---

14. Or the "Sea of Reeds": see the footnote to Ex. 10:19 in *The Voice* translation of the Bible.

serpent that had been Moses' rod swallowed their serpents, the message was clear: the God whom Moses served would "swallow" a pharaoh who would not acknowledge his sovereignty (compare Ex. 7:12 and 15:12). Several of the plagues were probably intended to be direct attacks on various Egyptian gods (Num. 33:4). These plagues clearly disrupted the cycles of nature that the gods were thought to preserve. The Nile god and the sun god were two of the most important Egyptian deities. The Nile god was the one believed to have brought Egypt into being and who, by the annual fluctuation of the river, continued to sustain its life. The sun god was the chief Egyptian deity. They believed he was the creator whose

> **By these mighty acts of deliverance God invites Pharaoh and all the people to acknowledge him as the true God and to submit to his sovereignty.**

daily rising represented life and resurrection. Thus God begins these plagues by turning the water of the Nile into blood in order to demonstrate his sovereignty over the god who gave Egypt existence (Ex. 7:14–25). The Lord is the true master of the Nile and thus of Egypt's life. In the ninth plague, God draws this contest toward a conclusion by blocking the light of the sun (Ex. 10:21–29). The palpable darkness that followed demonstrated that he was the Creator and the only true source of light and life. The death of the firstborn is the final plague that establishes the authority of *Yahweh* as the only true God (Ex. 11:1–10; 12:29–36). This attack is a direct defeat for Pharaoh's divine pretensions. His firstborn was also considered a god. Pharaoh was not able to protect the lives of the firstborn of all Egypt, much less of his own firstborn heir. Because Pharaoh would not let God's "firstborn," God's people, leave Egypt, God struck down his firstborn.

God began this substantiation of his deity by demonstrating his power over the Nile. He brings it to a conclusion by demonstrating his power over the Red Sea: he opens the sea so that his people can escape, and then returns it to its channel to accomplish Pharaoh's final destruction (Ex. 13:17–14:21). The Lord God has "swallowed" the one who clung to his own divine pretensions and refused to acknowledge God as the only true God. You can hear the songs of Moses and Miriam celebrating this great deliverance in Exodus 15:1–21.

Because God has been faithful to his promise and delivered his people with such power, he is to be their absolute Sovereign: "I am the Lord your God who brought you out of the land of Egypt" (Ex. 20:2). They are once again to live in obedient fellowship with him. The first four commandments (Ex. 20:1–11) emphasize this relationship. God's people must have "no other gods" besides him (Ex. 20:1–3). They must not try to manipulate God by making images of him or by using his name in incantations (Ex. 20:4–7). They must not disrespect his name. They acknowledge his lordship over all of their lives by keeping the Sabbath as a time of rest set apart to him (Ex. 20:8–11). They were called to follow the greatest commandment: "You shall love the Lord your God with all your heart, with all your soul, and with all your strength" (Deut. 6:5).

Living in this way under God's sovereignty would produce the exact opposite of Pharaoh's oppressive slavery. Under God's rule they would follow the second greatest commandment, "you shall love your neighbor as yourself" (Lev. 19:18). Thus they would live in harmonious fellowship with one another and enjoy the abundant benefits of the land he would give them. Best of all, he would be resident among them: "I will dwell among the children of Israel and will be their God. And they shall know that I am the LORD their God, who brought them up out of the land of Egypt, that I may dwell among them. I am the LORD their God" (Ex. 29:45–46). Thus this deliverance was an appropriate picture of the way in which Christ would deliver his people from the oppression of sin to live in fellowship with God, through the freedom of the Spirit, in anticipation of the final heavenly homeland. It also anticipates the final judgment when God will destroy all evil as he once destroyed the oppression of Pharaoh.

An Inadequate Deliverance. Yet almost from the beginning the limitations of this deliverance were evident. God's deliverance did not yet extend to "all nations" as God had promised Abraham. Furthermore, it did not yet adequately reach the depths of the human heart. There were those who lived in faithfulness to God; however, the people of God repeatedly turned away from him. This rebellion began even at Mount Sinai when they broke the newly given covenant at its most basic level by making an idol in the form of a golden calf (Ex. 32:1–35). This act of faithlessness was equivalent to committing adultery on the honeymoon. Faithless rebellion continued to characterize that first generation of people delivered from Egypt throughout their time in the wilderness. It raised its ugly head at Kadesh Barnea when they forfeited their inheritance by refusing to trust God and enter the land (Num. 14:1–45). It manifested itself again on the plain of Moab near the end of the wilderness wandering when they intermixed with the Moabites and began to worship their gods (Num. 25:1–18). The disobedience of that first generation was a warning to the generations to follow and an ominous sign of the way their children would follow the gods of the nations once they entered the promised land (Deut. 31:16; Judg. 2:17; 10:6; 13–17). The account of rebellion continues first in Judges and then throughout Samuel and Kings to the Exile. Surely the time will come when God, in faithfulness to his promise, will so redeem his people from sin that he destroys the power of evil that binds the human heart and establishes a people who live in harmony and in fellowship with him.

A Picture of the Deliverance Brought by Christ. Yes, God's delivering his people from Egypt anticipated what he would do in Christ both by its genuine effectiveness and by its inadequacy. Pharaoh claimed them as his. If Pharaoh was their master, they could not serve God. They could not live in fellowship with God as a society that reflected God's character. God delivered them from bondage to Pharaoh so that they could serve him. Christ would deliver them from the bondage of sin that still enslaved their hearts and thus would enable them to serve God "in spirit and in truth" (John 4:23). The deliverance he would provide would be offered to the nations of the world. By delivering his people from Egypt God demonstrated his mighty power over all the forces of evil and his faithfulness to his promise. By that same power he would conquer death and hell through the death and resurrection of Jesus.

The Passover. We have noted that the institutions God established for his redeemed people and the agents he used to deliver them also foreshadowed Christ. The Passover celebration that God instituted the night the people left Egypt is an example of the former; the great deliverer Moses, of the latter. God's people celebrated their freedom and reenacted this great deliverance every year by keeping the feast of the Passover (Ex. 12:1–13:16). God had commanded each household on the night they came out of Egypt to offer a lamb and put its blood over the door so that the angel who struck the firstborn of Egypt would "pass over" their firstborn. Then they ate the lamb roasted in anticipation of their imminent deliverance. The annual repetition of this meal reminded them that the Passover lamb stood not only for the firstborn of each household but also for the deliverance of the entire people of God, his own "firstborn," from slavery in Egypt. Christ would be the great Passover "lamb of God" (John 1:29, 36) who by offering himself would provide the necessary deeper deliverance from sin so that salvation could be offered to the nations

> God would offer his own 'firstborn' (Heb 1:6) to redeem for himself a 'firstborn' people (Heb 12:23).

of the world. God would offer his own "firstborn" (Heb. 1:6) to redeem for himself a "firstborn" people (Heb. 12:23). Through participating by faith in this great Passover lamb, all would be able to participate in this redemption just as God's people had once participated by eating the lamb in Egypt.

Moses. No other Old Testament persons loom larger than Moses. God delivered his people through Moses. God did mighty wonders through

Moses. God revealed himself in a unique way through Moses, with whom he communed "face to face" (Num. 12:6–8). It was Moses who went up Mount Sinai. It was Moses who received the tablets of the Ten Commandments. God's law was the "law of Moses." The first five books of the Bible are the "books of Moses." Deuteronomy, the last of these books, is Moses' speech to the second and following generations urging them not to imitate the disobedience of the generation delivered from Egypt. Thus it is no surprise that Moses is a picture or type of Christ as both revealer and deliverer. God may have spoken to Moses "face to face," but through the incarnate Son he has revealed his very "face" to all who will believe (John 1:14–18). Moses abandoned Pharaoh's palace and suffered with God's people in order to deliver them from bondage to Pharaoh and unite them as God's covenant people (Heb. 11:24–26). Christ descended from heaven and assumed our humanity in order to make this deeper deliverance a reality (Heb. 10:5–10). Moses built a tabernacle as a dwelling place for God among his unclean people. By providing for cleansing from sin Christ has made the people of God a tabernacle or temple indwelt by the Spirit of God (1 Cor. 6:19). Just as God's people of old were to reflect his character by their common life in accord with God's covenant, so we are to reflect that character by loving one another as Christ has loved us (John 13:34–35).

B. Part Two, the Sinai Covenant: "My People"

A Covenant That Establishes and Confirms the People of God. The harmonious life of God's people under his rule turns our attention to the second phase of God's inaugurated restoration. God brought the people to Mount Sinai in the wilderness and there made covenant with them. The covenant, of course, confirmed him as their God, but it also established the pattern for their common life together as the people of God. This common life was to be an expression of their unique relationship to God; note how God claims his people when he calls them "my son, my firstborn" (Ex. 4:22–23) and "a special treasure" (Ex. 3:7; 19:5), and affirms that they are to be a "holy nation" and a "kingdom of priests" (Ex. 19:6). If God is to dwell among them, then their life together must reflect his character. The Ten Commandments, found in Exodus 20:1–20, are the basic document of this covenant. Their significance is fleshed out in the other laws given in the books of Moses (see chap. 4). God used a type of covenant that would have been familiar to his people because it was widely used in their time. The rulers of contemporary empires would make this kind of covenant with the lesser kings who served them. The first stipulations of the covenant document would establish the exclusive sovereignty of the emperors over these lesser kings. We have seen above that this is what the first four commandments do (Ex. 20:1–11). The remaining stipulations, then, regulate the way the vassals treat each other. So commandments five through ten give an outline of how God's people are to treat each other so that they reflect his character (Ex. 20:12–17). The command to honor father and mother establishes proper respect for legitimate authority. The prohibition against murder is meant to teach self-giving love and kindness toward others; the forbidding of adultery teaches sexual purity; the ban against theft reinforces generosity; and the prohibition against false witness affirms the importance of integrity. Finally, "you shall not covet" shows that God is concerned about the heart. God forbids his people to nurture a selfish, greedy heart.

A Covenant Unable to Adequately Deal with Sin. Although this covenant embodied the purposes of God, it had no adequate remedy for sin. Sin prevents God's people from coming into his presence. Sin keeps them from reflecting God's character. This covenant was not able to overcome the hardness of the people's hearts. Furthermore, God's promise of blessing had not yet reached the nations of the world.

Nothing both demonstrates the saving purpose of God and betrays the inadequacy of the Sinai covenant like the sanctuary described in the Old Testament as the tent or the tabernacle. It was the most important institution of the Sinai covenant. This is the place where God would dwell among his people and they would have access to him. Much of Exodus describes God's plans for this tent-shrine (Ex. 24:12–31:18) and Moses' execution of those plans (Ex. 35:1–40:33). Thus it is no surprise that Exodus climaxes with the glory of God filling his dwelling place (Ex. 40:34–38). Leviticus, then, at the heart of the Pentateuch, describes the sacrifices and priesthood appropriate for approaching God at this tabernacle. It also catalogs laws of ceremonial and moral cleanliness that were required of the people among whom God would dwell. While God's people were in the wilderness this tabernacle was at the center of their camp. This was God's marvelous gift representing his presence among them. See **Figure 5**, a diagram of this tabernacle.

Figure 5

THE TABERNACLE

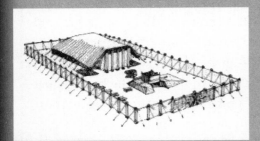

The tabernacle was to provide a place where God might dwell among his people. The term "tabernacle" sometimes refers to the tent, including the Holy Place and the Most Holy Place, which was covered with embroidered curtains. But in other places it refers to the entire complex, including the curtained court in which the tent stood.

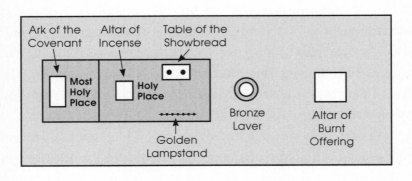

This illustration shows the relative positions of the tabernacle furniture used in Israelite worship. The tabernacle is enlarged for clarity.

Nelson's Complete Book of Bible Maps and Charts © 1993 by Thomas Nelson, Inc.

The inner sanctum of this tabernacle was the Most Holy Place, where God dwelt among his people. In here was the ark of the covenant, a gold-covered box approximately 131×79×79 cm (52×31×31 in) in size, which served as the throne of God. The outer sanctum, or Holy Place, was furnished with the golden altar of incense, the sevenfold golden lampstand, and a golden table. Twelve fresh loaves of bread were placed on this table each week. The golden altar was the place where God received the prayers of his people. The lampstand represented God as their light. The golden table signified his provision. His presence provided for them and showed them the way to live. His presence confirmed them in obedient fellowship and united them as his unique people who were to live in harmony and thus reflect his character.

The inadequacy of the Sinai covenant becomes clear when we turn to the outer court of the tabernacle. This outer court contained the altar of burnt offering and the sea or great basin filled with water for purification. The people of God could go no further than this court. God dwelt

> **The altar of burnt offering in the outer court helps us to understand why access to God was so limited. It was limited because of the sins of his people.**

in their midst, but they could not come into his presence. Only the high priest could enter that inner sanctum, the throne room of God—but only on one day each year, the great Day of Atonement (Lev. 16:1–34; see Heb. 9:1–11). The priests alone entered the outer sanctum or Holy Place. Here they ministered daily, unable to gain further access. The altar of burnt offering in the outer court helps us to understand why access to God was so limited. It was limited because of the sins of his people. God is absolutely holy. His people, however, are not holy. The altar of burnt offering was the place of offering for sin. The exact significance of the different sacrifices described in Leviticus 1:1–7:38 may not be fully clear.

There can be no doubt, however, that the burnt offering, sin offering, and guilt offering all pertained to the removal of sin. These sacrifices took the place of the worshiper and thus ceremonially removed the guilt and impurity of sin so that the worshiper could approach God so far as that was allowed in the tabernacle. The peace offering was a time of renewed fellowship with God and the grain offering an appropriate expression

> **The prophets emphasized this moral impurity and Jesus showed that it was the only true barrier to fellowship with God.**

of gratitude for God's provision. On the day of the high priest's annual entrance into the Most Holy Place, he had to prepare by sacrifice: first a sacrifice for himself and his family, then a sacrifice for the sins of all the people. The limited access provided by these sacrifices and their perpetual repetition showed their inability to adequately deal with the sin that separated God's people from him (Heb. 10:1–4). At the same time they pointed forward to a better sacrifice that would enable God's people to truly enter his heavenly presence.

It is true that many non-sinful things could make a person "impure" and thus bar them from tabernacle worship. Eating an unclean animal, touching a dead body, or menstruation and other bodily functions all kept people from approaching God in worship. These things were object lessons that taught people the need for care when coming into the presence of a holy God. However, the crucial barrier to approaching God was sin. These sins were the issues dealt with in the Ten Commandments, the ten fundamental "matters" that concern God. The prophets emphasized this moral impurity and Jesus showed that it was the only true barrier to fellowship with God (Mark 7:18–23). It was clear from these Sinai-covenant institutions of tabernacle, priesthood, and sacrifice: God's presence was central to what it meant to be God's people. And yet his people did not have free access to him. Their sin separated them from their God.

Animal sacrifices only reminded the worshipers that they needed a sacrifice adequate for the removal of sin.

An Anticipation of the Better Covenant. Thus, that covenant and its tabernacle prepared God's people for the fulfillment that he would accomplish in Christ. God dwelt among his people in the tabernacle of the Sinai covenant, but, as we have seen, sin severely limited their access. The provisions of that covenant for the removal of sin looked forward to what God would accomplish. By his obedient self-offering Christ would provide an adequate remedy for sin. He would "cleanse our conscience from dead works to serve the living God" (Heb. 9:14). By so doing he would become an effective High Priest able to cleanse his people from their sin and free them from its bondage. God's people would be able to "draw near" to God through him (Heb. 7:19, 25). Their High Priest would bring them not into an earthly Most Holy Place but into heaven itself.

The New Testament also uses this tabernacle imagery in another, complementary way. At the incarnation Christ became a new "tabernacle" (John 1:14). In the person of his Son, the God who once dwelt in the tabernacle assumed the humanity of Jesus. God's Son would purify that

> By his obedient self-offering Christ would . . . . 'cleanse our conscience from dead works to serve the living God' (Heb 9:14).

humanity by his own obedience so that all who are joined to him by faith would become the new, pure sanctuary indwelt by the presence of God through the Holy Spirit (2 Cor. 6:16).[15] Thus purified and indwelt, God's people would be a community called to reflect his character by living in holiness and by obeying Christ's command to "love one another as I have loved you" (John 13:34; 15:12).

---

15. Compare 2 Cor. 6:16 with Lev. 26:12; Jer. 32:38; Ezek. 37:27.

C. Part Three, the Conquest: "My Land"

God's dwelling among his people in the tabernacle leads naturally to a discussion of the promised land, for the land was the place where God's people were to live in unhindered fellowship with him. At the end of the Pentateuch, however, God's people have not yet entered the land. Two phases of this inaugurated restoration are complete. First, by delivering Abraham's descendants from Egyptian bondage, God has established himself as their God. He confirmed this new reality at Sinai by coming to dwell in their midst. Second, there at Sinai he established them as a great nation called to live in fellowship with him and reflect his character. God dwells among them but they still live as an armed camp in the alien world of the desert. The full blessings of life with God will not be theirs until they receive their inheritance in the promised land. There God will restore their relationship with the world lost through Adam's disobedience: "For the LORD your God is bringing you into a good land" (Deut. 8:7). This would be their new Eden, the place of blessing and fellowship with God. They were delivered from bondage to Pharaoh in Egypt so that they might live in blessed fellowship with God in the promised land.

> They were delivered from bondage to Pharaoh in Egypt so that they might live in blessed fellowship with God in the promised land.

The Promised Land as the Place of Blessing and Fellowship with God. The Lord chose the land of Canaan as the place where he would dwell in fellowship with his people. God alone could call it "my land" (2 Chron. 7:20; Jer. 2:7; 16:18). He would give it to his people as a gift (Deut. 3:18; 5:31; 12:1; 15:4; 19:2, 14; 25:19) in gracious fulfillment of his promise (Deut. 1:8, 35; 6:10, 18, 23; 7:13; 8:1; 9:5; 10:11; 11:9, 21; 19:8; 26:3, 15; 28:11; 30:20; 31:7; 34:4) on the condition that they faithfully keep his covenant. They would enjoy the blessing of this land as his tenants. This was to be their home—the place of stable, permanent, settled life in the presence of God. Thus it would be the place where his people would enjoy the abundant life that he would give to the faithful. It was, indeed, a new Eden. That is why God had instructed his people to keep it totally free of defilement once they had entered it. Thus Joshua was commanded to destroy the Canaanites whose iniquity was now full (Gen. 15:16). The sacrificial system was in place to deal with human weakness, but any member of the community who violated the covenant through idolatry, murder, or adultery must be put to death. Eden would not be Eden if anything were allowed to "pollute the land" and mar this holy environment.

The Promised Land as the Place of Disobedience and Failure. The book of Joshua recounts the story of how God brought them into their inheritance in the land. Various limitations, however, show that the promised land was only the preliminary place of fellowship. It was a type or picture of what was to come. First, we have already seen that the Sinai covenant provided only limited access to God. This limitation was not lifted when God's people entered the land. Second, the life of the faithful in the promised land might be long and good—but it was still temporal. This new Eden was less than the first Eden. The ultimate curse of death had not been removed. Third, the blessings of fellowship with God were not yet offered to the nations of the world. Finally, and most important, God's people failed to practice the obedient faithfulness appropriate for promised-land life in God's presence. The story of rebellion begun in the wilderness continues from Judges through the end of Kings. God had taken his people out of the wilderness, but he had not yet taken the wilderness out of them.

Throughout this history the consequences of disobedience were always exclusion from God's presence and loss of the land's benefits. During the time of the Judges people like the Midianites took the benefits of the land for themselves (Judg. 6:1–6). When Saul died the Philistines overran the whole land west of the Jordan (1 Sam. 31:7). During the time of the kings the land suffered dismemberment and diminution until the people were finally expelled through exile. The people returned from exile under Nehemiah and Ezra, but they did not regain their sovereignty over the land, nor did they rid themselves of the unclean practices that had led to their exile (Ezra 9:1–14; Neh. 13:1–31).

The Promised Land as a Picture or Type of the New Heaven and Earth. A proper understanding of the promised land as a type of the eternal destiny of the resurrected people of God will bring this chapter into perspective. The new heaven and new earth will be all that the earthly promised land longed for: an eternal place of the fullest fellowship with God, free of any uncleanness; a home for the people of God. There, freed at last from all sin, the common life of God's people will perfectly reflect his character. Nothing there will detract from their fullest well-being. Thus God's people at the end of the Pentateuch and the end of the Old Testament and throughout Scripture are a people anticipating this true promised land. God delivered his people of old from the bondage of Egypt and made them his people by coming to dwell among them in the tabernacle. So God has now delivered his people from sin through Christ and filled them with God's presence through the Holy Spirit. We, like those once delivered from Egypt, are on our way to the promised land (1 Cor. 10:1–13; Heb. 3:16–4:11). At Christ's return the faithful will enter the true homeland of the people of God, the heavenly Jerusalem, the new heaven and earth (Heb. 11:13–16; 12:22–24; Rev. 21:1–22:21).

CONCLUSION

God's delivering his people from Egypt, making covenant with them at Sinai, and bringing them into the promised land compose one great act of salvation: exodus, covenant, conquest. This powerful deliverance is fundamental to the people of God in the Old Testament. By this series of saving acts God inaugurated the restoration of his plan for the whole world in accord with his promise to Abraham. Thus, we should not be surprised that it foreshadows in manifold ways the fullness of salvation brought by Christ.

Figure 6 clarifies some of the main lines of thought in this chapter. Look first at the column entitled "Christ's First Coming." Just as God delivered his people from bondage to Pharaoh and from the gods of Egypt by Moses, so he has delivered us from bondage to Satan, sin, and death through the death and resurrection of Christ. At Sinai he came to dwell among his people in the tabernacle and thus gave them a covenant that would show them how to express his character. At Pentecost his people, through the work of Christ, were filled with the Spirit of God. Thereby they were empowered to reflect God's character by loving one another as Christ had loved them (John 13:34–35; 15:12). After Christ's first coming his people were still "waiting for the land." We are part of God's people who have received God's Spirit as a guarantee and foretaste of that future inheritance (Eph. 1:14), but we continue to live in a world polluted by sin.

Figure 6

THE TYPOLOGY OF EXODUS, COVENANT, AND LAND

	Christ's First Coming	Christ's Second Coming
EXODUS	**The Cross** Reconciled to God; delivered from sin	**The Judgment** Evil destroyed; righteousness established
COVENANT AT SINAI	**Pentecost** Filled with his Spirit; reflecting His character	Unhindered fellowship with God and his people
THE PROMISED LAND	Waiting for the fulfillment of our inheritance	**The New Jerusalem** Entering the fullness of our inheritance

At Christ's second coming (the next column of **Figure 6**) the victory won through the cross and empty tomb will be fully revealed. All evil will be destroyed. Righteousness will be fully established. As God was vindicated over Pharaoh and the gods of Egypt, so now he is vindicated before the world over all the forces of evil. God's people, who once had

God's tabernacle among them and then became the temple of the Living God, will now live in his direct presence. We have no title in the appropriate space because this fellowship can now be described as nothing short of life in the heavenly New Jerusalem. This Jerusalem is more real than any earthly city (Heb. 11:9–10). It is the dwelling place of God. All evil is excluded. It provides the context and gives shape and substance to the community of God's people in blessed fellowship with him. When Christ returns we enter the fullness of our inheritance. We will be forever at home with the family of God.

Every Old Testament person God uses to bring deliverance is, in some way, a type of Christ. Every divine intervention for the salvation of his people anticipates the work of Christ. Every Old Testament redemptive institution finds fulfillment in the salvation Christ provides. The way in which these individuals, interventions, and institutions are types of Christ is dependent upon the way God uses them in the Old Testament. It is not superficial details but substance that is determinative.

It is important to distinguish between the Example Principle and the Typological (Picture) Principle. The same person can be both an example for us to follow and a type of Christ. Insofar as God used Moses to deliver his people, Moses foreshadows Christ; insofar as Moses responded to God in faithful obedience, he is an example for us to follow. This book will help you gain a deeper understanding of this subject by suggesting other typological relationships in some of the following chapters. Meanwhile, in the next chapter we turn to the contemporary significance of the law that God gave Moses on Mount Sinai.

4

RESTORATION INAUGURATED
at SINAI, *Part B*

The Pattern Principle

Exodus to Joshua

It was Sunday night. The pastor had just risen to preach. He read Old Testament verses that pronounced the death penalty on such things as murder, adultery, and kidnapping (see, for instance, Num. 35:30; Lev. 20:10; Ex. 21:16). Others in the congregation were probably thinking what I was thinking: "How is he going to preach on these verses?" He began by saying something like this: "I believe in the death penalty for murder but nor for these other sins." I was shocked. How can we glibly say that one command in the Old Testament law still applies but deny the continuing relevance of other similar commands?

We won't find the answer to this question by a more detailed study of Hebrew grammar—as important as that may be. This pastor had studied Hebrew. Our answer lies elsewhere. We need a clearer understanding of the function of the Mosaic law for the people of God. We must grasp the distinctions that the Old Testament itself makes between several different kinds of laws and their functions. We must remember what we learned in chapter 3: God's Old Testament salvation was an anticipation of what he would accomplish through Christ. Our discussion of this issue will result in the formulation of our third principle for understanding the Old Testament. In chapter 2 we introduced the Example Principle. In chapter 3, the Typological (or Picture) Principle. In this chapter we will formulate the Pattern Principle.

I. GOD'S LAW AND GOD'S PEOPLE

Let's begin by looking at the function of God's law for the people of God. As we learned in chapter 3, God did not arbitrarily establish his law. His law is an expression of his holy nature. He gave his law to his people so that they would reflect the character of the God who dwelt among them. Just as he is distinct from the gods of the nations, so his people are to live an exemplary life before the peoples of the world (2 Sam. 7:22–24). The nations were to see—and be attracted by—the character of God in the common life of the people of God. The way God's people treated one another was to be a reflection of God's great love and grace toward them.

The situation of the people of God since the coming of Christ differs from the situation of God's ancient people in several ways. First, we no longer live in an ancient Canaanite environment. Second, during our present earthly pilgrimage to the heavenly city we are not a nation like ancient Israel: we are not a political or ethnic unity. The church of God is characterized by great ethnic diversity scattered throughout many lands. Third, as we saw in chapter 3, Christ has fulfilled the Old Testament sacrificial system and clarified the nature of true moral purity.

If, however, the Old Testament law was a reflection of God's character, we cannot simply disregard it because of these differences. The people of God since the coming of Christ have always affirmed the continuing relevance of the moral teaching found in God's law. They have continued to use the Ten Commandments as a basis for moral instruction. There are three classical ways in which this relevance has been described: The

Religious Use of the Law, The Civil Use of the Law, and The Moral Use of the Law. To these we add a fourth, which we have titled "The Evangelical Use of the Law." See **Figure 1** below.

Figure 1

FOUR APPLICATIONS OF THE LAW

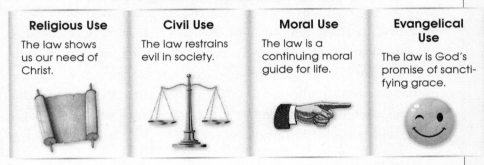

Religious Use	Civil Use	Moral Use	Evangelical Use
The law shows us our need of Christ.	The law restrains evil in society.	The law is a continuing moral guide for life.	The law is God's promise of sanctifying grace.

A. The Religious Use of the Law

The law shows us our desperate need for Christ. It shows us how far we fall short of God's holy character. Thus it exposes our need not only for forgiveness, but for the cleansing and transformation necessary for us to dwell in his presence. In this way the law is, as Paul says, a "schoolmaster" (Gal. 3:24 KJV). Martin Luther called it the "hammer" that drives us to Christ. We see God's moral law exposing the sinfulness of the human heart in Romans 7:1–23. God's law diagnoses our sinfulness and points us to the physician who can cure us.

B. The Civil Use of the Law

Good laws restrain evil in society. One of the purposes of the laws of any nation is to keep bad people from doing bad things. The laws of a nation may not be able to make bad people good, but they can deter bad people from doing evil. Thus many followers of Jesus throughout history have believed that the laws of the nations where they lived should reflect the moral teaching of God's Old Testament law. We should not seek to make laws that force people to believe in Jesus or to follow certain religious observances. There is, however, no reason why followers of Jesus should not encourage the nations in which they live to make laws that reflect the respect for persons, life, and property taught in the Old Testament.

C. The Moral Use of the Law

The law is a continuing moral guide for life. Many Christians believe that the law gives continuing moral guidance to those who have been transformed by Christ through the Spirit of God. The law provides guidance that keeps "walking in the Spirit" from degenerating into simply doing what I feel like I should do. One who walks in the Spirit, for instance, must never commit adultery or indulge in other forms of sexual impurity. The moral teaching of Paul's letters summarizes and applies much of the moral teaching of the Old Testament.

D. The Evangelical Use of the Law

The law is God's promise of sanctifying grace. What God commands us to do in the law, he will give us the grace to do. We said that we were going to add this use of the law to the previous three "classical" uses of the law. And yet this use of the law as God's promise has deep roots in the Christian tradition. This principle is expressed in Saint Augustine's prayer in his *Confessions*: "Lord, command [me to do] what you will, but will what you command" (*Confessions*, 202). This use of the law complements the first use of the law given above. The religious use shows us our need of God's grace in Christ, while the evangelical use assures us that God's grace is available.

II. BIBLICAL DISTINCTIONS WITHIN GOD'S LAW

If the moral teaching of the Old Testament law continues to be relevant in the ways given above, then what is that moral teaching? How, since we are not a nation in ancient Canaan and since fulfillment has come in Christ, does the Old Testament law continue to give us moral guidance? In order to answer this question, we must first observe some distinctions within the law. On the basis of the Old Testament we can discern three types of commandments. We have titled these The Greatest Commandments, The Ten Commandments, and The Everyday Commandments. See **Figure 2**.

Figure 2

THREE TYPES OF COMMANDMENTS

The Greatest Commandments	The Ten Commandments	The Everyday Commandments

The Greatest Commandments

Deuteronomy 6:4–6

⁴"Hear, O Israel: The LORD our God, the LORD is one! ⁵You shall love the LORD your God with all your heart, with all your soul, and with all your strength. ⁶"And these words which I command you today, shall be in your heart;"

Leviticus 19:18

"You shall not take vengeance, not bear any grudge against the children of your people, but you shall love your neighbor as yourself: I am the LORD."

The Ten Commandments

Exodus 20:1–11

1. "You shall have no other gods before Me."

2. "You shall not make for yourself a carved image—any likeness of anything that is in heaven above, or . . . the earth beneath or . . . the water under the earth."

3. "You shall not take the name of the LORD your God in vain, for the LORD will not hold him guiltless who takes his name in vain."

4. "Remember the Sabbath day, to keep it holy. Six days you shall labor and do all your work, but the seventh day Is the Sabbath of the LORD your God; in it you shall do no work . . ."

Exodus 20:12–17

5. "Honor your father and your mother, that your days may be long upon the land which the LORD you God is giving you . . ."

6. "You shall not murder."

7. "You shall not commit adultery."

8. "You shall not steal."

9. "You shall not bear false witness against your neighbor."

10. "You shall not covet . . . anything . . ."

The Everyday Commandments

Explanation:

The application of the *Greatest Commandments* as explained by the *Ten Commandments* to everyday life before Christ came.

Significance:

The way these commandments apply the more basic laws help us understand how to apply God's moral principles to our lives.

III. THE GREATEST COMMANDMENTS

There can be little disagreement about the central role of Deuteronomy 6:4–6 and Leviticus 19:18 in biblical faith or about the fundamental nature of their content. Their importance was affirmed not only by Jesus but by the scribe of his day (Luke 10:25–28). God's ancient people confessed their faith in the words of Deuteronomy 6:4–6. These verses expressed their complete loyalty to the living God alone. The Hebrew

> Thus the problem with these two Greatest Commandments is not their relevance but their generality. How do we love God and others in the course of our daily lives?

word for "heart" included both emotions and intellect. It encompassed the entire inward person. Thus when Jesus added the word "mind"—"you shall love the Lord your God with all your heart, with all your soul, with all your *mind*, and with all your strength" (italics added)—he was simply clarifying the verse's meaning (Mark 12:29–31). God's people are to serve him, and him alone, with their feelings, their intellect, their bodily strength, and with everything else that they are. This kind of love is not merely an emotion, but a commitment and devotion that results in obedience. Those who thus love God desire the "words" of God to be on their hearts so that they can obey with spontaneity. God's people were to love him wholly as the proper response to his great love for them—expressed in his delivering them from bondage and making them his own people.

The arrow in **Figure 2** points downward from Deuteronomy 6:4–6 to Leviticus 19:18. The command to love one's neighbor is an expression of love for God alone. This commandment is the fundamental principle underlying the way God's people are to treat one another and reflect God's character in their common lives. By his death and resurrection Jesus discloses the full significance of these commandments. He calls on us to love God in response to God's great love for us revealed in the cross. He commands us to love each other as he loved us when he went to the cross (John 13:34–35; 15:9–13).

Thus the problem with these two Greatest Commandments is not their relevance but their generality. How do we love God and others in the course of our daily lives? In order to answer this question, we turn first to the Ten Commandments, then to the Everyday Commandments.

IV. THE TEN COMMANDMENTS

For two thousand years Christian preachers and teachers have made the Ten Commandments the basis of their ethical teaching: the "top ten," or, as one author has called them, *The Perfect 10*.[16] But today, under the influence of secular culture, even some who call themselves Christians question the relevance of these commands.[17] After all, haven't these Old Testament laws been outmoded since the New Testament? Don't we understand things a lot better than they did in Old Testament times? Aren't these commandments a bit narrow in this age when we have to listen to everybody's opinion? No, the Old Testament context itself supports the fundamental importance and central role of the Ten Commandments, which are found in Exodus 20:1–17, and again in Deuteronomy 5:5–21.

A. Spoken by God

It was the most important moment in the Old Testament. God's people had been a ragtag bunch of slaves in Egypt. The Lord their God had delivered them with a "mighty hand" and an "outstretched arm" (Deut. 5:15) from abject slavery. God had plagued the Egyptians. God brought Israel through the Red Sea. He bore them "on eagles' wings"

---

16. Michael G. Moriarty, *The Perfect 10* (Grand Rapids: Zondervan, 1999).

17. Phillip Johnson captures the approach of the secular world when he says, "Thus modernist culture retains the prohibition of theft and murder, retains the sabbath merely as a secular day of recreation, discards the admonition to have 'no other gods before me' as meaningless, and regards ambivalently the prohibition of adultery and the command to honor parents." *Reason in the Balance* (Grand Rapids: Zondervan, 1998), 39.

to Mount Sinai (Ex. 19:4). He told them to prepare, for he was coming to meet them! Boundaries were marked around the mountain. No one could approach—on pain of death. God himself, in mighty power, was coming down to the mountain to meet with his people. With awesome, frightening thunder, lightning, smoke, and darkness God came. The mountain trembled. The people shook with fear.

> **These God-spoken words were then written on the two tablets of stone . . . . 'The Lord talked with you face to face on the mountain from the midst of the fire . . . '**

The sound of the trumpet grew louder, then God himself thundered the words of the Ten Commandments to his assembled people. The sight was so awesome that the people begged not to have to listen to God's voice again. God did not impress these words on someone's mind. He did not speak them privately to one person. God proclaimed them to all his people from the thunder and lightning of Sinai. These God-spoken words were then written on the two tablets of stone and preserved as the fundamental statement of God's relationship with his people: "The LORD talked with you face to face on the mountain from the midst of the fire . . ." (Deut. 5:4). "And God spoke all these words . . ." (Ex. 20:1). The word used for "commandments" can be translated "words." These are the "Ten Words" spoken by God. They are the things most important to him!

B. At the Heart of Biblical Faith

As we saw in the last chapter, these Ten Commandments were the basic stipulations of the covenant that God made at Sinai. They are fundamental statements of principle. The sixth commandment is a good example: "You shall not murder." This commandment does not clarify the meaning of murder by distinguishing it from the accidental taking of human life. Nor does it tell us what to do if someone commits a murder. It states a fundamental principle in no uncertain terms: "You SHALL NOT murder."

Figure 2 shows that the first four commandments (Ex. 20:1–11) explain what the Greatest Commandment means by loving God with all our heart, soul, and strength. The last six (Ex. 20:12–17) shed light on what Leviticus 18:19 means by loving one's neighbor as oneself. Sometimes the first four are called the commandments of the "first tablet," the last six, the commandments of the "second tablet." Furthermore, as we will see, many of the Everyday Commandments (see **Figure 2**) that make up so much of the Pentateuch apply these ten to life. The prophets call people to account for breaking these Ten Commandments (see, for example, Hosea 4:1–3; Jer. 7:6–10). Jesus assumed their foundational validity when he preached the Sermon on the Mount (Matt. 5:17–48). Paul affirmed their continued validity and relevance (Rom. 13:8–10; Gal. 5:14). Thus we can see that these commandments are at the very heart of the Bible. They are the very "words" that God urges his people to put on their hearts in Deuteronomy 6:6 so that they will be quick to obey him. Neither God nor the principles by which he wants his people to

> The Ten . . . were an expansion of the two Greatest Commandments and the fundamental principles upon which the old covenant was based.

live have changed. Under the new covenant, however, God himself writes these words upon our hearts so that we will be able and willing to obey him (Heb. 10:15–18; cf. Jer. 31:31–34).

C. A Place for God's People to Live

The Ten Commandments, then, were an expansion of the two Greatest Commandments and the fundamental principles upon which the old covenant was based. They were a clear expression of God's concerns and therefore of his character. Thus we would expect them to have a high degree of relevance for God's people of all ages. They begin to give specific content to love for God and love for one's neighbor. These commandments are a package. Together they show us the way of life of the people of God. We might say that they provide a place for God's people to live. It is helpful to compare them to a house in which God's people dwell. See **Figure 3**.

Figure 3

THE TEN COMMANDMENTS "HOUSE."

Every house must have a solid foundation. This house is built on the foundation of the first four commandments. These commandments are fundamental because they concern our relationship with God. The first commandment is the most important of all. The next three help us to understand its meaning.

Commandments five through ten concern our relationships with our neighbors. Obedience toward God determines the way we treat one another. The fifth commandment is the floor. Honor for father and mother is the basis upon which love and reverence for God become love and respect for others. Commandments six, seven, eight, and nine are the four walls that determine the boundaries of this house and regulate our conduct toward others. These four commandments prohibit certain behavior toward our neighbor and thus imply certain positive types of conduct. Finally, the tenth commandment shows that God is not just concerned with outward actions, but with the motivation of the heart that leads to those actions. When Jesus said that the commandment against murder was a command against hatred, he was explaining the implications of the sixth commandment in light of the tenth (Matt. 5:21–26)!

D. The Foundation of the House

The First Commandment. Let's begin by looking at the foundation commandments. The first is the most fundamental: "I am the LORD your God, who brought you out of the land of Egypt, out of the house of bondage. You shall have no other gods before Me" (Ex. 20:2–3). This first com-
mandment is a simplified restatement of the Greatest Commandment from Deut. 6:4–6: we are to give God our total and exclusive loyalty. "You shall have no other gods before me" can be translated "You shall have no other gods in my presence." When God enters our lives, there is room for no other. He banishes those things humans pursue most from the central place in our lives: fame, money, power, and pleasure. There are two important things to note about this first commandment. First, it is not theoretical belief in God, but complete loyalty to him that is important. Second, his call for our loyalty is based on the fact that he first loved us. Thus he addressed his people of old: "I am the Lord your God,

who brought you out of the land of Egypt, out of the house of bondage"; I delivered you from the worst slavery and set you free. Therefore, "You shall have no other gods before me." Today he reminds us: "For God so loved the world that He gave His only begotten Son . . ." (John 3:16). Because he first showed his love to us by going to the cross, we are to love him with all our hearts.

The prophets often use the marriage bond to make this kind of loyalty clear (Hos. 1:1–4:19; Ezek. 23:1–19). God is like a husband who has done everything to express love for his wife. His people are his wife and therefore are to love him and him alone in return. Paul develops this imagery in Ephesians 5:22–33. Christ is the bridegroom who gave himself in order that his people might be a spotless bride, loyal only to him.

The Second Commandment. I have heard it said that every groom thinks he has the best girl in the world, while every bride knows her husband is not the best—but with a little work he can be! We try to make others over in our own image. The second commandment forbids us to do this with God: "You shall not make for yourself a carved image—any likeness of anything that is in heaven above, or that is in the earth beneath, or that is in the water under the earth; you shall not bow down to them nor serve them" (Ex. 20:4–5). If we try to represent the Creator with anything that he has made, we limit him by highlighting certain characteristics and eliminating others. Thus we distort his character and usually make him the kind of God we want him to be. Most modern images of God are mental rather than physical: we want him to be "a higher power as we understand him." *God is just an idea, so he won't bother me; God is a benevolent grandfather who will indulge me; God is loving, so he will excuse me; God is an impersonal force that I can use; I have the potential in me to be God.* This second commandment adds steel reinforcement to the foundation laid by the first: not only must we embrace God alone; we must embrace him on his own terms and not ours. We must embrace him as he has revealed himself in the history of his people culminating in our Lord Jesus Christ—who is the God-given "image of the invisible God" (Col. 1:15).

Those who would distort God for their own ends distort the truth and introduce a legacy of deceit and destruction that follows them: "For I, the LORD your God, am a jealous God, visiting the iniquity of the fathers upon the children to the third and fourth generations of those who hate Me" (Ex. 20:5). But those who embrace God as he is release a thousandfold heritage of blessing: "but showing mercy to thousands, to those who love Me and keep My commandments" (Ex. 20:6). We must continually allow God to deepen our understanding of him. C. S. Lewis grasped this truth when he said, "The prayer preceding all prayers is, 'May it be the real I who speaks, May it be the real Thou that I speak to.'"[18]

The Third Commandment. The third commandment also reinforces the first: "You shall not take the name of the LORD your God in vain, for the LORD will not hold him guiltless who takes His name in vain" (Ex. 20:7). The God of the Bible has a name. His name is *Yahweh* (Jehovah). The Old Testament uses this name for God almost seven thousand times! Every time your English Bible uses the word LORD with all capitals, it is a translation of *Yahweh*, the personal Name for God. *Yahweh* is not a general word like "god," or even "lord," which could be used for someone other than the true and living God. It is the personal name for the God of Israel. God's people do not give him this name. As their sover-

eign Lord he reveals it to them because he wants to enter into a personal relationship with them. His name reveals his character.

Moses is trembling before the bush that burns but is not consumed (Ex. 3:3–22). He is overwhelmed by the awesome voice of God. God discloses his name to Moses and tells him what it means: "I am who I am." God's name distinguishes him from the gods of other nations. This is the

---

18. C. S. Lewis, *Letters to Malcolm: Chiefly on Prayer* (New York: Harcourt, Brace & World, 1963/1964), 82.

true and living God who is! He exists in himself, he is the creator of all, and he is active in the lives of his people. He is a faithful God upon whom his people can depend, for he will deliver his people from Egypt in fulfillment of his promise to Abraham, Isaac, and Jacob: "I am [*Yahweh*] your God who brought you out of the land of Egypt, out of the house of bondage" (Ex. 20:2). By disclosing his name God both reveals his sovereignty and establishes a relationship with his people as their faithful Redeemer. Because he loves his people he is a "jealous" God (Ex. 34:14). Those who reject his love must reap the consequences. The self-revelation that God granted in his Name finds completion in Jesus—whose name means "*Yahweh* is Salvation."

This command applies first of all to *Yahweh*, the Name of God. The Old Testament, however, extends its meaning to cover the respectful use of any word referring to God. The third commandment prohibits any attempt to manipulate God's name to get what we want. His name is not a charm that we can use for our own ends. This command forbids breaking an oath that was taken in God's name, venting one's anger by using God's name as a curse word, or any flippant reference to God. It encour-

ages thanksgiving, praise, and the proclaiming of God's name to the nations.

The Fourth Commandment. The fourth commandment directed God's people to set the seventh day apart for him: "Remember the sabbath day, to keep it holy" (Ex. 20:8). They set this day apart by resting from the work that characterized the other days: "Six days you shall labor and do all your work, but the seventh day is the Sabbath of the Lord your God. In it you shall do no work . . ." (Ex. 20:9–10a). The whole community was to observe this day of rest together. That is why those in authority were to grant rest to others: "your son, . . . your daughter, . . . your male servant, . . . your female servant, . . . your cattle, . . . [and] your stranger who is within your gates" (Ex. 20:10b). By participating in this sabbath rest God's people acknowledged him as the Creator: "For in six days the Lord made the heavens and the earth, the sea, and all that is in them, and rested the seventh day. Therefore the Lord blessed the Sabbath day and hallowed it" (Ex. 20:11). They also acknowledged him as the Redeemer of his fallen creation: "And remember that you were a slave in the land of Egypt, and the Lord your God brought you out from there by a mighty hand and by an outstretched arm; therefore the Lord your God commanded you to keep the Sabbath day" (Deut. 5:15).

By keeping the Sabbath, God's people participated as a community in his renewal of creation. Thus it is not surprising that the Sabbath became an anticipation of God's ultimate redemption yet to come: "There remains a place of rest, a true sabbath, for the people of God" (Heb. 4:9 *The Voice*). The prophets were insistent that God's people live as his redeemed people by honoring the Sabbath (Isaiah 58:13, 14; Ezekiel 20:12, 20). Jesus affirmed the benefit that comes by participating in God's renewal through keeping sabbath rest (Mark 2:27) and affirmed his own deity by claiming to be Lord of the Sabbath (Mark 2:28). Special forms of worship characterized the Sabbath day. Nevertheless, the first and primary characteristic of the Sabbath was rest from common labor.

Contemporary appropriation of this commandment is more difficult than the others. The earliest Christians began to worship on the first day of the week in honor of Jesus' resurrection (we see the beginning of this practice in Acts 20:7 and 1 Cor. 16:2). They gradually abandoned the Jewish Sabbath. The "rest" the Sabbath anticipated had begun in Jesus.

> Keeping the Lord's Day is an anticipation of and participation in God's restoration of creation.

They began to call this first day the "Lord's Day" because it was the day of the "Lord" Jesus' resurrection (Rev. 1:10). Many of them could not refrain from work on that day because they were slaves in the homes of those who didn't follow Jesus. Nevertheless, it appears that over the first several centuries Christians began to follow the example of the Jewish Sabbath by abstaining from common labor on the first day of the week. In AD 321 the Roman emperor Constantine passed a law forbidding work on the Lord's Day. Christians over the centuries have differed in the way they kept this day. The movement that sprang from the Great Awakening of the eighteenth century and encouraged the spread of Christianity around the world put a strong emphasis on keeping Sunday as a day of rest and worship. When God's people have set the Lord's Day apart for themselves and others they have experienced great blessing. Rightly understood, keeping the Lord's Day is an anticipation of and participation in God's restoration of creation. By so doing we acknowledge God as the Lord of history.

By calling for absolute loyalty to God, on his terms, as the sovereign Lord of creation and redemption, these first four commandments provide a solid foundation for the six following commandments that constitute the house in which God's people live.

E. The House

The Fifth Commandment. These last six commands are concerned not merely with the individual but with maintaining the integrity and purity

of God's redeemed community. God is interested in our life together. The integrity of his community rests on the fifth commandment: "Honor your father and your mother that your days may be long upon the land which the LORD your God is giving you" (Ex. 20:12). We refer to this commandment as the floor of the house because it rests directly on the foundation and is under all the rest of the house. God has given us parents to model his authority in our lives. They are to teach us the respect for God enjoined by the first four commandments. In turn, they are to instruct us in the way we should treat others according to the next five commandments. They are to provide us with an example of godly living. They, under God, have given us life. Respect for them is the foundation of respect for both divine and human authority and thus fundamental to our obedience as part of God's people.

When we are children, this respect takes the form of obedience (Eph. 6:1–3). When we are older, it is expressed in exemplary conduct that honors their teaching (Prov. 1:8–9; 6:20–23), in the way we speak of them, and in the thanks we render to them (Prov. 20:20; 30:17). It may take the form of support when they are old (Prov. 28:24; 1 Tim. 5:8). Parental respect means accepting responsibility for our own lives rather than blaming our problems on our parents.

That last statement raises the issue of abusive parents. What form does this respect take if our parents have been neglectful, abusive people who have set a bad example? None can deny the pain that many bear from the mistreatment received in childhood. Denial is not respect. We must fully acknowledge what has been done to us—and then, through the redeeming work of Christ, find the grace to forgive and to let go of bitterness (Matt. 6:12; 18:21–35). Only then can we become the people that God would have us to be.

This commandment is, then, an indirect exhortation for parents not to "provoke" their children "to anger" but to "bring them up in the discipline and instruction of the Lord" (Eph. 6:4 ESV). Example is so important. Do they see us cheating on our income tax? When we go into a restaurant that gives free food for children ages ten and under, do we say

> Respect for parents leads directly to the respect for others enjoined by the following five commandments . . .

to our eleven-year-old, "Son, remember, you are only ten"? One Sunday afternoon I was leaving for my office to complete an urgent piece of work. As I was going out the door my then five-year-old said to me, "Dad, we don't work on Sunday." The words kept ringing in my ears as I drove down the street. I turned around, came home, and said to her, "You are right, honey, we don't work on Sunday." One of my friends was teaching his daughter to drive. She failed to fully stop for a stop sign near their house. When her dad corrected her she said, "But Dad, that is the way you always go through that stop sign."

It is hard to overemphasize the importance of this commandment. Respect for parents leads directly to the respect for others enjoined by the following five commandments discussed below.

The Sixth Commandment. We turn now to the walls of this house. They provide boundaries and direction for the common life of the people of God. It is no surprise that the first of these "walls" is the command "You shall not murder" (Ex. 20:13). Some form of legal protection for

human life is basic to any society. And yet this command reflects a profound respect for God that accords well with the first four commandments. Human life is sacred because human beings have been made in the image of God (Gen. 9:6). The Old Testament context and the usage of the term translated "murder" make it clear that this com-

mandment is a prohibition of what we would call "murder" or "manslaughter." It is not, in itself, a prohibition of either capital punishment or defensive war. Whether the Bible as a whole condemns these things is a matter about which Christians differ and goes beyond the scope of this book. However, none can deny that this commandment prohibits the taking of innocent human life. This is a comprehensive prohibition covering young and old, male and female, born and unborn.

The Old Testament law recognizes the difference between intentional and inadvertent taking of human life, making provision for the redemption of the person guilty of the second. Yet it also recognizes that malice, envy, hatred, greed, anger, or a desire for personal advantage can cause a person to take the life of another although the act was not premeditated (Num. 35:16–21). In such cases the perpetrator is guilty of murder. Jesus, then, helps us to see what is latent in the Old Testament. This command is not merely a prohibition of the murderous act. It is a condemnation of those self-centered attitudes of the heart that lead to such a deed (Matt. 5:21–26). It is a call to seek reconciliation and to love others as ourselves by contributing to their life and well-being. Such love, which in olden times was called "charity," is the first wall that defines the life of the people of God.

The Seventh Commandment. In a large singles, Sunday school class of a mainline Texas church, the teacher stood and addressed the class in words like these: "God expects you to have sexual relations because he wants you to be happy. Of course you should only do it with the mutual consent of your partner and in a way that doesn't hurt anyone." The attitude of the secular world has infected the church. God, however, does not say, "You shall not commit adultery—unless it makes you feel good." He commands us to be more concerned with what is fundamental to a stable community and the well-being of its members—the sacredness of the marriage bond between a man and a woman—than with our own self-gratification. This commandment prohibits sexual relations between a husband or wife and anyone but his or her spouse (Lev. 18:20; 20:10; Deut. 22:22–27; Hos. 4:13; Ezek. 16:32). It also implies the need for abstinence among the unmarried (Deut. 22:28–29) and the

> God, however, does not say, 'You shall not commit adultery'—unless it makes you feel good.

illegitimacy of sexual perversions such as homosexuality, bestiality, and incest (Lev. 20:10–21). These kinds of behavior are also destructive of the marriage bond.

God established marriage to bring people into the closest union (Gen. 2:24) and for procreation (Gen. 1:27–28). Faithfulness in this area of our lives is fundamental to all of our commitments and is essential to social and personal well-being. Thus God often uses adultery as a metaphor for those who have been unfaithful to him (Jer. 3:7–9; Ezek. 16:31–33). The second wall that shapes the behavior of God's people is the wall of marital fidelity and sexual purity. Hebrews 13:4 says, "Let marriage be held in honor among all, and let the marriage bed be undefiled, for God will judge the sexually immoral and adulterous" (ESV).

The Eight Commandment. "You shall not steal" appears straightforward: do not take what belongs to someone else. And yet this command

is manifold. It forbids God's people to take advantage of others by depriving them of what is theirs through deceit, trickery, or manipulation, even if the means used are legal. This command forbids such things as failure to give a full day's work for a full day's pay, using one's position or office for personal financial advantage, or supporting laws that bring personal gain, but to the detriment of society. Instead of stealing, the Mosaic law calls on one to be concerned about a neighbor's physical welfare and to help others whenever possible. Paul summarizes the teaching of the Old Testament when he says, "Let him who stole steal no longer, but rather let him labor, working with his hands what is good, that he may have something to give him who has need" (Eph. 4:28). The third wall that shapes the people of God is the wall of generosity.

The Ninth Commandment. "You shall not bear false witness against your neighbor" (Ex. 20:16). This commandment, like the others, is not worded in individualistic terms. It is shaped to promote the unity and well-being of the people of God. Those who bear false witness against a neighbor fracture the harmony of the commu-

nity and promote injustice. This commandment prohibits perverting the truth about one's neighbor both in court and in private. It calls on us to speak the truth in all of our relationships. It is so easy for us to shade the truth for our own advantage. If we carefully select what we say to make a false impression, we are lying even if everything we have said is true. The opposite of perverting the truth for our own advantage is to follow Paul's exhortation: speak "the truth in love" (Eph. 4:15; cf. Col. 3:9). The fourth and final wall that shapes the life of God's people is integrity. God calls us to walk in truth through this world of deception, hypocrisy, and illusion. Those who deceive others live in self-deception.

The Tenth Commandment. "You shall not covet" (Ex. 20:17). This command is different from all but the first commandment. Both "You shall have no other gods before me" and "You shall not covet" are matters of the heart. The other commandments prohibit actions that can be observed: idolatry, vain use of God's name, Sabbath breaking,

dishonoring parents, murder, adultery, theft, and lying. But who can tell if one covets? Covetousness is a motivation of the heart. Thus this commandment has become the roof of the house. By calling for pure motives it keeps the rain from coming inside and spoiling everything.

Most people think of coveting as strongly desiring something that someone else has. This command, however, goes much deeper. To covet is to cultivate an obsessive desire for more. It is that greedy longing to garner more and more for the self, as John D. Rockefeller is reputed to have said when asked how much money was enough: "Just a little bit more." Covetousness is the opposite of generosity. It is a craving for an ever-increasing amount of what this world has to offer with the belief that it will satisfy. Notice how comprehensive this commandment is: "You shall not covet your neighbor's house . . . wife . . . manservant . . . maidservant . . . ox . . . donkey, nor anything that is your neighbor's."

The tenth commandment is closely related to the first. As Jesus said, "No one can serve two masters; for either he will hate the one and love the other, or he will be devoted to the one and despise the other. You cannot serve God and the things of this world" (Matt. 6:24 NKJV altered). Love for God and love for the things of this world cannot go together (1 John 2:15–17). Thus Paul was right when he referred to "covetousness, which is idolatry" (Col. 3:5). Just as love for God leads to keeping the other commandments, so covetousness leads to breaking them. For instance, because David coveted Bathsheba, he committed adultery with her, killed her husband, Uriah, took her as his wife, and then covered up Uriah's death (2 Sam. 11:1–27). He broke commandments six, seven, eight, and nine by murdering, committing adultery, stealing, and lying. In 1 Kings 21:1–16 Ahab's covetousness led to the murder of Naboth, the theft of Naboth's vineyard, and the use of false witnesses to cover the other crimes.

Thus the Ten Commandments provide a house where God's people can live a life that reflects his character. This is a life based on devotion to God as God, respect for parents and other proper authority, love for our neighbors, sexual purity, generosity, and integrity. It is a life freed from covetous desire by confidence in the goodness of God.

There can be little doubt about the continuing relevance of the Greatest Commandments and the Ten Commandments. They provide us with a solid moral foundation before we turn to the third part of the Mosaic law, the Everyday Commandments. These Everyday Commandments are often an application of the Greatest Commandments and the Ten Commandments to the life of God's ancient people.

V. THE EVERYDAY COMMANDMENTS
(SEE FIGURE 2)

As we saw in the last chapter, Jesus' own self-sacrifice has fulfilled the Old Testament sacrificial system; therefore, we are to no longer concern ourselves with the laws pertaining to the sacrificial system or with the laws regulating ceremonial cleanliness. Furthermore, he made it clear that God gave the laws of ceremonial purity in order to emphasize his own holiness and as an object lesson of moral purity. What remains, and what we are concerned with here, is the myriad of other commandments that, in large part, give us the details of how the Greatest Commandments and the Ten Commandments were to be carried out in the life of God's people living in ancient Canaan before the coming of Christ.

A. A Description of the Everyday Commandments

Sometimes these laws address issues of daily life not directly related to the Ten Commandments, such as slavery. In those cases they show us how the law of love for God and neighbor should be carried out in these situations. These laws are not, for the most part, statements of principle such as "You shall not murder." Rather they are instruction on how those principles are to be carried out in the affairs of everyday life. Some have called these Everyday Commandments "case law" because they apply the law in various cases.

It is not the purpose of this book to explain all of these individual laws. The significance of some of them remains a mystery or a matter for speculation. It is our purpose to explore how these laws can continue to provide moral guidance. We must also remember that the law of the Sinai covenant does not contain all that the Old Testament has to say

> **Some have called these Everyday Commandments 'case law' because they apply the law in various cases.**

about ethics. Jesus refers to the ordinances of creation (Mark 10:2–9). There are also the examples of Old Testament people and the teaching of the prophets.

Exodus 21:12–14 is an example of these everyday laws: "Whoever strikes a man so that he dies shall be put to death. But if he did not lie in wait for him, but God let him fall into his hand, then I will appoint for you a place to which he may flee. But if a man willfully attacks another to kill him by cunning, you shall take him from my altar, that he may die" (ESV). These laws apply the principle "You shall not murder" to everyday life. Note that they consider the circumstances of the act: "if he did not lie in wait for him . . . But if a man willfully attacks another to kill him by cunning . . ." They establish the punishment in accord with these circumstances: "I will appoint for you a place to which he may flee. . . . [Y]ou shall take him from my altar, that he may die." Much of the rest of Exodus 21 continues to apply "You shall not murder" to the circumstances of daily life. Numbers 35:1–34 continues this discussion. Leviticus 20:10–21 contains many Everyday Commandments that apply the seventh commandment, "You shall not commit adultery."

B. An Explanation of the Pattern Principle

Since these Everyday Commandments apply God's law to his people living in the promised land within the culture of ancient Canaan and before the coming of Christ, we cannot apply them directly to ourselves. Nevertheless, they continue to give us moral guidance. Laws reinforce a set of values in any society. God gave ancient Israel these laws in order to establish a certain set of values, to reinforce certain patterns of behavior. We can study these laws to determine what pattern of values and standards of behavior God wants for his people. These patterns of values/behavior cannot be ignored because they are an expression of the character of God. What is the pattern of values, for instance, that underlies Israel's economic life or Israel's sexual life? Then we can see how we can live by those patterns today. We are ready to present our third guideline for understanding the Old Testament: The Pattern Principle.

Figure 4

✓ **3RD GUIDELINE—THE PATTERN PRINCIPLE.**
(What the law says)

God gave his law at Sinai to show the kind of life he wanted people to live in fellowship with him and community with one another. Thus God's covenant with Israel is a pattern for our lives. We who live after Christ's coming may not be able to apply all the OT laws directly, but by studying them we can gain insight into the type of community God desires.

C. An Example of the Pattern Principle

Let's take a look at some of the laws regulating ancient Israel's economy to see what kind of "pattern" emerges. We must remember that every family/clan was to have an inheritance in the promised land. While houses in walled cities could be sold (Lev. 25:29–30), family farmland could not be transferred in perpetuity to another. Every seven years the land was restored to its original owners. Furthermore, in this seventh year the land was to be left uncultivated so that it could renew itself (Ex. 23:10–11; Lev. 25:4). If an Israelite had to sell himself or his family into slavery due to poverty, he too was to be released in the seventh year (Ex. 21:2, Deut. 15:7–11) or at least in the year of Jubilee (Lev. 25:39–46), which occurred every fifty years as a general year of release. When he was released his former master was to generously give him the provisions that he would need to start life on his own again (Deut. 15:12–15). The law encouraged those with means to give or lend to those in need (Deut. 15:7–11), but it absolutely forbade charging interest on any loan (Lev. 25:36–38). All were told to help those without resources: widows, orphans, and foreigners living in the land without property rights.

A complete understanding of the type of society shaped by these laws would take a more detailed study of these and other passages. Nevertheless, a pattern begins to emerge. These laws protect every family's share in the land that was a means of livelihood. A person would not need a loan unless he had suffered some difficulty: sickness, crop failure, or some other disaster. To charge him interest would only be to make the burden of his misfortune more grievous and to endanger his land. His next course of action, if need persisted, would be to sell some of his land. That, according to the law, would be returned to him in the seven-year release. If he still continued to sink in poverty, his only recourse would be to sell himself and his family to a fellow Israelite as slaves. In a sense this served as a type of welfare system, for the new master was required to provide the necessities of life for them. They, of course, found employment. However, when the seventh year or the year of Jubilee arrived they were to be set free and generously given the resources to begin again so that they would not immediately fall back into poverty. By guaranteeing everyone's share in the means of livelihood, these laws also prevented anyone from accumulating an inordinate amount of wealth. The seven-year release and the year of Jubilee forestalled the accumulation of large estates or numbers of slaves.

> Paul summarizes this truth when he says, 'Let the thief no longer steal, but rather let him labor doing honest work . . . so that he may have something to share.'

How can this pattern inform our own lives? It certainly calls us to a life of industry, freed from greed and characterized by generosity, especially toward those in need. Paul summarizes this truth when he says, "Let the thief no longer steal, but rather let him labor, doing honest work with his own hands, so that he may have something to share with anyone in need" (Eph. 4:28 ESV). If we have not lived in this way, it calls us to repentance (the religious use of the Law). It assures us that God will give us grace to live this life of industry and generosity (the evangelical use of the Law). And it provides moral guidance for how we should live in the Spirit (the moral use of the Law). It also has implications for the civil use of the Law. It suggests that we should seek to establish laws and structures that protect the share of all in the means of livelihood, restrict the unlimited accumulation of wealth by a few, and encourage productive labor for all. The Bible, of course, does not tell us how this should be done in the modern context.

We have already interpreted the seventh commandment, "You shall not commit adultery," in light of these other Everyday Commandments. We have seen that they restrict sexual intimacy to a husband and wife united by the marriage bond. These laws assume that the man will usually be the initiator, and thus they protect the woman innocently violated. They forbid a man having relations with either a married (Lev. 18:20; 20:10; Deut. 22:22–27) or single woman (Deut. 22:28–29) who is not his wife, though the punishment for the latter is less since it is not a direct violation of the woman's marriage bond. They forbid incest, thus protecting those living in the same household from molestation. They also forbid homosexuality and bestiality (Lev. 20:10–21).

The Sinai law did allow for divorce and it did not prohibit polygamy. Jesus, of course, showed us that divorce was not in God's original plan by citing the conclusion of the creation account: "Therefore a man shall leave his father and mother and be joined to his wife, and they shall become one flesh" (Gen. 2:24). He declares that God allowed divorce only because of the hardness of the human heart (Mark 10:2–9). But even within the Old Testament God declared through the prophet Malachi (2:16): "I hate divorce." The two becoming one flesh in Genesis 2:24 also excludes polygamy from God's plan for humanity. Old Testament examples do not glorify polygamy. By insisting that church leaders have only one wife, the New Testament sets an example for others (1 Tim. 3:12).

Failure to maintain the integrity of marriage and to live up to the sexual purity required by God's law drives us to Christ for forgiveness (the religious use of the Law). God's demand for sexual purity, despite the human propensity for sensuality, is possible, for God will supply the grace

> **God's demand for sexual purity, despite the human propensity for sensuality, is possible, for God will supply the grace necessary.**

necessary (the evangelical use of the Law). The Old Testament's teaching on faithfulness and sexual purity is reinforced by the New and provides a guide for Spirit-filled living (the moral use of the Law). Finally, the Old Testament's teaching on fidelity in marriage and sexual purity suggests that we should promote laws and structures in our own society that protect the integrity of the marriage bond (the civil use of the Law).

D. Problems with the Everyday Commandments

These two examples—the Sinai law's economic and sexual regulations—must suffice to show how the Pattern Principle works. Before concluding this chapter, however, we must turn to scriptures like those with which we began. The Everyday Commandments of the Sinai law pronounce the death penalty for sins like idolatry (Lev. 20:2), blasphemy (Lev. 24:16),

> **The death penalty for these sins reminded people of God's uncompromising holiness and of their need to be holy if they lived in his land.**

Sabbath breaking (Ex. 31:14; 35:2), murder (Num. 35:30), adultery (Lev. 20:10), and sorcery (Lev. 20:27), but not for theft, except for theft of persons—kidnapping (Ex. 21:16). All of these violations put one outside the bounds of God's covenant. What are we to make of this—to us—harsh penalty?

To address this problem, we must keep two things in mind. First, we must remember the significance of the promised land. Second, we must look at how this death penalty was actually applied throughout the Old Testament.

As we saw in the last chapter, the promised land was to be the place where God's people lived in the presence of their holy God and in harmony with one another through obedience to his law. By this obedience they would reflect his character. This land was the new Eden of fellowship with God. It was a type and picture of the heavenly Jerusalem to come that would be the place of perfect fellowship with him. Mistakes could be remedied. However, any violation that broke God's covenant endangered not only the violator, but the entire community with the judgment of God. The violator must be removed to protect the purity of the community and its life in the land. The death penalty for these sins reminded people of God's uncompromising holiness and of their need to be holy if they lived in his land. The land must be kept clean in order to be a proper type of the heavenly Jerusalem to come.

Second, we must look at how this death penalty was carried out. It may seem harsh to have executed the man in Numbers 15:32–36 who picked up sticks on the Sabbath day. However, his violation was flagrant. The command had just been given. In brazen disregard of the command and the holy God who made it, he picked up these sticks in front of other members of the congregation. Often—in fact most of the time—God had mercy and did not exact this punishment. David is an example in point (2 Sam. 11:1–12:15). When he sinned against Bathsheba, he broke three commandments that had the death sentence: murder, adultery, and theft (of another man's wife). He also bore false witness, which, in this case, would also have been a capital offense, since it led to Uriah's death (Deut. 19:18–19). When David confessed, the first words out of the prophet Nathan's mouth were, "The LORD also has put away your sin; you shall not die" (2 Sam. 12:13). In fact, God's great mercy is shown by the way in which he spared the nation of Israel throughout its history. His people were continually turning to idolatry, adultery, and all of the other sins that called for the death penalty. Yet he continually spared them; he would send nations to oppress them in order to bring them back to himself, but he did not destroy them. In fact, if God had enacted the provisions of the law, he would have destroyed his people in Exodus 32:1–35 when they committed gross idolatry by making the golden calf.

One thing we learn from the penalty assigned to these sins—even if, in God's mercy, his people were often spared its execution—is their seriousness in the sight of God. Those who commit them show great disregard for God and/or violate other human persons. God considers our consideration of others, our faithfulness, our sexual purity, and our integrity to be nonnegotiable. Contrast God's view with the prevalent modern view: if it feels good, or is to your immediate advantage, then just do it. Even if the death penalty is not exacted, the long-term consequences of violation are tragic in terms of violence, broken homes, neglected children, and the breakdown of the social order.

The apostle Paul taught that people publicly guilty of gross sins, some of which incurred the death penalty under the old covenant, should be excluded from the church (1 Cor. 5:1–13). But even then, penitence could lead to re-inclusion among the people of God (2 Cor. 2:5–13).

As we have seen, then, capital punishment was pronounced on idolaters, murders, adulterers, kidnappers, and others in order to protect the promised land as the place of fellowship with God. The purity demanded by these laws was a reminder of the Jerusalem to come in which there would be no sin. Even within this context, however, God usually had mercy and spared his people, giving them a chance to repent. We cannot, then, say that these laws that applied God's principles to the ancient promised land require us to institute capital punishment for the same crimes today. What we can say is this: God takes these violations (murder, adultery, perjury, kidnapping, etc.) very seriously. The consequences for a society characterized by these things is terrible. We would do well, then, to establish laws and build structure in our societies that protect such things as human life, marriage, and integrity (the civil use of the Law).

We have already indicated that God's Old Testament people repeatedly failed to live in obedience. The next chapter will look at that failure and God's response to it. He responded by giving his people institutions that would encourage them to obey: the Davidic kingship and the great city of Jerusalem with its temple.

5

RESTORATION INSTITUTIONALIZED
in the CHOICE *of* DAVID

"My King," "My City"

Judges to 2 Kings

The book of Joshua ends well. God's people are living in the promised land, enjoying obedient fellowship with God and harmony with each other. God has fulfilled his promises (Josh. 23:15). However, the promise of blessing for the whole world is still to come. Furthermore, we have already seen the repeated disobedience of God's people in the wilderness. Moses has forebodingly warned of disobedience yet to come (Deut. 32:1–52). Judges 2:7 reads, "So the people served the LORD all the days of Joshua, and all the days of the elders who outlived Joshua, who had seen all the great works of the LORD which He had done for Israel . . ." (cf. Josh. 24:31), but what happened then? After all that God had done for his people, they did not remain true to his covenant.

I. A BROKEN COVENANT

The book of Judges chronicles the descent into this condition of disobedience with its accompanying social and moral deterioration. All three of the fundamental relationships that constituted God's plan for his people were in disarray; God's disobedient people were not living in fellowship with him. They were not enjoying a harmonious society. The surrounding peoples often oppressed them and deprived them of the benefits of the promised land. The God who had made covenant with them at Sinai was their King, yet "everyone did what was right in his own eyes" (Judg. 17:6; 21:25), ignoring authority human and divine. God called "judges" and empowered them by his Spirit to deliver his people from oppression and lead them in obedience. Their function, then, was much broader than modern judges. They were the instruments through which God exercised his rule over a disobedient people.

Figure 1

THE STORY OF JUDGES
. . . everyone did what was right in his own eyes.
(Judg. 17:6; 21:25).

Judges 1:1–2:7	The beginning of disobedience
Judges 2:8–16:31	The descending cycle of disobedience
Judges 17:1–21:25	The tragic results of persistent disobedience

Judges 1:1–2:7 describes the beginning of this disobedience. Chapters 2:8–16:31 chronicle the repeated story of disobedience-oppression-deliverance by a judge: Othniel, Ehud, Deborah, Gideon, Jephthah, and Samson. These judges provide examples of both faithfulness and failure that can inform our own lives. The long narrative about Gideon is a good example of courage and deepening trust (Judg. 6:1–8:21). Gideon's refusal of kingship but compromise with idolatry at the end of his life forebodes what his son, Abimelech (Judg. 9:1–57), will do. Abimelech is the opposite of what a judge should be. By trickery and violence he claims

the kingship for himself. Samson's life mirrors the fickle, undisciplined life of the people as a whole (Judg. 13:1–16:31). Indeed, the disobedience of the nation is a warning-example to the people of God throughout their earthly journey. Judges is fertile ground for the Example Principle presented in chapter 2.

We referred to the repeated story of disobedience above. Each time God's people fell into sin, God allowed another nation to oppress them and then, when they cried for help, sent a judge to deliver them. For the remainder of his lifetime, each judge would lead the people in obedience. Oppression by these other nations was a reminder that God's people could enjoy the blessings of the promised land only when they lived in faithful obedience to God and thus in harmony with each other. Domination by these nations was a foreshadowing of the exile that would come for persistent disobedience. This cycle of disobedience and restitution is represented in **Figure 2**. It was a deteriorating cycle. Each time, it seemed, the people sank lower. Even the last judges—Jephthah and Samson—lacked a clear understanding of the ways of God.

Finally, Judges 17:1–21:25 describes the depth of the moral, spiritual, and social chaos into which God's people had sunk. Their common life was characterized by idolatry, sexual immorality, faithlessness, and vio-

> The book of Ruth provides a ray of hope in the midst of this faithlessness. A young, non-Jewish Moabite woman is faithful to the God of Israel . . .

lence, with little residual true knowledge of God. The book of Ruth provides a ray of hope in the midst of this faithlessness. A young, non-Jewish Moabite woman is faithful to the God of Israel—and through her, God produces none other than King David.

Figure 2

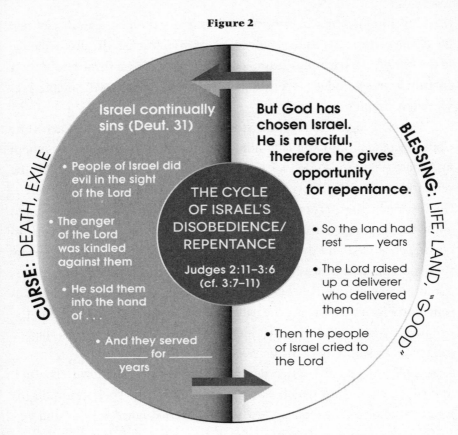

First Samuel 1:1–8:22 continues the time of the judges by relating the stories of Eli and Samuel (see **Figure 3**). We move easily from faithful Ruth to faithful Hannah in 1 Samuel 1:1–2:10. She, like Ruth, out of the difficulties of life, throws herself upon the mercy of the God of Israel and receives his blessing. She responds in both praise and obedience. As with Ruth, God not only blesses her faithfulness but uses it to deliver his people through the birth of Samuel. Samuel, called and obedient from his childhood, is a welcome relief to judges like Jephthah and Samson. Faithful Samuel is a crucial transition figure, often called the last of the judges and the first of the prophets (though in a broader sense people like Abraham and Moses can be called prophets). He was also the one who established kingship in Israel.

Figure 3

1 & 2 SAMUEL
The Lord has sought for Himself a man after His own heart . . .
(1 Sam. 13:14)

1 Sam. 1:1–8:22	The ministry of Samuel, the last judge and the first prophet.
1 Sam. 9:1–15:35	The disobedience of Saul, Israel's first king.
1 Sam. 16:1–31:13	The rise of David and the demise of Saul.
2 Sam. 1:1–10:19	God establishes David as king in Jerusalem.
2 Sam. 11:1–20:22	David's sin and its consequences.
2 Sam. 20:23–24:25	Concluding information about David's reign.

Eli the priest judged Israel but he did not discipline his sons (1 Sam. 2:12–21). They typified the moral state of the nation by desecrating God's sacrifices and living lives of gross immorality. They tried to use the ark of the covenant as a charm to guarantee the defeat of the Philistines. But God will not be used. They were killed, the ark was captured, and Eli died of the shock (1 Sam. 4:5–21). We have certainly reached a low point in the people's relationship with God. God, however, has prepared Samuel to judge his people. He himself demonstrates his sovereignty by restoring the ark (1 Sam. 5:1–6:21).

The climax of the people's disobedience comes in 1 Samuel 8:1–9 when the people demand that Samuel give them a king so that they can be "like all the nations" (1 Sam. 8:5). From a worldly point of view their request made sense. The Philistines were oppressing them. They needed someone to organize them and provide strong leadership. This "judges system" wasn't working. Eli's children had disobeyed God. Samuel is old, and his sons are disobedient (1 Sam. 8:1–3). The people refused to trust God as their King to deliver them and to raise up appropriate people to lead them. This demand had been long in coming. The people had wanted Gideon to begin a royal dynasty, but he had refused in no uncertain terms: "The LORD will rule over you" (Judg. 8:23 ESV). His son Abimelech, whose name means "My father is king," tried by violence to establish the dynasty refused by his father (Judg. 9:1–21). Now the people themselves reject God's direct rule by demanding a king. These people who were to be God's own "chosen nation" and a "royal priesthood" want to become like "all the nations."

Samuel is displeased at their faithlessness and warns them of the oppression that a king will bring upon them (1 Sam. 8:10–22). By taking

> These people who were to be God's own 'chosen nation' and a 'royal priesthood' want to become like 'all the nations.'

their children, land, and produce, a king will disrupt the harmony God intended for them as free people in the promised land. If they had only recollected their history they would have remembered the taste they had of this oppression under Abimelech. Nevertheless, God instructs Samuel to give them a king.

First Samuel 9:1–15:35 narrates the choice, disobedience, and rejection of Saul, the first king of Israel (see **Figure 3**). He was handsome, head and shoulders taller than anyone else. He had a regal bearing. God gave them the kind of king they thought they wanted in order to show them the tragedy of their choice. This king's self-will and disobedience led to his defeat and the overwhelming domination of the land by the Philistines (1 Sam. 31:7). Then God gave them the person no one would have considered kingly material: David, the little shepherd boy, youngest son of Jesse (2 Sam. 16:1–13). He was a king after God's own heart, who, despite his failures, retained a humble, submissive heart before his God.

First Samuel 16:1–31:13 begins with the choice of David and ends with the death of Saul (see **Figure 3**). These chapters chronicle Saul's attempts to destroy David and David's patient reliance on God to bring him into his kingship. We are encouraged to follow David's faith and warned by Saul's conduct of the consequences of disobedience.

II. GOD'S ANSWER: "MY KING," "MY CITY"

God does not leave his people in disobedience. He takes their sinful request for a king and uses it for their benefit. He gives them two institutions to stabilize them in obedience: the Davidic dynasty and Jerusalem with its temple, the Holy City. That is why we have entitled this chapter "Restoration Institutionalized." Due to their frailty and inconsistent obedience, God will institutionalize his rule over them and his presence among them.

A. "My King": David and His Descendants

God established David and his "house," his sons (2 Sam. 7:8–14) to "plant" his people (2 Sam. 7:10) by leading them to follow God's covenant and by delivering them from their enemies. What God was doing through David and his house was not something different from the Mosaic covenant. David was to lead the people to obey that covenant so they could enjoy the blessings of fellowship with God, harmonious life, and the benefits of the promised land. All of this was, of course, in fulfillment of God's promise to Abraham. Who, then, was this David? What did God expect his descendants to be? God's conversation with David in 2 Samuel 7:8–14 helps us to answer these questions. God calls him "my servant David" (2 Sam. 7:8). David has the great privilege of being singled out as God's own servant. He will be king, but he will be the servant and regent of

> David . . . will be king, but he will be the servant and regent of the Great King. It will be his responsibility to obey the voice and law of his Lord.

the Great King. It will be his responsibility to obey the voice and law of his Lord. He is God's "chosen" (1 Sam. 16:1–10) one. David was not elected or chosen by the people to be king. He did not attain this position by his own strength or merit. Through Samuel, God clearly chose David and gave the kingship to him. Samuel, at God's instruction, went to the house of Jesse, David's father, to anoint a new king for Israel. God told him to pass over David's seven older brothers, though they were kingly in appearance, and to choose the youngest, a shepherd boy whom none

> **David would be empowered to carry out his office by the Spirit's power. That is . . . why, with nothing but a sling, he was able to slay Goliath.**

had thought to call from tending the sheep (1 Sam. 16:1–13). Upon his anointing, David did not seize the throne. First Samuel 16:1–31:13 shows how he waited for God to give it to him. By God's choice David became a man "after [God's] own heart" (1 Sam. 13:14; Acts 13:22).

God also called David "my anointed" (Ps. 132:17). Samuel had, of course, anointed David with oil. That anointing, however, was a bestowal of God's Spirit upon David. David would be empowered to carry out his office by the Spirit's power. That is why he was able to kill the lion and the bear as a shepherd boy and why, with nothing but a sling, he was able to slay Goliath (1 Sam. 17:37). As the one anointed by God's Spirit he was God's special representative.

In fact, this relationship with God was so intimate that God could call the Davidic king "my Son" (Ps. 2:7; compare 2 Sam. 7:14) and even address him as "O God" (Ps. 45:6). These titles, in particular, anticipated great David's greater son, our Lord Jesus Christ, in whom they would find an even deeper meaning (Heb. 1:5, 8–9). The Davidic king, then, was an institution that God established to lead his people in obedience to the Mosaic covenant. By so doing the Davidic king would restore to them those three relationships lost by sin, promised to Abraham, and enjoyed initially under the Mosaic covenant: obedient fellowship with God, harmonious fellowship among the people of God, and enjoyment of the promised land.

B. "My City": Jerusalem and the Temple

Jerusalem, often called Zion after one of the prominent hills on which it is built, is closely linked with David. David conquered this city and made it the nation's capital. Though it became known as the "City of David" (2 Sam. 5:6–12), Jerusalem was God's city. God chose this city to give to his chosen one, David. He chose it as the place for his temple, the place where he would put his Name, the place that would embody his dwelling among his people (1 Kings 11:36; 14:21). The fact that he would not let David build his temple underscored both his ownership of this city and the priority of grace. God would first build David a "house" by putting his son on the throne. Then, that son would be able to build God's "house," the place that represented his presence among his people (2 Sam. 7:1–14). Thus Jerusalem and its temple became an institution that visibly represented God's presence with his people in the land. The regular worship and annual pilgrimages to this place made it the physical embodiment and reminder of every aspect of God's covenant. Thus it encompassed all three of the relationships that constituted God's plan for his people: First and foremost, it institutionalized God's presence among his people and thus reminded them of their obligation of obedience. Here was the place where God dwelt. Second, as the visible symbol of God's covenant with his people, the temple was the focal point of their national life and a call for the harmony that would reflect God's character. Third, it was God's promise of continued blessing in the promised land. In fact, Zion/Jerusalem, the city of God, came to embody all that the land had represented. "Zion" became a symbol for God's presence, God's people, and God's heritage. Finally, it was also a guarantee of God's promise to David (2 Sam. 7:1–14).

Figure 4 shows how the Davidic kingship and Jerusalem with its temple were established to support the three basic relationships that had been restored by the Mosaic covenant. As related in previous chapters, these three relationships constituted God's original plan that was marred through disobedience. Their restoration was promised to Abraham. Compare **Figure 4** with the charts in the previous chapters and with the master chart at the end of this book.

Figure 4

RESTORATION INAUGURATED AT SINAI AND INSTITUTIONALIZED AT ZION

THE OLD COVENANT

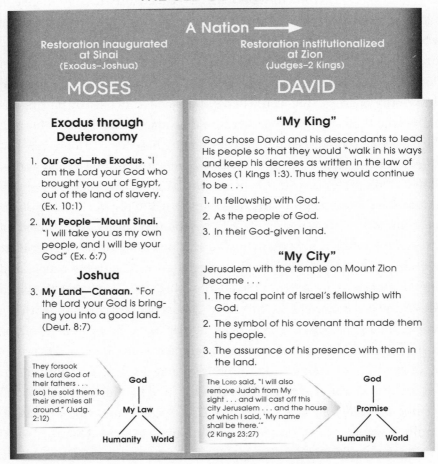

A Nation ——→

Restoration inaugurated at Sinai
(Exodus–Joshua)

Restoration institutionalized at Zion
(Judges–2 Kings)

MOSES

DAVID

Exodus through Deuteronomy

1. **Our God—the Exodus.** "I am the Lord your God who brought you out of Egypt, out of the land of slavery. (Ex. 10:1)

2. **My People—Mount Sinai.** "I will take you as my own people, and I will be your God" (Ex. 6:7)

Joshua

3. **My Land—Canaan.** "For the Lord your God is bringing you into a good land. (Deut. 8:7)

They forsook the Lord God of their fathers . . . (so) he sold them to their enemies all around." (Judg. 2:12)

God
|
My Law
/ \
Humanity World

"My King"

God chose David and his descendants to lead His people so that they would "walk in his ways and keep his decrees as written in the law of Moses (1 Kings 1:3). Thus they would continue to be . . .

1. In fellowship with God.

2. As the people of God.

3. In their God-given land.

"My City"

Jerusalem with the temple on Mount Zion became . . .

1. The focal point of Israel's fellowship with God.

2. The symbol of his covenant that made them his people.

3. The assurance of his presence with them in the land.

The LORD said, "I will also remove Judah from My sight . . . and will cast off this city Jerusalem . . . and the house of which I said, 'My name shall be there.'" (2 Kings 23:27)

God
|
Promise
/ \
Humanity World

III. THE PEOPLE'S RESPONSE: DISOBEDIENCE AND EXILE

During David's reign and son Solomon's early years as king, God's people lived under God's blessing in God's land more fully than ever before. This was their golden age, when they occupied the full extent of the promised land and lived in prosperity. This was the age of David, the sweet singer of Israel who wrote many psalms, and of Solomon, the wisest man who ever lived, who wrote proverbs instructing people how to live according to the "fear of the Lord" (Prov. 1:7).

And yet the disobedience that had been so characteristic of God's people began to rear its head again in Solomon's reign. Instead of leading the people in obedience, most of the kings who followed Solomon became corrupt. The people themselves remained prone to unfaithfulness. The temple was sometimes used for self-serving political or economic ends, was polluted by the worship of false gods, and even became a source of comfort amid disobedience. Some people came to believe that because the temple was there it guaranteed the preservation of the nation even if they lived in faithless disobedience (Jer. 7:8–15). Thus an institution meant to encourage faithfulness was perverted into an excuse for continued disobedience. Such behavior led ultimately to the covenant curse anticipated by the oppression of other nations during the time of the judges: exile from the land and all the blessings for which it was the context. We will enumerate some of the important steps in this decline into greater and greater faithlessness below. The Sin-o-Meters in **Figures 5–10** depict this decline.

A. "All That the Lord Says We Will Do"

God gave his people his covenant, including his law, at Mount Sinai. In gratitude for his mighty deliverance from Egypt and for this covenant, his people answered, "All that the Lord says we will do" (see **Figure 5**). They promised the obedience necessary for fellowship with their gracious Savior-God. We have already seen how they struggled with this commitment from the beginning. While they were still at Mount Sinai, they grew impatient waiting for Moses to come down the mountain and made a golden calf idol, breaking this covenant at its most fundamental level (Ex. 32:1–35). The generation that came out of Egypt died in the wilderness (Num. 14:20–35), but their children inherited the promise and, under Joshua, entered the promised land.

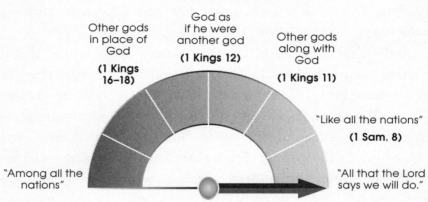

Figure 5

SIN-O-METER

Other gods in place of God

(1 Kings 16–18)

God as if he were another god

(1 Kings 12)

Other gods along with God

(1 Kings 11)

"Like all the nations"

(1 Sam. 8)

"Among all the nations"

"All that the Lord says we will do."

B. Like All the Nations (1 Samuel 8:1–9)

The disobedience of God's ancient people took a significant turn for the worse in 1 Samuel 8:1–9: they rejected divine rule by asking for a human king so that they could "be like all the nations" (1 Sam. 8:5). See **Figure 6.** Instead of trusting God they wanted to trust in an established human ruler with a dynasty. They blamed God for the fact that other nations were oppressing them rather than admitting that this oppression was the result of their own unfaithfulness. By seeking to be like "all the nations" they were denying their unique status as God's special posses-

> They blamed God for the fact that other nations were oppressing them rather than admitting that this oppression was the result of their own unfaithfulness.

sion and his royal priesthood. God had intended for them to reflect his character to other nations by living as his own special people, but God granted their request and told Samuel to appoint a king for them. After giving them a king who showed the folly of their request, he gave them David to lead them in obedience.

Figure 6

SIN-O-METER

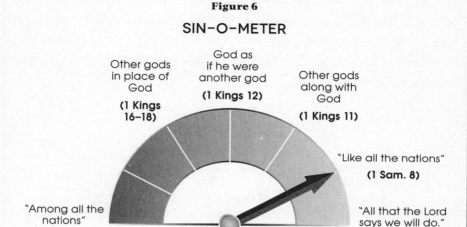

Other gods in place of God
(1 Kings 16–18)

God as if he were another god
(1 Kings 12)

Other gods along with God
(1 Kings 11)

"Like all the nations"
(1 Sam. 8)

"Among all the nations"

"All that the Lord says we will do."

C. Other Gods Along with God (1 Kings 11:1–13)

The kingdom flourished under David, despite problems with his children. After God put David's son Solomon on the throne, the kingdom reached new heights of sophistication and prosperity. Solomon began auspiciously by seeking God's wisdom (1 Kings 3:1–15). Then, however, Solomon followed the practice of other kings by marrying many foreign women, something contrary to God's law. He built temples for the gods of these wives, and then he began to worship them himself (1 Kings 11: 1–13). As we saw in the last chapter, the first commandment states the most fundamental principle of God's covenant: "You shall have no other gods besides me" (Ex. 20:3 ESV). Solomon broke this commandment by worshiping the gods of his wives. Even though he was still worshiping *Yahweh*, whose temple remained the shrine for the nation, Solomon set an example for the entire nation when he began to worship other gods along with God (see **Figure 7**). How easy it is to worship the gods of this world—whether power, pleasure, fame, money, ease—while still professing to worship the true God. Solomon's unfaithfulness was accompanied by immorality and by heavy oppression of the people. All the things that

Samuel told the people a king would do—take their property and their produce and put them to forced labor—Solomon did with a vengeance (1 Sam. 8:10–22). Faithlessness toward God inevitably leads to oppression and social disintegration. At Solomon's death his son Rehoboam was left with only a small part of the kingdom: the tribes of Judah and Benjamin (1 Kings 12:1–25). God left those tribes "for the sake of my servant David" (1 Kings 11:32).

Figure 7

SIN-O-METER

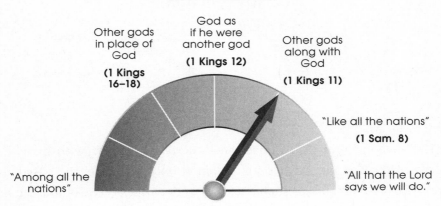

Other gods in place of God

(1 Kings 16–18)

God as if he were another god

(1 Kings 12)

Other gods along with God

(1 Kings 11)

"Like all the nations"

(1 Sam. 8)

"Among all the nations"

"All that the Lord says we will do."

D. God As If He Were Another God (1 Kings 12:25–33)

The next step in this spiral of disobedience occurred immediately after Solomon's death. His son Rehoboam foolishly insisted on continuing—even increasing—his father's oppression. The people rebelled, following one of Solomon's capable leaders, Jeroboam (1 Kings 12:1–18). Through the prophet Ahijah, God had promised Jeroboam ten of the twelve tribes as his kingdom (1 Kings 11:29–39). However, after the prophecy was fulfilled, Jeroboam refused to trust God. He was afraid that people would turn back to Rehoboam if they kept going up to Jerusalem to worship *Yahweh*, the God of Israel. So, on his own authority, he set up two other shrines—one at Dan in the far north of his kingdom, the other at Bethel on the very road to Jerusalem. He violated a multitude of God's instructions. He made golden calves for his gods. He established feasts that paralleled the Jerusalem feasts but were at different times. He appointed priests who were not Levites (1 Kings 12:25–33). He claimed, however, to be worshiping the true God. When he presented his golden calf, he declared, "Behold your gods, O Israel, who brought you up out of the land of Egypt" (1 Kings 12:28 ESV). When people want to be like the unbelieving world and begin to worship other gods along with God, they soon begin to worship God as if he were like these other gods (see **Figure 8**). They lose sight of God's unique holy character. They begin to worship God on their own terms. This is exactly what the second commandment forbids: "You shall not make for yourself a carved image" of anything in the universe as a representation of God. Jeroboam's legacy echoes throughout the annals of the Northern Kingdom: he is "Jeroboam the son of Nebat who made Israel sin" (1 Kings 22:52; 2 Kings 3:3; 10:29, 31; 13:2; 14:24; 15:9, 18, 24, 28; 23:15).

Figure 8

SIN-O-METER

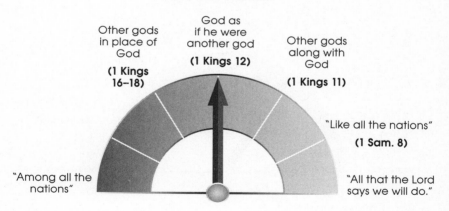

Other gods
in place of
God

**(1 Kings
16–18)**

God as
if he were
another god

(1 Kings 12)

Other gods
along with
God

(1 Kings 11)

"Like all the nations"

(1 Sam. 8)

"Among all the
nations"

"All that the Lord
says we will do."

E. Other Gods in Place of God (1 Kings 16–18)

The Northern Kingdom, made up of the ten tribes that God gave Jeroboam, never recovered from the pattern established by Jeroboam's sin. There were some faithful people among these tribes, but the nation as a whole turned away from God. It was only a short step from worshiping God as if he were another god to worshiping other gods in place of God (see

Figure 9). After all, if there isn't any distinction between God and other gods, what difference does it make whom one worships? King Ahab took this step. He married Jezebel, the daughter of the king of Sidon. She introduced the worship of Tyrian Ba'al as the official religion of the state and attempted to root out all worship of *Yahweh* (1 Kings 16:29–17:24). Marrying an idolatrous wife, contrary to God's law, was again taking its toll. Ba'al was a fertility god who was supposed to bring abundance of crops, flocks, herds, and children. His worship reinforced the self-centered, oppressive rule begun by Solomon, as evidenced by Jezebel's behavior when she blatantly stole Naboth's vineyard for her husband through murder and false witnesses (1 Kings 21:1–16). Only Elijah's great victory over the prophets of Ba'al at Mount Carmel (1 Kings 18:1–46) prevented the virtual extinction of *Yahweh* worship in this Northern Kingdom.

Figure 9

SIN–O–METER

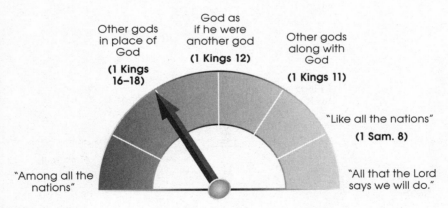

Other gods in place of God
(1 Kings 16–18)

God as if he were another god
(1 Kings 12)

Other gods along with God
(1 Kings 11)

"Like all the nations"
(1 Sam. 8)

"Among all the nations"

"All that the Lord says we will do."

F. Among All the Nations

God's people began the path of disobedience by wanting to be "like all the nations." That path led to their being scattered "among all the nations." The ministry of the prophets Elijah and his successor Elisha saved the Northern Kingdom from coming completely under the dominion of Ba'al and postponed its final destruction. God used Elisha to eliminate the rest of Ahab's wicked house (2 Kings 1–10). The coming doom was masked by a brief time of power and prosperity under the rule of Jeroboam II (2 Kings 14:23–29). Yet within a hundred years after Ahab's death the Northern Kingdom was taken into exile by Assyria, never to return (2 Kings 17:1–41). The Assyrians brought in other nations who intermarried with the remnant of the Israelites to make a mixed, idolatrous people (see **Figure 10**).

Figure 10

SIN-O-METER

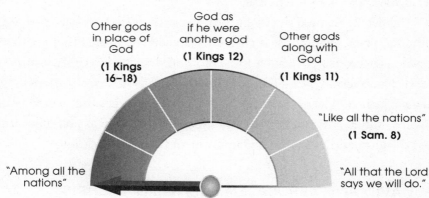

The nation of Judah, still under the rule of a son of David, lasted another 150 years (2 Kings 18:1–25:30). Judah had several faithful kings, most notably Hezekiah (2 Kings 18:1–20:21) and Josiah (2 Kings 22:1–23:30). Nevertheless, most of her kings were lukewarm to the worship of *Yahweh* or, like Manasseh (2 Kings 21:1–18), positively hostile. The kings and people of Judah repeatedly returned to and persisted in idolatry and immorality. Instead of trusting God they formed alliances with idolatrous nations and their gods. Some, as noted above, derived a false sense of security from the temple, thinking, *Since God's temple is here, God will take care of us no matter how we live.* Finally Judah, the Southern Kingdom, is also taken into captivity—this time by Babylon (2 Kings 25:1–26).

This exile from the land was the inevitable consequence of disobedience. God had given them the land as the place where they could live in obedient fellowship with him and in harmony with one another in accord with his covenant. If God's people would live with their holy God they must obey his voice and reflect his character. Faithlessness and disobedience polluted the land. Thus disobedience led to expulsion from God's presence. Through Moses and the prophets God had been warning them from the beginning. When they sinned he often sent other nations to rule over them and to diminish their land as a foretaste of the exile to which disobedience would lead. Finally their unrepentant, persistent disobedience took its toll in exile.

The people wanted the institutions that other nations had, such as a king. By giving them those institutions God demonstrated that political/social institutions were unable to overcome the disobedience of the human heart. However, as we will see below, God used these institutions—the Davidic king and Jerusalem/Zion—as pictures or types that would point toward and help us understand the salvation that he was going to bring and the glorious destiny he had in mind for the people of God.

IV. DAVID AND JERUSALEM FULFILLED IN CHRIST

Some may ask, what is the importance of God's choice of David and Jerusalem for believers today? What is the continuing significance of this narrative that stretches from Judges through 2 Kings? How does this story of divine mercy, human faithlessness (with occasional repentance), and final judgment impact the lives of God's people today? Let's reflect on what we have been saying in light of the three guidelines articulated in earlier chapters: the Example Principle, the Pattern Principle, and the Typological Principle.

A. The Example Principle and the Pattern Principle

We have put these two together because there is little more to say about the Pattern Principle from this part of Scripture. It is important to remember that the Davidic king did not establish a new law. His mission was to lead people in obedience to the Mosaic covenant. Thus, observing how

God actually held his people accountable before the law in this history of their disobedience brings clarity to the Pattern Principle by emphasizing the moral aspect of the law. The prophet did not confront David over something trivial but over adultery, murder, theft, and false witness (2 Sam. 12:1–31)! Furthermore, this narrative helps us understand what seem to be the harsher aspects of the law. God maintained the seriousness of his law by executing judgment for disobedience on both individuals and the nation. And yet he repeatedly showed mercy by delaying judgment and providing an opportunity for repentance. The mercy of God thus revealed helps us to put the death penalty required by the law for idolatry, murder, adultery, and other sins in perspective. God considered these sins such a violation of his relationship with his people and of their common life that they incurred the death penalty. Yet in practice he often delayed judgment in hope that the guilty would repent—and then suspended the judgment altogether if they repented. Israel's long history of idolatry and immorality bears witness to the mercy of God.

This part of Scripture is fertile ground for the Example Principle. Remember, Old Testament characters are not examples in everything they do. They are examples we should emulate when they respond to

> Old Testament characters are not examples in everything they do. They are examples we should emulate when they respond to God with faith and obedience.

God with faith and obedience, and they are examples we should shun when they respond with faithless disobedience. Thus the whole narrative of God's disobedient people that stretches from Judges through 2 Kings is a powerful example that warns us of the consequences of disobedience. It is important to remember that Jerusalem and the land are types or pictures of the eternal destiny of God's people (see chap. 4 and the discussion of typology below). This narrative warns us against that persistent disobedience that results in eternal exclusion from God's presence (compare Heb. 3:1–4:13).

Many persons within this narrative furnish us with examples positive and negative. As we would expect, King David, so prominent in this story, provides a wealth of examples. David's simple confidence in God

> David's humble penitence when confronted with his sin is the prime scriptural example for how we should react when confronted with our disobedience . . .

before the threat of Goliath gives us courage before every seemingly insurmountable difficulty that challenges God's people and defies his name (1 Sam. 17:31–51). David's patient refusal to take things in his own hands and seize the throne from Saul exemplifies the kind of faith that waits on God to fulfill his promises in his own time. David's humble penitence when confronted with his sin is the prime scriptural example for how we should react when confronted with our disobedience (2 Sam. 12:13–18). Although David had the power, he did not destroy God's messenger, explain away God's convicting word, or indulge in self-justification.

David's fall into sin is also a stern warning—especially for the leaders of God's people. David had reached the pinnacle of success and was enjoying his ease (2 Sam. 11:1). How easy it was to fall into temptation, to think, almost unconsciously, that he was above God's law, to engage in one sin, adultery, which quickly led to murder, theft, and deceit. Although he was forgiven, the consequences of his act continued to infect his family and, through them, to plague the people of God for generations. David's fall calls us to practice careful accountability. We might also point to David's failure to discipline his children—compare both Eli (1 Sam. 3:11–14) and Samuel (1 Sam. 8:1–3)—as an example to avoid. Solomon began with trust and with humility before the Lord (1 Kings 3:1–13), but through the corrupting power of fame, wealth, and influence came to rely upon his own resources and to practice oppression (1 Kings 11:1–43).

Jeroboam's determination to make God over for his own ends set in motion a course of destruction that resulted in the demise of the Northern Kingdom. King Josiah of Judah provides us with an example of one wholly devoted to God. The prophets Samuel, Nathan, Elijah, and Elisha are examples of faithfulness to the word of God, courage, and integrity.

These are some of the more important applications of the Example Principle to the books of Judges through 2 Kings. A more detailed study of the text would provide further insight into these and other examples. However, it is time to turn from the Example Principle to the Typological Principle. Scripture develops the rich typological significance in God's choice of David and of Jerusalem.

B. The Typological Principle

David and His Descendants. God's disobedient people made the sinful request to be "like all the nations" by having a king (1 Sam. 8:5). They did this because they blamed God for the oppression they were suffering rather than admitting that it was the result of their disobedience. They did not trust God to protect them. God granted their request by instituting the Davidic monarchy. The Davidic dynasty was to be an eternal institution (2 Sam. 7:13, 16, 24–26, 29) that would establish God's people in obedience and thus allow them to live in fellowship with God, free from the oppression of their enemies. The king was to be God's special representative, called "the Lord's Anointed" (1 Sam. 16:6; 24:6–10; 26:9, 11, 16, 23; 2 Sam. 1:14, 16; 19:21) and empowered by God's Spirit for his God-given task.

In actual fact, the kings more often than not fulfilled the people's desire rather than God's purpose. They did not confirm God's people in obedience as the unique people of God who reflected his holy character. Rather they led the people to be "like all the nations." Rather than rely on the faithfulness of God they did the things that kings did in order to be effective in the world. They developed bureaucracies that oppressed the people with taxes, tribute, forced labor, and slavery just as Samuel had said they would (1 Sam. 8:10–22). They protected themselves by making alliances with idolatrous nations sealed by marriages to foreign women and cemented by idolatrous worship. Their rule began to reflect the character of the gods of the nations rather than the God of heaven and earth.

As the disparity between the person seated on the throne in Jerusalem and the coming King promised by God deepened, the writers of the Old Testament began to look forward to a greater David, a true "Lord's Anointed One" who would fulfill God's purpose. "Anointed One" is *Messiah* in Hebrew, *Christ* in Greek. The demise of kingship after the Exile only fueled expectations of this "Messiah," who would deliver God's people once and for all from oppression and establish them in obedient fellowship with God. King David became the type or picture of this one who would come.

We have seen how God's delivering his people from Egypt was a type of the deliverance Christ would bring (chap. 3). He is the perfect priest, the effective sacrifice, and the deliverer/revealer/prophet like Moses par excellence. All of these functions, however, come to focus in his role as Messiah, for it is the anointed representative of God who would deliver God's people from disobedience and establish them as faithful subjects of the kingdom of God. Yes, as the Psalms and Prophets make clear (see the following chapters), he will accomplish this by suffering as an atoning sacrifice for the sins of the world; but it is he, the Messiah, great David's greater son, who will accomplish this redemption for the people of God. That is why the term *Christ* is so prominent in the New Testament.

Who can fill this role? The story began with the rejection of divine rule and the request for a human king. No merely human king, even of David's line, was able adequately to restore that divine rule. Divine rule can only be reestablished when the eternal Son of God assumes the human seed of David—when God's Son and David's son are one and the same (see **Figure 11**). Then the cry goes out: "Your God reigns" (Isa. 52:7). God the Father can, in the fullest sense, address this Messiah as "my Son" (Ps. 2:7; see Heb. 1:5) and as "God" (Ps. 45:6; see Heb. 1:8).

This Messiah has assumed the broken humanity of David's line and taken his seat, not on a throne in earthly Jerusalem but at the right hand of the throne of God (Ps. 110:1). By so doing he has redeemed an obedient people who live in God's kingdom eagerly awaiting its full revelation at Christ's return.

Figure 11

THE SON OF GOD BECOMES THE SON OF DAVID

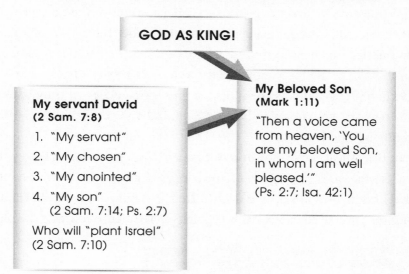

GOD AS KING!

My servant David (2 Sam. 7:8)

1. "My servant"
2. "My chosen"
3. "My anointed"
4. "My son"
   (2 Sam. 7:14; Ps. 2:7)

Who will "plant Israel" (2 Sam. 7:10)

My Beloved Son (Mark 1:11)

"Then a voice came from heaven, 'You are my beloved Son, in whom I am well pleased.'"
(Ps. 2:7; Isa. 42:1)

Let's not miss the fact that Christ has done more than "save" individuals. He has redeemed a people of God who live in obedient fellowship with God and are called to live in love with one another (John 13:34–35; 15:12–14). It is fitting that we now turn to the significance of Jerusalem as the ultimate home of God's people.

Jerusalem/Zion. We have seen that by choosing Jerusalem as the place where he would dwell with his people God made it a concrete, institutionalized embodiment of all the relationships that constituted his plan for humanity. It represented his presence among them. It was the focal point of their common life. Above all, it was the centerpiece of the land he had given them. Thus it is not surprising that a manifold typology and symbolism developed around the image of Jerusalem/Zion. The Psalms and the Prophets use this imagery for God's dwelling among his people, for the people of God, and for the restored place of their abode in God's presence. The New Testament continues this development—as does Christian hymnody.

Jerusalem/Zion with its temple incorporates some of the tabernacle imagery that we talked about in the last chapter. Jesus himself is the new Temple (John 2:13–21). The God who dwelt in the Jerusalem temple became incarnate in Jesus in order to remove the barrier of sin that restricted his people's approach to him under the previous regime. That barrier has been removed! Therefore Christ's extended body, the church, is now the temple of God indwelt by the Spirit (1 Cor. 3:16–17; 6:19; Eph. 2:21). This is the glorious present privilege of the people of God: to be the new temple, the new Zion, indwelt corporately and individually by God himself.

In the fullest sense, however, Jerusalem/Zion is a picture/type of the New Jerusalem, the heavenly Mount Zion, the city of the living God, the eternal home of God's people (Heb. 12:22–29; Rev. 21:9–22:5). The Old Testament prepared well for this typology. Jerusalem/Zion was the place

> The God who dwelt in the . . . temple became incarnate in Jesus . . . to remove the barrier of sin . . . Therefore Christ's . . . body, the church, is now the temple . . .

that God chose to put his name, to live among his people. It was the focal point of their fellowship with him. It drew into itself the symbolism of the promised land as the place where God dwelt with his own. Because of its significance the Psalms and Prophets describe Jerusalem in the most extravagant terms: "Great is the Lord, and greatly to be praised in the city of our God, in His holy mountain. Beautiful in elevation, the joy of the whole earth, is Mount Zion on the sides of the north, the city of the great King" (Ps. 48:1–2). To approach God in Jerusalem was to experience unbounded joy. Temporal Jerusalem, with its solid foundation and strong walls, became a type of the city "which has foundations, whose builder and maker is God" (Heb. 11:10) and of the full restoration of all three aspects of God's plan for humanity. See **Figure 12**.

Figure 12

THE TYPOLOGY OF JERUSALEM/ZION

Old Zion, Jerusalem

1. God's guarantee of his presence

2. The visible symbol of God's covenant with his people

3. The guarantee of the land, the new "Eden" God had given his people

The incarnate Zion, Jesus

1. "God with us"

2. The twelve and other disciples formed the new community.

3. They enjoyed the blessings of the kingdom.

New Zion, the Body of Christ

1. Infilled by God's Spirit

2. The people of the new covenant in Christ

3. Partakers of the heritage of God's people

Heavenly Zion, The New Jerusalem

1. Living in God's immediate presence

2. Living as his people

3. Living in a re-created world

According to both Hebrews (Heb. 12:22–29) and the Revelation (Rev. 21:9–22:5), this city is the "heavenly Jerusalem"; it already exists as the dwelling place of God. And yet the "New" Jerusalem is a future city: it will be fully revealed at Christ's return as the eternal home of God's people. In both Hebrews and the Revelation this city and the Most Holy Place (represented of old by the inner sanctuary of the temple) embody the same reality. As the Most Holy Place it is the place where God's redeemed people as the new humanity will enjoy the deepest and most direct fellowship with him. As the city of God it is the place where the community of God's people will enjoy the richest common life.

This city is the opposite of the human city represented at the beginning of Scripture by Babel (Gen. 11:1–9) and at the end by Babylon

(Rev. 17:1–18:24). That city was based on rebellion against God and thus on human selfishness, greed, and oppression. And yet the eternal city is the fulfillment of everything the human city was intended to be. Hebrews 12:22–24 describes the joyous fellowship and celebration of God's people in this city. The extravagant description of this city in the Revelation, with gates, precious stones, streams, fruit, and healing leaves, pushes our imagination to the limit: we know that life in this city with God will be better than anything we could imagine, and yet it will be the fulfillment of our deepest longings. In this city God's original plan for humanity—fellowship with him, love for one another, and enjoyment of the environment—will be complete.

Thus Jerusalem/Zion is a type and picture of the glorious hope of the people of God. In company with Abraham and the faithful of all time, we are looking forward to the city "which has foundations, whose builder and maker is God" (Heb. 11:10). That city is the "homeland" where our citizenship lies (Heb. 11:13–16). "We're marching to Zion,/Beautiful, beautiful Zion;/We're marching upward to Zion,/The beautiful city of God" (Isaac Watts).

John Newton's description of this city in his great hymn based on Psalm 87 whets our appetite to enter its gates:

> Glorious things of thee are spoken, Zion, city of our God;
> He whose word cannot be broken Formed you for His own abode;
> On the Rock of Ages founded, What can shake your sure repose?
> With salvation's walls surrounded, You may smile at all your foes.

The last verse of his hymn helps us on the pilgrim way:

> Savior, if of Zion's city, I through grace a member am,
> Let the world deride or pity, I will glory in your name;
> Fading is the world's best pleasure, All its boasted pomp and show;
> Solid joys and lasting treasure None but Zion's children know.

The narrative that begins in Judges and runs through 2 Kings ends in exile. The institutions that God established during this time—the Davidic king and Jerusalem/Zion—were not able to overcome the persistent disobedience and rebelliousness of God's people. This story of their rebellion demonstrates the great need for God to bring about the salvation typified by David and Zion. These institutions were powerful pictures of the one who would deliver the people of God from their disobedience and of the glorious destiny that God has for the redeemed community.

The rest of the Old Testament awaits this coming salvation with anticipation. First Chronicles through Esther shows how the history of God's people looked forward to this restoration. Job through the Song of Songs helps us to see how the experience of God's people anticipated its arrival. Through the Prophets, God promises his people that it will come and stimulates their desire by describing the form it will take.

In the next two chapters we will look at some of the most neglected (Isn't Chronicles just a rehash of Samuel and Kings?) and the most treasured (Psalms, Proverbs) books of the Old Testament. These books took their final shape after the Exile. They bring us hope even in the darkest times.

6

RESTORATION ANTICIPATED *in the* HISTORY *of* GOD'S PEOPLE

"My Anointed One"

1 Chronicles to Esther

INTRODUCTION

Why should we have a separate chapter on 1 and 2 Chronicles, Ezra, Nehemiah, and Esther? Don't 1 and 2 Chronicles retell the story of Samuel and Kings? Why not include these books with the previous historical books? Then we would have the complete story of God's people in the promised land from the time of the Judges through the Kings to the Exile and return. If we take all of these historical books together, Ruth and Esther complement each other. Ruth tells about a faithful pagan woman who comes to the promised land in the time of the Judges. Esther tells about a faithful Jewish woman living in the land of exile during the time of the restoration.

A. 1 Chronicles Through Esther and the Other Historical Books

There are, however, several important reasons for studying 1 Chronicles through Esther as a separate group of books. First, as noted above, 1 and 2 Chronicles do not continue the story of Samuel and Kings; they retell it. Second, 1 Chronicles does not begin with King Saul, with the judges, or even with the Exodus from Egypt, but with creation and with God's promises to Abraham. Third, Ezra and Nehemiah are closely related to the Chronicles. Ezra begins where 2 Chronicles ends, with the decree of Cyrus. All of these clues help us to see that 1 Chronicles through Ezra is not simply a continuation of the Judges-Samuel-Kings narrative. It is a new narrative. That earlier narrative ran from the time God's people entered the promised land under Joshua to their exile. If we include the Pentateuch, from the creation to the Exile. The narrative in 1 Chronicles-Nehemiah also retells the whole story but in a way that addresses those who have returned from exile. Thus it begins again with creation but extends beyond the Exile to the return from captivity. The story of Esther complements the return of the exiles in Ezra and Nehemiah just as Ruth anticipates the account of David in Samuel. Judges, Samuel, and Kings recount the history of God's people as a warning. They show how their persistent sin in the face of God's continued mercy led to the judgment of exile. Chronicles through Ezra addresses those who have suffered this judgment and who continue, despite their repentance, to face discouragement and opposition. These books offer a message of hope based on God's present deliverance and the magnitude of his past blessings. If we include them with the previous books we will miss their distinct contribution. In fact, our tendency will be to skip Chronicles and go directly from 2 Kings to Ezra.

B. First Chronicles Through Ezra and the Poetic Books

Furthermore, 1 and 2 Chronicles, Ezra, and Nehemiah share several emphases with the poetic books that follow and thus provide a smooth transition to Job, Psalms, Proverbs, Ecclesiastes, and the Song of Songs. The book of Psalms contains hymns and prayers for worship. Job,

Proverbs, Ecclesiastes, and the Song of Songs, often called the "Wisdom Literature," deal with the experiences of everyday life.

We have seen that 1 Chronicles through Esther addresses those who have returned from exile with a message of hope. It is also probable that Psalms, Proverbs, Ecclesiastes, and the Song did not receive their final form until after the return from exile. It is difficult to determine with certainty the time when Job was written. However, Job's emphasis on the suffering of the righteous makes it appropriate reading for God's people who were searching his ways because they continued to suffer though they had repented and returned from the captivity.

Furthermore, both the historical narrative of 1 Chronicles through Ezra and the "poetic" books, with the exception of Job (that is, Psalms, Proverbs, Ecclesiastes, and the Song), venerate David and Solomon. In chapters 1–9, the author of 1 Chronicles uses genealogies to prepare for the coming of David by linking his family and the people of God as a whole to creation and to the promises God gave Abraham. It may be tempting to skip these genealogies when reading through the Bible, yet these first nine chapters are important because, among other things, they put the reigns of David (1 Chron. 10:1–29:30) and his son Solomon (2 Chron. 1:1–9:31) in universal perspective as central to the work and people of God. The chapters in 2 Chronicles that describe events after the time of Solomon continue this emphasis on David and Solomon by omitting the all but universally disobedient kings of north Israel and focusing only on the descendants of David who ruled Judah (2 Chron. 10:1–36:23). The territory of the former Northern Kingdom is now inhabited by a mixed, idolatrous people who entice those returned from exile to compromise their faithfulness and who hinder their progress. It is the line of David and Solomon that has preserved the remnant who have become the faithful people of God and who now have returned from the Exile. Yet they live under the dominion of great empires as they wait for God to fulfill his promises.

The poetic books mentioned above continue this emphasis on David and his son Solomon. These books contain much that was handed down from the days when kings ruled in Israel and Judah. David, the sweet singer of Israel, is credited with a large number of the psalms. Solomon was the fountain and source of the wisdom in Proverbs, Ecclesiastes, and the Song. Thus this group of books focuses on David (Psalms) and Solomon (Proverbs, Ecclesiastes, the Song of Songs) just as did the historical narrative of 1 Chronicles through Ezra. The first group of books describes the glory of David's and Solomon's reigns; the second group, their legacy of worship and insight for daily living.

Thus these two groups of books—Chronicles through Ezra and Job through the Song of Songs—share the perspective of those who have returned from the Exile with great admiration for the past glories of David and Solomon. Furthermore, these two groups of books complement each other. Chronicles through Ezra puts the historical context of this post-exilic era into perspective for the returned people of God. God's great blessings in the age of David and Solomon assure God's suffering but penitent people that his promises for the future are certain. The Psalms and the Wisdom Literature focus on the daily experience of those who live in the time between God's great mercies of the past and his promises for the future. The Psalms teach them how to sing and how to pray. Through these hymns and prayers God's people bring their experience—their suffering and their joys—to God. Proverbs, Ecclesiastes, and the Song pertain to everyday experience in the sphere of human relationships within this world. From these books God's people learn how to conduct their daily affairs aright according to "the fear of the Lord." Anticipation for God's future salvation, for his Messiah who will establish his kingdom, runs through both the history and the experience of these returnees. Thus we have included both groups of books, along with the Prophets, under the heading "Restoration Anticipated." In different ways both groups of books point forward to the Christ and help us to understand him.

As long as the people of God continue to face suffering while awaiting the return of Christ, these books will continue to sustain us just as they did those who returned to their homeland from the Exile long ago. There is still need for return, for repentance, for instruction in and obedience to God's word, for rebuilding walls, for confidence that God is at work in a hostile world, for sustained hope in God's returning Messiah.

Let's look first at the historical context of God's returned exiles as described in Chronicles, Ezra, and Nehemiah, and Esther before turning to the more popular Psalms and Wisdom Literature in chapter 7.

I. THE HISTORICAL CONTEXT OF GOD'S PEOPLE AFTER THE RETURN FROM EXILE

We have already pointed out the way in which the Chronicles focus on David and Solomon. In fact, with some justification, we can say that they idealize the days of these two kings as the golden age of the people of God. See **Figure 1**.

Figure 1

THE HISTORICAL CONTEXT OF THOSE REDEEMED FROM EXILE

The Idealized Past

1 Chron. 1–9	Prologue: Adam through Saul
1 Chron. 10–29	David, Torah
2 Chron. 1–9	Solomon, Temple
2 Chron. 10–36	Epilogue: the later kings of Judah

The Diminished Present

Temple	Ezra 1–6
Torah	Ezra 7–10 Neh. 8–10
City walls	Neh. 1–7, 11–13

God's Universal Power

Esther 1–10

CHRONICLES ⟶ EZRA, NEHEMIAH ⟶ ESTHER

A. An Idealized Past: 1 and 2 Chronicles

First Chronicles 1:1–9:44. This magnification of David and Solomon's age begins with the genealogies of 1 Chronicles 1–9. These genealogies put the history of David, Solomon, and the nation of Judah within the context of creation and of God's promises of redemption to Abraham (1 Chron. 1:1–54). As we would expect, special attention is given to Judah (1 Chron. 2:3–55; 4:1–43, including the tribe of Simeon that joined Judah), to the family of David (1 Chron. 3:1–24), and to the Levites (1 Chron. 6:1–48) who would play such an important part in the temple that David's son Solomon would build in Jerusalem. The prominent list of those dwelling in Jerusalem (1 Chron. 9:1–34) anticipates the central role that city will play in David's life and in the nation's destiny. First Chronicles 8:1–40 and 9:35–44 recount the tribe and family of Saul in preparation for his defeat (1 Chron. 10:1–14) and the rise of David. The author of 1 and 2 Chronicles, whom we will call the Chronicler, mentions Saul's sin as the cause

> The Chronicler is not warning people who face the imminent threat of exile. He is encouraging those who have now returned from that exile.

for his destruction (1 Chron. 10:13–14), but is uninterested in the details of Saul's disobedience or the struggle between Saul and David. He and his readers are well aware of the disobedience that led to their exile, as recorded in Judges through 2 Kings. The Chronicler is not warning people who face the imminent threat of exile. He is encouraging those who have now returned from that exile. That is why he emphasizes the goodness God showed them by giving them king, temple, and city. He wants them to remember the heritage of faithfulness that they receive from those kings who were obedient. Thus, the Chronicler is very concerned with God's establishing the line of David to lead his people in law-obedience, with David's establishment of Jerusalem as the city where God would dwell among his people, and with David's preparation for and Solomon's building of the temple in Jerusalem as the house of God. Yet the Chronicler will not let his hearers forget God's judgment (2 Chron. 7:19–22), lest they fall back into old practices.

Figure 2

1 AND 2 CHRONICLES—PART ONE

I. Prologue (1 Chron. 1:1–9:44)

II. David (1 Chron. 10:1–29:30)

A. David becomes king. (10:1–12:40)

B. David brings the ark to Jerusalem. (13:1–16:43)

C. God makes a covenant with David. (17:1–27)

D. David's conquests. (18:1–20:8)

E. David prepares for the temple. (21:1–27:34)

F. David instructs his son Solomon. (28:1–29:30)

1 Chronicles 10:1–29:30. These emphases continue throughout the twenty chapters dedicated to the reign of David (1 Chron. 10:1–29:30). This section begins with the death of Saul (1 Chron. 10:1–14) and ends with the coronation of Solomon (1 Chron. 29:21–30). There is no mention of David's adultery, of the rebellion of Absalom, or of Adonijah's attempt to preempt Solomon's accession to the throne. David's prideful census of the people for which he suffered divine judgment was, through God's mercy, the occasion for establishing the site of the temple. Thus the Chronicler could not avoid giving considerable space to this event (1 Chron. 21:1–30). Yet he softens David's responsibility by attributing this census to the incitement of Satan (1 Chron. 21:1). The Chronicler focuses on God's establishing David, on the extent and glory of David's reign, and on the things he did that prepared for the temple in Jerusalem.

God established the Davidic dynasty when he made his covenant with David in 1 Chronicles 17:1–27. This covenant is central to the

Chronicler's interest in the Jerusalem temple and obedience to the law of God. God has graciously established the Davidic line forever. God's temple will be a sign and seal of this grace, for it will be built by the first son of David's line. God will dwell in this temple among his people. The Davidic king will "plant" (1 Chron. 17:9) them in God's land by leading them in obedience to God's law so that they can live in God's holy presence.

First Chronicles describes the magnitude of David's reign. We are told about his mighty men and his army (1 Chron. 11:10–12:40), his fame (1 Chron. 14:1–17), his military victories, and the extent of his kingdom (1 Chron. 18:1–20:8).

The Chronicler is very concerned about all that David did to prepare for God's dwelling place among his people. He begins by telling us that David established Jerusalem, the place where the temple would be built, as his capital (1 Chron. 11:1–9). David brought the ark of God, which would be the centerpiece of the temple, to Jerusalem (1 Chron. 13:1–14; 15:1–16:43). He acquired resources and personnel that Solomon would use to build the temple (1 Chron. 22:1–19). Perhaps most important of all in the Chronicler's eyes, he organized and assigned duties to the priests, Levites, gatekeepers, and musicians who would serve in the temple (1 Chron. 23:1–26:28). The temple would be the place in which the law of Moses was put into practice (2 Chron. 8:12–15). This golden age of David and Solomon was the time of the Torah, God's law given through Moses, in the temple, the place where God lived among his people (see **Figure 1**).

Rebuilding God's dwelling place and living according to the law were issues that deeply concerned the redeemed exiles (see **Figure 1**), even as they longed for an heir to David's line. The house of God had been burned and their fathers and mothers had been expelled from the promised land because they refused to reflect God's character by living according to the precepts of his law. By God's grace, the returned exiles were going to rebuild the temple and live obediently in his presence.

Second Chronicles 1:1–9:31. The first nine chapters of 2 Chronicles continue this idealization of the past by focusing on the glory of Solomon's reign. Solomon's building the temple for which David had so carefully prepared was central to this golden age in the history of the people of God. According to 2 Chronicles 1:1–12, Solomon began his reign by seeking God and asking him for wisdom. Second Chronicles 1:13–17 introduces his great wealth. Second Chronicles 8:1–9:31 describes the extent of his kingdom, his worshiping of the Lord, his wisdom (including the visit of the Queen of Sheba), and the extent of his wealth. There is no mention of Solomon's sin. The division of the kingdom after his death is, on the one hand, attributed to Rehoboam's folly (2 Chron. 10:1–17), and on the other, to God's fulfilling his word given through the prophet Ahijah (2 Chron. 10:15). The deterioration of Judah and its oppression by Egypt during Rehoboam's latter reign is attributed to Rehoboam's sin (2 Chron. 12:1–16).

Figure 3

1 AND 2 CHRONICLES—PART TWO

III. Solomon (2 Chron. 1:1–9:31)

    A. Solomon receives wisdom from God. (1:1–17)

    B. Solomon builds the temple. (2:1–4:22)

    C. Solomon dedicates the temple. (5:1–7:22)

    D. The glory of Solomon's reign. (8:1–9:31)

IV. The kings of Judah (1 Chron. 10:1–36:23)

Above all, 2 Chronicles focuses on Solomon's building (2 Chron. 2:1–4:22) and dedication (2 Chron. 5:1–7:22) of the temple. As David began his preparation by bringing the ark of God to Jerusalem, so Solomon begins the dedication of the temple by bringing the ark of God, representing God's presence, into the new house of God (2 Chron. 5:1–14). Solomon next affirms the presence of the Lord in his house (2 Chron. 6:1–2), and then turns to the people and announces the faithfulness of God: God has fulfilled his promises by coming into his temple (2 Chron. 6:3–11).

Solomon's prayer is the centerpiece of this service of dedication (2 Chron. 6:12–42). He opens his prayer by affirming the faithfulness of Israel's promise-keeping God. He admits that no house could contain the God of the universe, but entreats God to keep his eyes on this house. He asks God to hear the prayers of his people when they turn toward this house with any need or in any crisis (2 Chron. 6:18–31, 34–35); he even asks that God will hear the prayer of the foreigner who acknowledges the God of heaven by turning toward this house (2 Chron. 6:32–33). As his prayer draws to a conclusion he implores God to forgive his sinful people if they turn in repentance toward this house—even if they have sinned

> The prayer climaxes when God occupies his house . . . God has filled this house with his presence as he once filled the tabernacle erected by Moses . . .

to the point of exile from the land (2 Chron. 6:35–40). The prayer climaxes when God occupies his house in response to Solomon's invitation (2 Chron. 7:1–3). God has filled this house with his presence as he once filled the tabernacle erected by Moses long ago (Ex. 40:34–38).

After the prayer came celebration: Solomon offered many sacrifices and kept a feast to the Lord (2 Chron. 7:4–11). If Solomon's prayer is the centerpiece of this dedication, God's answer in 2 Chronicles 7:12–22 is its conclusion. God promised to look on this house and to hear his people's prayers if they would turn from their wicked ways. He promised to establish Solomon's line if Solomon would walk in obedience. But if God's people would not obey, then he would uproot them from the land and leave his house in ruins as a testimony to their disobedience. God's warning in 2 Chronicles 7:19–22 assures us that the Chronicler has not forgotten the disobedience of God's people recorded in Samuel-Kings, though he chooses not to dwell on it. The returned exiles have experienced the reality of this divine judgment with which God's answer concludes. They have, however, also experienced the mercy of God on repentant exiles for which Solomon pleaded at the end of his prayer (2 Chron. 6:36–39). Since they are the answer to the great Solomon's prayer, the heritage of this golden age is theirs. Yet they must remember not to succumb to the disobedience that destroyed their fathers and mothers. They look forward to the time when God will again establish his people in glory.

2 Chronicles 10:1–36:33. After the division of the Davidic kingdom in the time of Rehoboam (2 Chron. 10:1–12:16), the worship of God was sustained and passed on by the nation of Judah centered in the temple at Jerusalem and ruled by a son of David. However, many faithful people from the Northern Kingdom became part of Judah, including the displaced Levites (2 Chron. 11:13–16). Many others from the north followed at the time of King Asa's revival (2 Chron. 15:9), and still more came at the invitation of Hezekiah (2 Chron. 30:1, 11, 18, 25) after the fall of Samaria. Josiah's reform also reached into the area of the former northern tribes (2 Chron. 34:1–9). Judah is heir to God's covenant with "all Israel" and contains within it representatives of the other tribes. The integrity of God's promises to his people remains unbroken.

Second Chronicles 13:1–36:23 tells the story of the subsequent kings of Judah. The golden age of David and Solomon shines brighter in its glory when compared with the story of these lesser kings and with the eventual tragic demise of the nation due to its sin.

The Chronicler is well aware of the wicked kings (Jehoram, 2 Chron. 21:1–20; Ahaziah, 2 Chron. 22:1–9; Ahaz, 2 Chron. 28:1–27; Manasseh, 2 Chron. 33:1–20; Amon, 2 Chron. 33:21–25; Jehoiakim, 2 Chron. 36:5; Jehoiachin, 2 Chron. 36:9; and Zedekiah, 2 Chron. 36:12), of those who served God partially (Joash, 2 Chron. 23:16–24:27; Amaziah, 2 Chron. 25:1–28; and Uzziah, 2 Chron. 26:1–23), and of the sin of the nation that led to exile (2 Chron. 36:11–21). The story of these kings enhances his description of the glorious David-Solomon golden age from which he has omitted mention of royal shortcomings.

Yet the Chronicler dedicates thirteen of these twenty-six chapters to Judah's four best kings: Asa (2 Chron. 14:1–16:14), Jehoshaphat

(2 Chron. 17:1–20:37), Hezekiah (2 Chron. 29:1–32:33), and Josiah (2 Chron. 34:1–35:27). Their faithfulness offers hope. It is an example for the returned exiles and for the people of God of all time. In fact, the Chronicler even uses the ruthlessness of Athaliah to describe the way in which the faithful priest Jehoiada bravely preserved the royal seed (2 Chron. 22:10–23:15). He has made the worst king of Judah, Manasseh, a positive example by describing his repentance (2 Chron. 33:1–20). Manasseh's life embodies the experience of the nation: he was taken as a captive to Babylon, turned to the Lord in repentance, and then returned to his kingdom.

The golden age of David and Solomon shines brightly in contrast to the persistent sin of kings and people that led to exile. And yet the faithful kings and people like Jehoiada have passed on the heritage of that golden age to the returned exiles and to the generations to come. The narrative of 1 and 2 Chronicles ends on a note of hope. The same God who announced the Exile (2 Chron. 36:15–21) through the prophets has also announced the return (2 Chron. 36:22–23). At his instigation, Cyrus the Persian king has not only given permission for the return, but has ordered God's people to rebuild God's house. God will hear Solomon's prayer that he grant mercy on exiled sinners (2 Chron. 6:36–39). The return of penitent Manasseh (2 Chron. 33:10–13) will be repeated by the repentant nation.

B. A Diminished Present: Ezra and Nehemiah

Ezra and Nehemiah bring the narrative of Chronicles to its conclusion by describing the return from exile, the rebuilding of the temple, the restoration of the people according to the law of Moses, and the construction of the walls of Jerusalem. The completion of this process took about 140 years. It began with the first return in 537 BC under Zerubbabel. The second return under Ezra did not happen until 458 BC. Even then the walls of the city were completed only when Nehemiah came to Jerusalem with firm intent to construct them. This restoration was real. God restored the city of David and replaced the destroyed temple of Solomon.

The law of Moses became more firmly entrenched than ever as the basis for life. Yet God's people lived in what we might call a "diminished present" (see **Figure 1**). Neither the temple nor the city was as grand as it once had been. The number of those who returned was small by comparison. The province of Judah was only a fraction of what had been the nation of Judah—and it was only a province. God's people were under the dominion of foreign kings. There was no one to sit on the throne of David. Furthermore, despite the prominence given the divine law, God's people kept needing reformation because of their compromise with the surrounding pagan nations.

Figure 4

EZRA AND NEHEMIAH

I. The return of the exiles under Zerubbabel. (Ezra 1:1–2:70)

II. The rebuilding of the temple. (Ezra 3:1–6:22)

III. The return of the exiles under Ezra. (Ezra 7:1–8:36)

IV. The first reformation under Ezra. (Ezra 9:1–10:44)

V. The return of Nehemiah. (Neh. 1:1–2:8)

VI. The rebuilding of the wall. (Neh. 2:9–6:19)

VII. The second reformation under Ezra and Nehemiah. (Neh. 7:1–10:39)

VIII. The repopulation of Jerusalem. (Neh. 11:1–12:26)

IX. The dedication of the wall. (Neh. 12:27–43)

X. The third reformation under Nehemiah. (Neh. 12:44–13:31)

When compared with the past glories of David and Solomon, this reduced present fueled the longing for God to fulfill all his promises and the expectation that he would. Technically the Exile had ended; they were back in the land. Their reduced circumstances, however, made them feel like, in fact, it had not ended. Zerubbabel, a descendant of David, was the leader of the first return. He, however, soon disappears. The books of Ezra and Nehemiah make no mention of a coming royal son of David, perhaps because the restoration and their part in it was permitted and supported by the Persian throne. Yet this diminished present must have fueled a deep desire in many for God to liberate his people by sending a son of David to restore the monarchy. The leadership of this coming Messiah would restore the three lost relationships integral to God's plan for humanity: obedient fellowship with God, harmonious fellowship among the people of God, and responsible enjoyment of the land.

Ezra and Nehemiah were shocked at the continued propensity of the people to compromise with the pagan world. These people had not only suffered the judgment of exile, but they had also been thoroughly instructed in the law. This propensity shows that the greater fulfillment still intended by God must provide for the transformation of the human heart. Thus the diminished state of God's people after the Exile points

> **Thus the diminished state of God's people after the Exile points forward to Christ, the great Son of David, who has taken his seat at God's right hand.**

forward to Christ, the great Son of David, who has taken his seat at God's right hand. He has established the new covenant and thus enables his people to obey by filling them with God's Spirit. In this way he prepares them to live with him forever in the New Jerusalem.

A more detailed look at these books confirms this analysis of their message and importance. Ezra begins where 2 Chronicles ended: with the decree of Cyrus ordering God's people to return and rebuild the temple (Ezra 1:1–4). The exuberant return under Zerubbabel (Ezra 1:5–2:70) led quickly to the building of the altar and the restoration of regular sacrifices (Ezra 3:1–6). Soon thereafter the returnees laid the foundation for the temple (Ezra 3:7–13). Yet those who could remember Solomon's temple wept at the small size of this foundation. The diminished present was plain to see. Little did they realize that by the time this temple was completed twenty years later most of those who could remember Solomon's temple would be dead. The opposition of the surrounding peoples and their manipulation of the Persian kings caused this delay (Ezra 4: 1–24). Finally, through the urging of the prophets Haggai and Zechariah and the restored approval of the Persian monarch, the temple was completed (Ezra 5:1–6:22). The people celebrated this event by keeping the Passover.

The return of Ezra, the priest and scribe of the law (Ezra 7:1–8:36), led to a restoration of the community on the basis of the Mosaic law (Ezra 9:1–10:44). Ezra's shock at the people's sin followed by his humiliation before God and his intense prayer of repentance brought the people to their senses. They agreed to annul their intermarriages with the surrounding pagan people and to separate themselves from their ungodly customs so that they could be faithful to God's law. His law became the constitution of their community.

If the book of Ezra focused on the rebuilding of the temple and the reformation of the community according to the Mosaic law, Nehemiah is concerned with the rebuilding of Jerusalem's walls (Neh. 2:–6:19; 12:27–43) and the reformation of the people (Neh. 7:1–10:39; 12:44–13:31). The rebuilding of the walls was a greater threat to the surrounding people and thus generated even more resistance than the construction of the temple. Nevertheless, under Nehemiah's brave leadership the walls were completed in fifty-two days. The rebuilding of the physical walls and the reformation of the people were closely related. Instruction in the law and renewal of the covenant took place between the completion of the walls (Neh. 6:15–19) and their dedication (Neh. 12:27–43). God's renewed city was intended for God's renewed people. Thus the dedication of the walls celebrated the restoration of both city and people. Yet in Nehemiah's absence the people fell back into compromise with the sinful practice of the surrounding nations. They neglected God's house and disregarded his Sabbath. Thus the book of Nehemiah concludes with Nehemiah's consternation at the people's persistent unfaithfulness and with his instituting once again the needed reforms (Neh. 12:44–13:31). Though they fall away, the people who returned from exile seem to have a desire to follow God and be more ready to repent than many of their ancestors. Yet the ending to this long story that began at 1 Chronicles 1:1 confirms the need for God to change his people's hearts.

C. God's Universal Power: Esther

Those returned from exile living in the tiny province of Judah recognized their diminished state even as they rejoiced in their return:

> Here we are, servants today! And the land that You gave to our fathers, to eat its fruit and its bounty, here we are, servants in it! And it yields much increase to the kings you have set over us, because of our sins; also they have dominion over our bodies and our cattle at their pleasure; and we are in great distress. (Neh. 9:36–37)

The story of Esther unfolds far away in the corridors of power at Susa, the capital of the Persian Empire. This book assures us that God is in control of the affairs of empires and nations even when they are unaware of his presence or have excluded him from their thought (see **Figure 1**). God's people may be diminished, but he is not.

Figure 5

ESTHER

I. The choice of Esther as queen. (Est. 1:1–2:23)

II. The plot of Haman for the destruction of the Jews. (Est. 3:1–15)

III. The courage of Esther before the king. (Est. 4:1–5:8)

IV. The downfall of Haman. (Est. 5:9–7:10)

V. The deliverance of the Jews. (Est. 8:1–10:3)

Throughout this account of Esther, God has been excluded from public life as thoroughly as in any modern secular or even atheistic state. The book of Esther never mentions God, his covenant, or his mighty acts. It says nothing about such persons as Abraham, Moses, or David. The pedigree of Haman, the enemy of the Jews, is the only clear reference to people known elsewhere in Scripture: he is an "Agagite" (Est. 3:1), a descendent of an ancient king of the Amalekites who were traditional enemies of God's people (1 Sam. 15:1–9, 32–35).[19] The heroine and the hero of the book are named after Babylonian gods: Esther after Ishtar, Mordecai after Marduk. The book of Esther does not tell us that Mordecai refused to bow to Haman because of his loyalty to God (Est. 3:1–6). On the surface Mordecai's refusal appears to be sheer stubbornness—and that is exactly how it must have appeared to his contemporaries. Even the hero and heroine do not mention God. Mordecai tells Esther that "deliverance will arise . . . from another place" (Est. 4:14) if she does not take her stand. Esther calls on Mordecai to fast but does not ask him to pray (Est. 4:16). It is as if they speak in this roundabout way because of the influence or pressure of their godless environment.

And yet God's hand is providentially at work in every part of this story for the deliverance of his people. He uses the lusts and pride of a pagan emperor to bring Esther to the throne (Est. 1:1–2:20). Mordecai did not just "happen" to expose a plot on the king's life (Est. 2:21–23). It did not just "happen" that his actions were recorded in the king's chronicles or that those chronicles were read to the king just at the right time for the king to embarrass Haman by honoring Mordecai (Est. 6:1–14). It did not just "happen" that the king showed Esther favor when she approached him (Est. 5:1–8). This book intends us to see God's hand behind all of these events. God's people can be confident in a secular world that excludes God. He is still at work as the Lord of rulers and nations accomplishing his purposes. He will deliver and he will fulfill his promises—even in contexts that forbid the mention of his name. This book does not condone living as the secular world around us lives. It does invite God's people to imitate the courage of Esther and Mordecai and to take their stand even when they are alone in an environment that excludes God from its reckoning.

---

19. In Esther 2:5–6 Mordecai is identified as a Benjamite, the son of Jair, the son of Shemei, the son of Kish. While the name "Kish" is suggestive, there is no clear indication that this is a reference to Kish, the father of King Saul (1 Sam. 9:1–2; 10:21).

II. THE MESSAGE AND CONTINUING RELEVANCE OF 1 CHRONICLES THROUGH ESTHER

It will be helpful to review some of the things we have said about how 1 Chronicles through Esther fits into the rest of Scripture and about how its message is perennially applicable to God's people. At a very fundamental level God's fulfillment of his promise to bring his people back from the Exile assures us that he keeps his promises. Despite appearances, he is using the nations of the world to accomplish his purposes

As we saw in chapter 5, the typological significance of David and Jerusalem was already present in the Samuel-Kings narrative. Yet the contrast between the idealized past of David and Solomon and the diminished present of the return from exile intensifies this typological signifi-

> **1 Chronicles through Esther joins the rest of the Old Testament in anticipating . . . the coming of Christ and the . . . destiny of the people of God in the . . . heavenly Jerusalem.**

cance. This contrast anticipates the coming of the King from David's line, God's "anointed" one, who will do even more than David and Solomon did. He will truly enable God's people to live in obedience and "plant" them in God's presence. This contrast also anticipates a much greater Jerusalem where his people will truly and permanently live in fellowship with him. Thus 1 Chronicles through Esther joins the rest of the Old Testament in anticipating both the coming of Christ and the ultimate destiny of the people of God in the new or heavenly Jerusalem. God's people will then live in obedient fellowship with him, in harmony with each other, and in enjoyment of the place God has prepared for them—just as he intended from the beginning. I have used the word *anticipate* deliberately. The prophets, as we will see, speak explicitly about the one who would come. It is, however, the direction of the narrative in 1 Chronicles through Esther that implicitly points toward his appearance. **Figure 6** visualizes the way in which these books anticipate God's coming salvation. A look at how **Figure 6** fits into the master chart in Appendix 2 will help you to see how 1 Chronicles through Esther relates to the earlier parts of the Old Testament that we have already studied.

Figure 6

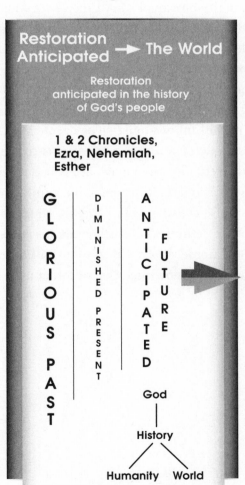

This narrative provides many opportunities to apply the Example Principle. If we have fallen into sin, we should follow the example of the repentant exiles with the confidence that God will restore us. The people who returned to the land lived faithfully despite suffering and opposition, patiently awaiting God's greater deliverance to come. We are called to follow their example as we await the return of Christ. The faithfulness of Judah's good kings, the repentance of Manasseh, Ezra's devotion to the law, Nehemiah's passion for both the restoration and renewal of God's people, and Esther's courage in a pagan world inspire us to imitate the patterns of their lives. Nehemiah's rebuilding the walls has provided an appropriate example for many who have sought the spiritual renewal of God's people or the establishing of a church or institution that would advance his kingdom.

If we would be faithful, we must be as devoted to Christ and to the Scripture that bears witness to him as Ezra was to the law of his God. We, like those who returned from exile, are called to separate from the godlessness around us and make a personal commitment that results in obedience. We are also called to wait patiently with the confidence that God is the Lord of the nations who is achieving his purpose in the world. We, like Esther and Mordecai, are called to be faithful even if we live in societies that refuse to acknowledge God or forbid us to name the name of Christ.

CHAPTER 7

RESTORATION ANTICIPATED *in the* EXPERIENCE *of* GOD'S PEOPLE

"My Anointed One"

Job, Psalms, Proverbs, Ecclesiastes, Song of Songs

INTRODUCTION:
THE DISTINCT CHARACTER OF THESE BOOKS

"The Lord is my Shepherd, I shall not want" (Ps. 23:1). "The fear of the LORD is the beginning of wisdom, and the knowledge of the Holy One is understanding" (Prov. 9:10). In this section of the Old Testament we find two of our most beloved books: Psalms and Proverbs. Throughout the ages the followers of Jesus have found much joy and comfort in the Psalms. The Proverbs have long provided guidance for daily life. As we have noted, this group of books is focused on the daily experience, rather than the history, of God's people. Thus it differs from both the historical narratives that have preceded it and the Prophets that follow. The prophetic books, as we will see, are intimately involved with the ongoing story of the history of the people of God as recorded in 1 and 2 Kings and retold in Chronicles through Ezra.

And yet, although these books are not historical record, they are not detached from the story of God's dealing with his people. The very facts that so many of the Psalms are attributed to David and that Proverbs, Ecclesiastes, and the Song are associated with Solomon identify

> The Proverbs tell us that the foundation for wise living is the 'fear of the Lord'. . . the same Lord that delivered his people from Egypt . . . and . . . returned them from exile.

these books with the Old Testament golden age of David and Solomon. The Proverbs tell us that the foundation for wise living is the "fear of the Lord": this is the same Lord that delivered his people from Egypt, brought them into the promised land, and has now returned them from exile. The Psalms in particular look forward to God's coming deliverance and anticipate his Messiah. Even the opening and closing chapters of Job use *Yahweh* (LORD), the name by which God revealed himself to his people.

I. THE EXPERIENCE OF GOD'S PEOPLE: THEN AND NOW

As we pointed out in the last chapter, both Psalms and Proverbs include much that comes from the time of the monarchy. Nevertheless, they probably assumed the form in which we have them today after the return from exile. Thus these books, as they are, were first read and heard by the returned remnant of the people of God. They address the people of God who, as we saw in the last chapter, live in the diminished present of the return but anticipate a glorious future fulfillment of the promises of God. Their lives were often characterized by suffering and by opposition from unbelievers. It is not difficult for God's people today to identify with their situation and hear the word of God that was addressed to them. We enjoy the great privileges of salvation brought by our Lord Jesus Christ in fulfillment of the hope expressed in the Psalms. And yet we look forward to his return when the faithful will enter once and for all the new, heavenly Jerusalem that God has prepared for his people. Thus we, too, are called to wait in patience. We who follow a crucified Lord often face suffering and opposition as we long for the glorious hope of the people of God. It is not surprising that Psalms and Proverbs continue to mean so much to the faithful today.

There is nothing superficial in the way these books address human experience. They are very aware that human life in this world is often characterized by suffering and injustice. And yet they help us maintain our hope in God and our assurance of his ultimate deliverance. Therefore it is not surprising that this section is introduced by a book like Job that is so concerned with the conflict between the suffering of the righteous and the goodness of God.

The Psalms, then, provide the vehicle for God's people to bring their experience to him in worship through complaint, petition, thanksgiving, and praise. God addresses his people in Scripture. In the Psalms he graciously gives them the words to answer him. Proverbs, Ecclesias-

> **God addresses his people in Scripture. In the Psalms he graciously gives them the words to answer him.**

tes, and the Song of Songs, however, deal with the experience of God's people in everyday life. How do we conduct our affairs so that we live well according to "the fear of the Lord"? **Figure 1** diagrams this relationship between these books. The harp in this diagram reminds us that David, the sweet singer of Israel, is the fount of the Psalms. The boldfaced word

WISDOM represents Solomon, the source of wisdom in Proverbs, Ecclesiastes, and the Song of Songs.

Figure 1

THE EXPERIENCE OF GOD'S PEOPLE—THEN AND NOW

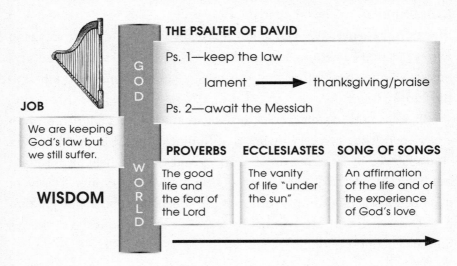

We will begin by looking at the way in which Job introduces this section. Next we turn to the experience of God's people as it is offered to God in worship through the Psalms. Then we will look at this experience as it is lived in daily life according to Proverbs, Ecclesiastes, and the Song.

A. Job: the Suffering of the Righteous

Job is a great and righteous man who worshiped the one true God before God's covenant with Israel. The author of Job is a member of God's covenant people, as evidenced by his use of the divine name in the prologue and epilogue. Job, however, lived in primeval times. This is a world story, a story about the righteousness of God's governance. It addresses the universal question of God's goodness and the suffering of the righteous. Thus this first book of the Wisdom Literature, like the Chronicler, reaches back to the beginning of time, not to trace a genealogy, but to address this question that is so important to all who affirm both the power and goodness of God. It was a question of special significance to the repentant exiles who had experienced God's favor but were still suffering, facing opposition, and living under oppression. It is a question for the people of God today.

The prologue reveals to us something Job did not know: God has allowed Satan to strip Job of wealth, family, and health in order to prove Job's loyalty to God (Job 1:1–2:13). Job does not deny God, but he curses the day of his birth and wishes that he were dead (Job 3:1–26). Three cycles of speeches follow in which his three "friends" try to comfort him by attempting to substantiate the received, though simplistic, wisdom that the truly righteous always enjoy God's material blessings while the wicked always suffer material pain and loss (Job 4:1–26:14). They base their argument on mystical experience, on the tradition of the wise, and on experience in the world, what we might call "common sense." Job responds after each cycle unflinchingly maintaining his innocence. As their speeches progress, they becoming increasingly caustic in their insistence that Job must have sinned in light of his suffering. The more intense the speeches of Job's friends become, the more obviously absurd their argument.

At one point Job comes close to denying the goodness of God (Job 9:1–35; 10:3–7), though he never repudiates divine authority. He wants God to give him the opportunity to place his complaint in court. Then he appears to regain the confidence that God will vindicate him (Job 13:13–19). After two extended speeches by Job (Job 27:1–31:40), his three friends are silenced. A young man, Elihu, shamelessly takes the floor in order to do what his elders failed to do. He succeeds in adding nothing to their argument but in making their case even more absurd (Job 32:1–37:24).

God then appears in overwhelming majesty (Job 38:1–42:6). How can mere mortals judge his righteousness or comprehend his ways? Just as God has allowed room in his creation for the chaotic and destructive forces of nature, so he has allowed room for the wickedness of proud human beings. Both, however, are bounded by his sovereignty and used for his purposes. Job accepts this more profound understanding of God's sovereignty and goodness. God has allowed evil because he is using it to achieve his own good purposes for his creation. Job has become a truly wise man (Job 42:1–6).

Through Job's intercession his superficial friends are restored to relationship with God (Job 42:7–17). Yet this book makes it clear that evil and God's use of it are temporal. The bountiful restoration of Job at the end to twice the expected life span (140 years) and to twice what he had before assures us that ultimately God—not humanity—will establish all things in righteousness. Job 19:25–27 appears to affirm the resurrection of the righteous. Thus in its own way the book of Job joins the rest of the Old Testament in looking forward to God's coming great salvation. Job introduces the following books that deal with human experience by addressing the crucial question of the suffering of the righteous and the righteousness of God.

B. The Psalms: the People of God at Worship

The Psalter (a traditional name for the book of Psalms) is the prayer-hymn book of those living in covenant with God. The first psalm invites all whose "delight is in the law of the Lord" to enter the world of prayer and praise opened before them in the following psalms. The five books into which the Psalter is divided (Pss. 1–41; 42–72; 73–89; 90–106; 107–150) parallel the five books of Moses. God graciously gave his people the Psalter so that they would know how to speak to him in the experience and circumstances of their lives.

The great variety of psalms reflects the varied circumstances of the lives of the people of God. Psalm 23 is a psalm of assurance and comfort for those who are distressed. Psalm 51 is a psalm of penitence for those who have fallen into sin. Psalm 103 is a great song of praise for those who rejoice in the majesty and mercy of God. Some psalms instruct us in how to live if we would please God, such as Psalms 1, 24, 37, 49, 73, 112, 127, and 128. It is, however, the movement from petition (complaint) to thanksgiving and praise that constitutes the music and rhythm of the psalms. This music encompasses the misery and suffering of human life with a firm faith in the goodness and "steadfast love" of the God who has created the world and is in the process of its redemption through his people.

Many have divided the majority of the psalms into three large categories: psalms of petition (Pss. 3, 5, 6, 7, 13, 22, 26, 28, 31, 35, 36, etc.); psalms of thanksgiving (Pss. 8, 18, 21, 30, 32, 34, 92, 103, 107, 116, 118, 124, 138); and hymns of praise (Pss. 33, 103, 113, 117, 145, 146, 147, 150). The music of petition, thanksgiving, and praise that begins in the first type finds resolution and climax in the third. In the first the psalmist comes to God with need, often in great distress. In the second the psalmist thanks and praises God for specific deliverance from that great need. Sometimes this is called "declarative praise" because the singers declare to others what God has done for them. Finally, in the hymns of praise the psalmist praises God for who God is and for his great works of creation, deliverance, and redemption. This is often called "descriptive praise," since the psalmist describes God as worthy of praise due to the faithfulness of his character, his majesty, and his boundless power. The rhythm of petition (complaint), thanksgiving, and finally praise runs through all three types. The petitions look forward to thanksgiving, which culmi-

> The movement from petition . . . to thanksgiving and praise . . . constitutes the music of the psalms.

nates in pure praise. The psalm that introduces the final book of the Psalter, Psalm 107, clearly presents this movement from distress to praise. It begins with a call to give God thanks (vv. 1–3). Then it describes a series of situations characterized by distress (vv. 4–5; 10–12; 17–18; 23–27), petition (vv. 6a, 13a, 19a; 28a), deliverance (vv. 6b–9, 13b–16, 19b–22, 28b–32) and call for thanksgiving (vv. 8–9, 15–16, 21–22, 31–32).

The psalms of petition are often the cry of those in deep distress—sickness (real or metaphorical), persecution by the wicked who are unjustly flourishing, false accusations from the unfaithful, military defeat at the hands of God's enemies—distress that leaves the one praying without resource. Sometimes the son of David, as representative of the people, is the singer of these psalms. Sometimes the people of God as a whole are in great anguish while their idolatrous oppressors appear to enjoy prosperity. These psalms begin with a direct address to God, acknowledging that he alone is the one who can meet the petitioners' need (Pss. 3:1; 5:1; 6:1). Then comes the lament or complaint in which the petitioners describe their great distress and often complain of God's delay in delivering (Pss. 5:2–7; 13:1–4; 22:6–18). They often feel alienated from God (Pss. 13:1; 22:1). Finally, after emptying their distress and bitterness before the Lord, the worshipers reach a point of confidence in the God who is both faithful without exception and great beyond measure (Ps. 3:3). Some psalms, like Psalm 23, are entirely psalms of confidence.

> The worshipers reach a point of confidence in the God who is both faithful without exception and great beyond measure (Ps. 3:3).

After address, complaint, and confidence, these psalms of petition reach the petition itself (Pss. 6:4–5; 13:3–4): the psalmist asks for divine favor and for deliverance. Finally, in confidence that God is going to answer prayer, the psalmist ends with praise for the anticipated deliverance (Ps. 13:5–6; 22:22–23; 26:12; 28:6–7)—because God is "good," and his "steadfast love endures forever."

If the petitions/laments were to be offered in times of distress, the psalms of thanksgiving were composed for the time of deliverance. The worshipers who once petitioned now give thanks for the deliverance they sought. They begin by affirming their intention to thank and praise the

Lord (Ps. 116:1–2). Then in the main body of the psalm the worshipers tell the wonderful story of the Lord's great deliverance for all to hear (Ps. 116:3–9). In conclusion, those singing these psalms testify once again to the Lord's gracious act of salvation and address the congregation urging them to offer an appropriate response to such a God (Ps. 116:10–19).

The petition that has turned to thanksgiving reaches full flower in the hymns of descriptive praise. The psalmist is no longer thanking God for some particular personal or corporate deliverance in the recent past. The worshipers who sing these psalms thank and praise God for his works of creation, sustenance, and redemption in general and especially for his character: for his "unfailing love," his "kindness," his "mercy," and his "faithfulness" toward his covenant people and toward his creation. Psalm 117, the shortest psalm in the Psalter, illustrates the basic form of these hymns: a call to praise ("Praise the Lord, all you Gentiles! Laud Him, all you peoples!" Ps. 117:1) is followed by a description of the cause for praise ("For His merciful kindness is great toward us, and the truth of the Lord endures forever," Ps. 117:2a), and finally by a concluding call to praise ("Praise the Lord!" Ps. 117:2b). Compare also Psalm 118:1: "Oh give thanks to the Lord, for He is good; because His mercy endures forever!"

The arrangement of the psalms demonstrates the finality of praise. Each book of the Psalter concludes with a doxology of praise (Pss. 41:13; 72:18–19; 89:52; 106:48; 150). There is a steady movement in the book of Psalms from petition/complaint to thanksgiving and praise (see the arrow in **Figure 1**). Though one can find laments toward the end (God's people still suffer), they predominate near the beginning. As the Psalter reaches a climax it is filled with psalms of thanksgiving and hymns of praise. Psalm 150 brings the fifth book and the entire Psalter to an ecstatic climax with a great call to praise the Lord in every way possible.

The Psalter's litany of petition, thanksgiving, and praise reaches out to the whole world and moves forward with anticipation to the full redemption of God's people and God's creation. Since God is the universal

Creator, faithful to his purposes of redemption, the psalms call all the nations (Pss. 33:8; 47:1–2; 66:1, 8; 67:4–6; 96:1–3; 97:1; 98:4; 100:1; 145:21; 148:11) and all creation (Pss. 19:1–4; 69:34; 97:6; 98:7–8; 145:10–11; 148) to praise him. His people know that all petitions lead to thanksgiving and ultimately to praise because God is going to bring final

> **His people know that all petitions lead to thanksgiving and ultimately to praise because God is going to bring final redemption to this sinful, corrupt, suffering world.**

redemption to this sinful, corrupt, suffering world. Thus the movement toward praise in the psalms anticipates the time when all will be put right because God reigns. When that time comes, God the mighty warrior (Ps. 118:15; 48:10; 98:1–2) will have vanquished evil, he will visibly establish his reign over all (Pss. 47:6; 99:4; 103:19; 145:13; 146:10), and he will judge individuals and nations aright that injustice and oppression might be no more. The—to us—harsh language of passages like Psalm 139:19–24 remind us that the establishment of God's reign requires the judgment of the wicked. Righteousness cannot prevail if wickedness remains.

The Psalter also reminds us of the part the Messiah, God's "Anointed One" (Ps. 45:7; 84:9; 89:20; 132:17) will play in the restoration of God's rule. Many psalms written by David or by his assistant Asaph were part of the worship instituted by David in anticipation of the temple his son would build. Some psalms are associated with incidents in David's life (Pss. 3, 18, 34, 51, 52, 54, 56, 57, 59, 60, 63, 142) and others with the victory, rule, and majesty of David's descendants (Pss. 2:7–8; 3; 72; 89). The king of David's line is either the speaker or is addressed in many psalms. The king speaks both as God's designated regent who establishes the people in covenant obedience with all its blessings and as representative of God's sometime suffering people. In Psalm 2 God announces the universal rule of his regent, David's son, whom God then addresses as his "Son" in anticipation of Christ. As noted above, the collection and arrangement of the Psalter after the return from exile enabled the returned but still oppressed remnant to identify with the suffering and to find hope in the praise of these psalms. The extravagant description of the king of David's line found in many psalms became a type of the great descendant of David who would come. In Psalm 110:1 David himself affirmed that God would invite his greater son to sit on the right hand of God's own throne. The sinfulness of the kings before the Exile and the failure to reestablish kingship after the return only whetted the appetite of many for the one who would fulfill these expectations.

The royal psalms in the first two books of the Psalter (Pss. 1–72) fueled expectation of the time when God would establish his ultimate reign and bring his final redemption through his anointed one, great David's greater Son. The psalms of the third book (Pss. 73–89), seem to lose faith in David's coming heir. There is, however, hope. The fourth book (Pss. 90–106) firmly proclaims the fact that God himself will establish his reign (Pss. 93–99). Hope for David's line returns in the fifth and final book (Pss. 107–150). God will establish his rule through great David's greater son who is also the Son of God.

Since the fully obedient incarnate Son of God exercised the fullest "delight in the law of the Lord" (Ps. 1:2), he is the speaker who fulfills

> Since the fully obedient incarnate Son of God exercised the fullest 'delight in the law of the Lord' (Ps. 1:2), he is the speaker who fulfills all of the psalms.

all of the psalms. When Jesus claimed Psalm 22 as his own by quoting its opening line on the cross—"My God, my God, why have you forsaken me" (compare Matt. 27:46; Mark 15:34)—he became the righteous sufferer of the psalms par excellence. By taking that suffering unto himself he atoned for sin, took his seat at the right hand of God's throne (see Ps. 22:22 in Heb. 2:12), and secured the deliverance and divine rule for which the psalmists praised God.

We sing and pray the Psalter in harmony with the righteous remnant of God's people who returned from exile. As they persevered in faith amid suffering in anticipation of the Messiah's first coming, so we persevere as we await his second and final coming. As they identified in hope with the King of David's line who would establish God's rule, so we identify with the one who fulfills God's promise to David. As they identified with the righteous sufferer awaiting God's deliverance, so we identify with the righteous sufferer who has procured our redemption. This anticipation of the coming Messiah in the worship of God's people complements the anticipation of his coming in the narrative of their history recorded in 1 and 2 Chronicles, Ezra, and Nehemiah.

C: Wisdom: The People of God in Daily Life

Proverbs. Together Psalms and Proverbs encompass the world of human experience (see **Figure 1**). The first, as we have seen, pertains to the worship of God, the second to wholesome conduct in the everyday world of

> [The Psalter] pertains to the worship of God, [Proverbs] to wholesome conduct in the everyday world of people and nations.

people and nations. The goal of the book of Proverbs is the possession of true wisdom and the practice of wise living. As David shaped the worship of God's people through the Psalms, so his son Solomon is the great instructor of wisdom for daily living (Prov. 1:1). Proverbs calls on God's people to pursue God's gift of wisdom as Solomon did (1 Kings 2:3–30; 2 Chron. 1:2–13). Solomon's fall reinforces Proverbs' many warnings against the temptations of folly (1 Kings 11:1–43).

Figure 2

PROVERBS

I. Introduction—pursue wisdom! (Prov. 1:1–7)

II. The proverbs of Solomon
to youth (Prov. 1:8–9:18)

III. The proverbs of Solomon
concerning the godly and the wicked (Prov. 10:1–22:16)

IV. The proverbs of Solomon
concerning various situations (Prov. 22:17–24:34)

V. The proverbs of Solomon
copied by Hezekiah's men (Prov. 25:1–29:27)

VI. The words of Agur (Prov. 30:1–33)

VII. The words of King Lemuel (Prov. 31:1–31)

Many peoples, both ancient and modern, have used proverbs: short, concrete observations that convey insight about people and situations. I learned many proverbs during my years in Africa. Here are a couple of favorites: "One finger can't pick up a stick"; "If every tree you climb has ants, check your own pants." With a little thought, you understand them. No one needs to explain their meaning. The book of Proverbs, however, is not just a collection of the best wit and wisdom that Israel had to offer. By themselves the partial, and sometimes apparently contradictory (Prov. 26:4–5), proverbs do not convey the wisdom necessary for right living. Solomon and other contributors to the book of Proverbs are insistent: "The fear of the Lord is the beginning of wisdom" (Prov. 9:10, cf. 1:7; 15:33). Wisdom begins with and is founded on proper awe and humility before and obedience to the Lord—he who created the world will redeem it through his promise to Abraham, his covenant with Abraham's descendants, and his choice of David's line. The truly wise make and study proverbs by observing the world from the vantage point of those who reflect the character of this God by living in accord with his covenant. Only this Creator-Redeemer God can grant wisdom, because only he has all knowledge (cf. Prov. 3:19–20; 8:22–31). All human observation is limited and partial, and thus grants true wisdom only within the framework provided by the self-revelation of the living God. Apart from this perspective, a proverb can be used to justify wrong ("foolish") behavior. Thus it is appropriate that Psalms precedes Proverbs; the proper relationship to God cultivated by the worship of the psalms is foundational for the right conduct of life according to the wisdom of Proverbs.

Within this context the proverbs do not supplant, but reinforce, supplement, and apply the moral principles of the law. Covenant law clearly prohibits certain actions and enjoins others, but it cannot cover every life situation. The proverbs reinforce God's law by reflecting on the natural consequences of behavior. God has so structured the world that diligence in work tends toward human good while carelessness leads to poverty (Prov. 13:4). Adultery may appear to be pleasurable, but it leads to poverty and death (Prov. 5:1–23). A teachable spirit brings success, but self-sufficient pride leads to failure (Prov. 16:19; 28:25). Heeding counsel brings wisdom (Prov. 12:15; 15:7, 12, 31). If you associate with the wise you will be like them (Prov. 13:20). Truthful, wholesome, restrained speech (Prov. 10:19–20, 31; 12:18–19; 15:1–4) and discreet silence both bring blessing (Prov. 17:28). The proverbs help the wise apply God's moral principles in the varied situations of life.

The end of the wise and the fate of the foolish is the same as the reward of those who keep and the punishment of those who violate God's covenant. Folly and disobedience to God's law result in death. Wisdom and obedience bring life (Prov. 11:19; Deut. 30:15, 19. See also Prov. 4:13; 8:35; and 10:16). The wise, however, are aware that this sequence is not always apparent or immediate. Taken alone, some proverbs sound like retribution visibly and immediately follows folly (Prov. 10:2–5, 23–27; 11:31; 12:7, 12; 14:11–12). Proverbs, however, cannot be taken alone. Other proverbs admit that the wicked may appear to prosper while the righteous suffer injustice (Prov. 16:8, 19; 17:1; 19:1, 22; 21:9; 24:19–20; 25:24–26). This seeming contradiction must be addressed on two levels. First, the suffering of the wise/righteous does not negate the fact that in themselves the virtues encouraged by the proverbs—such as integrity, diligence, and purity—produce wholesome living. Second, according to the proverbs mentioned above, the present prosperity of the wicked and suffering of the righteous is not final. Death awaits the foolish and wicked. Even if the wise/righteous now suffer, God has a fullness of life in store for them. The abundance of life God promises to the wise is based on their relationship to him and thus extends beyond physical death to eternal life in the presence of God (Prov. 2:21–22; 10:2; 11:4, 19; 13:14; 14:27, 32; 15:24; 23:17–18). This is the life lost by sin in the Garden of Eden, foreshadowed by the covenant promise of life in the promised land (Deut. 30:15, 19), and fulfilled through the work of Christ: "I have come that they might have life, and that they might have it more abundantly" (John 10:10).

This wisdom is so fundamental to life that both father and mother are to teach it to their children (Prov. 4:3; 6:20; 23:24–25; 31:1–2, 26–28; cf. 10:1; 15:20; 23:22; 29:15). Wisdom is learned through both instruction and imitation (Prov. 13:20). In fact, the wise person always assumes the teachable spirit appropriate for a child (Prov. 3:7; 26:12). The book of Proverbs, then, confirms what is implied by the order of the Ten Commandments: respect for parents (the fifth commandment) is the means by which the fear of God (commandments one through four) is made concrete in behavior (commandments six through ten).

Wisdom is not only to be taught, it is to be pursued. The first four chapters of Proverbs are largely concerned with urging the pursuit of wisdom, as are many other passages. Solomon knows that the human heart, left alone, tends toward folly. Thus he zealously urges those he is instructing to pursue wisdom and shun folly. Wisdom is personified as a virtuous woman inviting those who would be wise to follow her ways (Prov. 8:1–9:6). By contrast, Dame Folly is the adulteress who would seduce her victims and lead them to death (Prov. 7:6–27; 9:13–18). Marital unfaithfulness has become the paradigm for all folly. Solomon and others who have contributed to the book of Proverbs are very urgent: we must begin to pursue wisdom when we are young and persevere in our quest throughout our lives because wisdom is the only way to abundant living! Falling into folly leads to nowhere but "death."

This wisdom for right living is, then—like the law before it, like the Davidic king, like the psalms—the gracious gift of God. Apart from God we are left in folly. That is why we pursue wisdom by absorbing the teaching of the wise. Many have read and reread the book of Proverbs without pursuing wisdom. If we meditate on these proverbs within the context of reverence for God and a commitment to humble obedience, he will use them to make us wise. We will learn how to live life in its fullness, both now and in eternity. Those who live wisely will enjoy obedient fellowship with God and joyful harmony among the people of God in the place of blessing that he has prepared for his own. The instruction of Proverbs is of perennial relevance to the people of God as they await the fullness of God's salvation at the return of Christ.

Ecclesiastes. A book that begins with the words "Vanity of vanities" (KJV); "Meaningless! Meaningless!" (NIV); or "Useless! Useless!" (NCV) is not likely to be the most popular book in the Bible. We worship joyfully with the psalms and are instructed by the proverbs, but we seldom read Ecclesiastes in our devotions—unless we are reading the Bible through; and then we get through this book as quickly as possible. Who wants to

> This wisdom for right living is, then—like the law before it, . . . like the psalms— the gracious gift of God. Apart from God we are left in folly.

hear, "Better to go to the house of mourning than to go to the house of feasting, for that is the end of all men; and the living will take it to heart" (Eccl. 7:2)?

And yet, rightly understood, this book makes an important contribution to the life lived according to wisdom. The "Preacher" (Eccl. 1:1), the author's self-designation, is a teacher of wisdom (Eccl. 1:15–16). He agrees with the book of Proverbs that wisdom is better than folly (Eccl. 2:13–14; 7:11–12; note his wisdom-teaching in such places as 5:1–17;

10:1–20). His concern includes, but is broader than, the suffering of the righteous addressed by the book of Job. He is burdened by the transitory and uncertain character of the good life lived by the wise (Eccl. 2: 14b–16). Even the life of the wise is fraught with uncertainties. Furthermore, even if one lives a wise life and enjoys all of its benefits, its end is death. Both the wise and fools die. The word translated by various versions as "vanity," "meaningless," or "useless" is, literally, *vapor*. Even the well-lived life of the wise is as transitory as vapor, and therefore, from this temporal world's point of view, it seems "meaningless." The Preacher uses the phrase "under the sun" to describe this temporal point of view (Eccl. 1:3, 9, 14; 2:11, 17–20, 22; 3:16; 4:1, 3, 7, 15; 5:13, 18; 6:1, 12; 8:9, 15, 17; 9:3, 6, 9, 11, 13; 10:5). He describes himself as one who has experienced all the good things of this life in abundance: pleasure, wisdom, wealth, and achievement. In the end he finds that none of these transcend life's temporal boundaries and thus provide the key to its meaningfulness (Eccl. 1:12–2:26).

God has made human beings so that they want to understand the meaning of life, but the uncertain and temporal character of their earthly existence prevents them, on their own, from doing so (Eccl. 3:11; 8:16–17). From this temporal perspective—under the sun—the life of wisdom is relatively better than a life of folly. Yet even the wise are soon forgotten. Due to life's brevity and uncertain character, the best way to live is to enjoy the fruit of one's labor as it is given daily by God: food, drink, family, and so forth (Eccl. 5:18–20; 9:9–10). This is the best human beings can do from the point of view of their ephemeral existence under the sun.

By their observation of the world, human beings on their own cannot escape this "under the sun" perspective. It is only as the eternal God has revealed himself and the eternal destiny planned for his own that this temporal life takes on ultimate meaning (Eccl. 3:17; 12:1–14). In light of that destiny the wise not only enjoy the fruit of their temporal labor but live from their youth in a way that honors God and his commands. The "fear of the Lord" is not only the "beginning" but the end of wisdom. The book of Proverbs teaches that living according to wisdom results in abundant life in fellowship with God. Ecclesiastes reminds us that without the eternal dimension implied by fellowship with God, the life of wisdom is of limited value and the meaning of life is inscrutable. Thus these books anticipate the fuller disclosure of the eternal destiny of God's people that will be revealed in Jesus Christ.

The author does not directly claim to be Solomon, though he describes himself in Solomon-like terms (Eccl. 1:1, 12–17) as one who is wise and who has enjoyed an abundance of what this temporal life has to offer. It is because he has experienced these blessings that he is qualified to assert the temporal and thus meaningless character of life under the sun. It would be strange, however, for Solomon to say, "I have attained greatness and have gained more wisdom than all who were before me in Jerusalem," since he was only the second Israelite king to rule from Jerusalem. Many believe that, at least in its completed form, this book was written after the return from exile. Its message was certainly appropriate for those returnees, or for those who still suffered in the land of exile. The truth of this book, however, is perennial for all the people of God as we seek to understand the meaning of our lives from within our finite existence.

The Song of Songs. This section of Scripture that focuses on human experience began with the problem of suffering in the book of Job. It concludes with this collection of poems celebrating the beauty and purity of human love when pursued with integrity between a man and a woman in accord with God's plan for marriage (Gen. 1:27–28; 2:21–25). The Shunamite woman expresses her love to her beloved who responds in turn, admiring her beauty and proclaiming his love for her. The "daughters of Jerusalem" are a chorus that provides background for this dialogue. Though many have tried, it is unlikely that we can find a plot in this collection of poems. It is the beauty of their imagery and the intensity of their emotion that provide unity.

"The voice" of "the bride" and "the bridegroom" in the street was an occasion for and symbol of great joy (Jer. 7:34; 16:9; 25:10; 33:11). This section on human experience may have dealt extensively with suffering and with the transitory nature of human life, but it ends on a note of exuberant joy. Thus indirectly by its location the Song reinforces those elements in Job, Psalms, Proverbs, and Ecclesiastes that anticipate God's great salvation. Elsewhere the Bible often compares God and his people (Jer. 2:1–9; Ezek. 23:1–49; Hos. 1:1–3:5) or Christ and his church (Eph. 5:22–23) to the bridegroom and the bride. Thus believers throughout the ages have seen in this book a picture of the church as the bride of Christ: a "marriage" that will be consummated at his return in the "marriage supper of the Lamb" (Rev. 19:9).

CONCLUSION

These books deal with the experience of God's people. They begin with the unavoidable question of the suffering of the righteous in Job. The Psalms provide a way for the people of God to offer their experience to him in worship. Proverbs and Ecclesiastes provide instruction for wise living in daily life. The Song concludes this section on a note of great joy by celebrating the God-given delight of love within the marriage bond.

The experience of God's people anticipates the future full restoration of God's plan for humanity. Job affirms a future vindication of the suffering righteous. The prayers and hymns of the Psalter anticipate the establishment of God's visible rule through the Messiah. Proverbs implies that death cannot terminate the abundant life of fellowship with the God that is the reward of the wise. The Preacher of Ecclesiastes reminds us that apart from God's eternal purposes human life remains an enigma. The story of God's dealing with his people as recounted in 1 Chronicles through Esther looked forward to God's restoration. So does the experience of God's people according to Job, Psalms, Proverbs, Ecclesiastes, and the Song of Songs. **Figure 3**, part of the master chart in Appendix 2, brings these two sections together. Comparison with the rest of the chart shows how these books fit into the overall movement of the Old Testament.

Figure 3

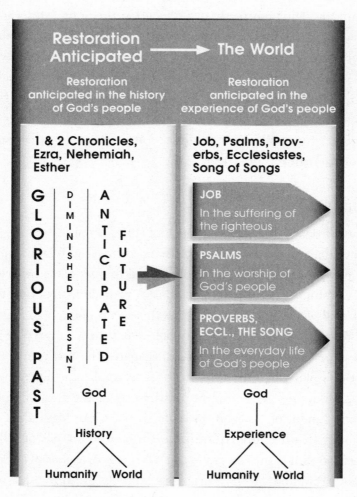

As we turn in chapter 8 to the prophets, we reenter the world of history. The prophets warned a disobedient people of the coming judgment of God in the form of exile from the promised land. But they also proclaimed a future restoration of God's plan that would reach beyond the Exile and remake the people of God by addressing the root cause of their disobedience.

8

RESTORATION ANTICIPATED *in the* PROMISES *of the* PROPHETS

"My Servant," "My Spirit"

Isaiah—Malachi

INTRODUCTION

A: Who Were the Prophets?

If you go into any Christian bookstore, you will find pictures and wall plaques inscribed with Jeremiah 29:11 and Isaiah 40:31: "'For I know the plans I have for you,' declares the LORD, 'plans to prosper you and not to harm you, plans to give you hope and a future'" (Jer. 29:11 NIV); "[T]hose who wait on the LORD shall renew their strength; they shall mount up with wings like eagles, they shall run and not be weary, they shall walk and not faint" (Isa. 40:31). Sometimes you might see Isaiah 1:18: "'Come now, and let us reason together,' says the LORD, 'Though your sins are like scarlet, they shall be as white as snow; though they are red like crimson, they shall be as wool.'" We draw great encouragement from these verses. The Prophetic books, however, are much more than a source of uplifting quotations. They are an integral part of the Old Testa-

> The Prophetic books . . . are an integral part of the Old Testament, a source of instruction, and a crucial link to the coming of Christ in the New Testament.

ment, a source of instruction, and a crucial link to the coming of Christ in the New Testament.

Sometimes the term *prophet* is used for anyone through whom God revealed himself in the Old Testament. In this sense Abraham, Moses, and David can be called prophets. The Bible, however, usually uses this term to describe those special people whom God anointed with his Spirit and commissioned to call his people to repentance. They often began their messages with "Thus says the Lord . . ." to show that God spoke directly through them. They preached God's coming judgment on unrepentant Israel and proclaimed his promised salvation for the people of God if they would turn from sin with a contrite heart. Their predictions of the future were closely tied to these messages of judgment and salvation. The line of the prophets began with Samuel and ran throughout the time of the kings to the era of Zechariah and Malachi after the return from exile. The historical books Samuel through Kings (and also 1 and 2 Chronicles) introduce us to a number of these prophets who did not commit their prophecies to writing: Samuel, Gad, Nathan, Ahijah, Elijah, Elisha, and others. Some prophets, however, did, under the inspiration of the Holy Spirit, record their prophecies. Sometimes their disciples faithfully collected, organized, and preserved their words. The Old Testament contains the writings of four "major prophets" and twelve "minor prophets." The major prophets—Isaiah, Jeremiah, Ezekiel, and Daniel—are so-called simply because their books are longer. And the books of the minor prophets—Hosea, Joel, Amos, Obadiah, Jonah, Micah, Nahum, Habakkuk, Zephaniah, Haggai, Zechariah, and Malachi—are shorter. Before bookbinding, these twelve were often circulated together because they were written on one scroll. Thus they became known collectively as "The Book of the Twelve." The small book of Lamentations appears after Jeremiah because it was accredited by many to have been written by him and because its anguish at the fall of Jerusalem fits well with the final chapters of Jeremiah.

B. How Do the Prophet Books Fit in with the Rest of the Bible?

The message of the prophets was based on the covenant God made with his people at Sinai through Moses. God sent the prophets again and again to call his disobedient people back to this covenant. Thus the message of judgment looms ever larger in the prophetic writings. As God's people persisted in sin, the threat of imminent judgment intensified. That judgment would take the form of exile from the land that God had given them as the place for fellowship with him. If God's people persisted in violating his covenant, they could no longer fellowship with him in the covenant land. The prophets, however, also promised God's blessing if his people would repent. When it became evident that exile was inevitable for this persistently unrepentant people, the prophets announced that God's deliverance would go beyond the Exile. First, he would restore his people through providing a salvation that overcame their habitual disobedience by changing their hearts. Second, he would reestablish Jerusalem on a scale far grander than ever before. The nations would join in the worship of God. These promises are fulfilled by Christ at his first and second comings. Reestablished Jerusalem is the New Jerusalem and the new heaven and earth of Revelation 21:1–22:21. Thus the prophets addressed the disobedience of God's people recorded in the historical books (1 Samuel through Ezra) by calling them back to the covenant established in the Pentateuch. Their message anticipates fulfillment in Christ. **Figure 1** helps us to visualize the role the Prophets play in the biblical canon.

Figure 1

THE PROPHETS AND THE REST OF THE OLD TESTAMENT

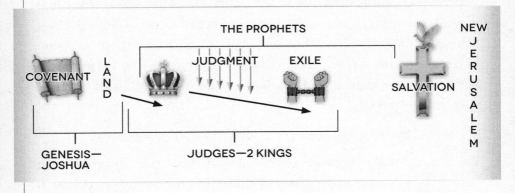

In Genesis through Joshua God makes covenant with his people (represented above by the scroll) and brings them into the promised land. Next the book of Judges describes their disobedience (the short slanted arrow in **Figure 1**). In Samuel, God instituted the Davidic kingship (the crown in **Figure 1**) with the purpose of establishing his people in obedience. The two books of the Kings continue the story of the persistently disobedient people of God (the longer slanted arrow in **Figure 1**) until the Exile. Repeatedly throughout this long period of disobedience (punctuated by short times of obedience) the prophets proclaimed God's coming judgment—in the form of exile—on this stubbornly unrepentant people. The downward vertical arrows in **Figure 1** represent this prophetic message. However, their message also promised that God would bring a future salvation beyond the Exile. This coming salvation is accomplished in the cross of Christ and the coming of the Holy Spirit (represented in **Figure 1** by the dove). It finds consummation, as noted above, in the New Jerusalem (and the new heaven and earth).

I. AN OVERVIEW OF THE PROPHETIC BOOKS

It might be helpful to have a brief overview of the Prophet books before a more detailed discussion of their place in the Bible and their continuing relevance. The order in which the Major Prophets appear in our Old Testament is also their chronological order. Isaiah prophesied during the reigns of Uzziah, Jotham, Ahaz, and Hezekiah, four kings of Judah (ca. 760 to 695 BC). He lived through the destruction of the Northern Kingdom by Assyria (721 BC) and predicted both the exile of Judah (chaps. 1–39) and a coming glorious deliverance that would follow that exile (chaps. 40–66). He called the people to covenant faithfulness and condemned the kings for their tendency to depend on military strength and political alliances rather than on God. His oracles against the nations assert God's supreme lordship over history and the world. Isaiah contains many prophecies of the coming Messiah. The four songs of the Suffering Servant (Isa. 42:1–9; 49:1–7; 50:4–11; and 52:13–53:12) clearly describe the work of Christ. God's divine Servant will establish justice, restore God's people, and be a light to the nations. Though innocent he will "bear the sins of many" and thus make atonement through his suffering and death. God, however, will raise him from the dead and give him "a portion with the great" (Isa. 53:12, cf. 53:10).

Figure 2

ISAIAH

I. Judgment on an unfaithful people. (Isa. 1:1–39:8)

A. The Lord is the God of Israel. (1:1–12:6)

B. The Lord is the Master of nations. (13:1–23:18)

C. The Lord is the sovereign Judge and Redeemer. (24:1–27:13)

D. The Lord is the One his people must trust. (28:1–39:8)

II. Consolation for a judged people. (Isa. 40:1–55:13)

III. Warning and promise for a redeemed people. (56:1–66:24)

Jeremiah ministered from about 625 to 586 BC. He began during the reforms of King Josiah and continued to prophesy through the final tragic reign of Zedekiah and the destruction of Jerusalem (586 BC). His call for repentance was persistently rejected by the people and by these last kings of Judah. Despite this rejection, he proclaimed God's coming restoration of his people and the establishing of the new covenant (Jer. 31:31–34). Jeremiah is known as "the weeping prophet" because of his grief over the unremitting disobedience of God's people and the consequent destruction of their nation. His career ended with his being carried into Egypt against his will by the remnant of the people who, despite Jeremiah's reassurances from the Lord, feared Babylonian reprisal (Jer. 43:1–13). The five psalms of lament in the book of Lamentations accord well with Jeremiah's deep grief. The author of these psalms acknowledges the justice of God's judgment, but, like the other prophets, is confident of God's future renewal and restoration (Lam. 3:22–23, 61–66; 4:22). We learn from the book of Jeremiah that Baruch, the scribe, recorded and copied Jeremiah's prophecies (Jer. 36:4, 17–18, 32). Other prophets may have had such scribes or followers as well. The prophecies in the book of Jeremiah as we have received it follow neither a chronological nor a thematic order.

Figure 3

JEREMIAH

I. God calls Jeremiah. (Jer. 1:1–19)

II. Jeremiah announces present judgment. (Jer. 2:1–29:32)

III. Jeremiah promises future restoration. (Jer. 30:1–33:26)
(added information. Jer. 34:1–35:19)

IV. Jeremiah suffers persecution for his message. (Jer. 36:1–38:28)

V. The fall of Jerusalem and the continual rebellion of God's people. (Jer. 39:1–45:5)

VI. Jeremiah pronounces judgment on the nations. (Jer. 46:1–51:64)

VII. The people persist in disobedience. (Jer. 52:1–34)

Ezekiel's ministry lasted from about 593 to 571 BC. He had been carried away into Babylon at the time of the first deportation (605 BC). Therefore, unlike Isaiah and Jeremiah, he prophesied from Babylon, though he often addressed the idolatry and unfaithfulness of those living in Judah. About halfway through this book Ezekiel receives the news of Jerusalem's destruction (Ezek. 33:21). Since the predicted judgment has come to pass, he begins to give the exiles hope by describing his God-given visions of future restoration. The visions of the dry bones coming to life (Ezek. 37:1–14) and of an idealized and restored temple, city, and land (Ezek. 40:1–48:35) look forward to God's coming salvation—as does his prophecy that God will change his people's hearts by putting his Spirit in them (Ezek. 36:24–28). He, like Isaiah, affirmed the universal sovereignty of the Lord in his prophecies against the nations (Ezek. 25:1–32:32).

Figure 4

EZEKIEL

I. God's judgment on his people. (Ezek. 1:1–24:27)

II. God's judgment on the nations. (Ezek. 25:1–32:32)

III. God's glorious restoration of his people. (Ezek. 33:1–48:35)

Daniel and his friends were among the youth of Judah who were taken to Babylon during that first deportation (Dan. 1:1–7). Daniel's ministry, however, extended beyond 539 BC into the beginning of the Persian period (Dan. 6:1–5). He and his companions exemplified faithful living in the godless environment of a foreign land. Daniel's visions (Dan. 7:1–12:13) affirm God's lordship over history and anticipate the future restoration of God's plan. The vision of the divine Son of Man in Daniel 7:13–14 finds its fulfillment in Jesus who often called himself the "Son of Man."

Since the predicted judgment has come to pass, [Ezekiel] begins to give the exiles hope by describing his God-given visions of future restoration.

The twelve Minor Prophets cover a period of more than four hundred years and address a variety of situations before and after the Babylonian exile and the destruction of Jerusalem in 586 BC. Hosea, Amos, and Micah come from the period of Assyrian domination (850 to 700 BC). During the prophecies of Nahum, Habakkuk, and Zephaniah, Babylon's power was on the rise (630 to 610 BC). Obadiah appears to have been written soon after the destruction of Jerusalem. God spoke through Haggai, Zechariah, and Malachi after the return from exile (520 to 400 BC). Joel and Jonah are of uncertain date.

Hosea and Amos were contemporaries of Isaiah, though they proclaimed God's word in the Northern Kingdom before the fall of Samaria to the Assyrians in 721 BC. The period of great prosperity under Jeroboam II at the beginning of their ministries was a time of excessive luxury, oppression of the poor, and of Ba'al worship. Many professed to be worshiping the Lord but worshiped him as if he were an immoral fertility god like Ba'al. This era of indulgence and unfaithfulness led to the rapid deterioration of the nation and the destruction of Samaria by the Assyrians in 721 BC. Amos was particularly concerned with the debased worship of the golden calves that Jeroboam I had established in Bethel and with the oppression of the poor by a luxury-loving elite. The adulterous behavior of Hosea's wife, Gomer, was a poignant picture of the nation's persistent abandonment of the Lord in pursuit of Ba'al (Hos. 1:1–3:5). Hosea announced God's coming judgment on Samaria, but he also envisioned a future restoration (Hos. 14:1–9). Amos ends on a note of hope: God will restore David's house and give David's descendant sovereignty over the nations

(Amos 9:11–15). Micah was a southern contemporary of Hosea and Amos who joined Isaiah in addressing the corrupt worship of God in Judah. Like Amos, he was indignant at those who oppressed the poor. He also rebuked the sins of north Israel and predicted the imminent destruction of Samaria and the coming demise of Jerusalem. Micah affirms the vision of future restoration by promising a great ruler and deliverer of God's people whom God would raise up after judgment was complete (Mic. 4:1–5:15).

Figure 6

HOSEA

I. Hosea's unfaithful wife. (Hos. 1:1–3:19)

II. Hosea's message to unfaithful Israel. (Hos. 4:1–13:6)

III. Hosea's promise of divine restoration. (Hos. 14:1–9)

AMOS

I. God's judgment on the Nations. (Amos 1:1–2:16)

II. God's judgment on Israel. (Amos 3:1–6:14)

III. Visions of judgment. (Amos 7:1–9:10)

IV. God's promise of salvation. (Amos 9:11–15)

MICAH

I. God's judgment on the people is followed by a promise of restoration. (Mic. 1:1–2:13)

II. God's judgment on the leaders is followed by the promise of God's restored Reign. (Mic. 3:1–5:15)

III. God will preserve a remnant who will live in victory over sin. (Mic. 6:1–7:20)

As noted above, dates for the composition of Joel and Jonah are uncertain. Joel is the most beautifully crafted prophetic book. Joel saw the great locust plague of his time as the judgment of God and a call for repentance (Joel 1:1–2:17). He also looked forward to the time when God would restore his people by pouring out his Spirit upon them (Joel 2:28–32).

Then, on the great Day of the Lord, God would judge his enemies and bring full restoration to his own (Joel 3:1–21). The short book of Obadiah pronounces God's judgment on the Edomites for the way they treated the people of Judah when Jerusalem was destroyed by the Babylonians. While the other prophetic books may contain brief biographical elements, the story of Jonah's life is the message of the book that bears his name. His only prophetic oracle is the warning to Nineveh: "'Yet forty days, and Nineveh shall be overthrown!'" (Jonah 3:4). Stubborn Jonah learns that the sovereign Lord of the universe has chosen Israel as a messenger of God's mercy to the nations. The story of Jonah is set in the eighth century BC, though the date of the book's composition is disputed.

Figure 7

JONAH
I. Jonah stubbornly flees God's call. (Jonah 1:1–2:10)
II. Jonah reluctantly obeys God's call. (Jonah 3:1–4:11)

JOEL
I. A call to repentance—the past day of the Lord. (Joel 1:1–20)
II. The outpouring of God's Spirit—before the coming day of the Lord. (Joel 2:1–32)
III. The vindication and restoration of God's people—on the coming day of the Lord. (Joel 3:1–21)

As noted above, the seventh-century prophets Nahum, Habakkuk, and Zephaniah lived in an age of threatening Babylonian expansion. Nahum affirms the justice of God's moral government by pronouncing divine judgment on Nineveh and announcing the downfall of Assyria (612 BC) due to its cruel treatment of the nations. The book of Habakkuk does not record the prophet's preaching; it records his complaints (Hab. 1:1–4, 12–17), God's answers (Hab. 1:5–11; 2:1–3:15), and Habakkuk's final response of faith (Hab. 3:16–19). Habakkuk is appalled by God's failure to judge his wicked people, and even more appalled when

God tells him he will use the wicked Babylonians to judge them. Habakkuk recovers his trust in God after God affirms his justice and infinite glory. Zephaniah, a contemporary of Nahum and Habakkuk, directed his prophecy during the early reign of Josiah against the sinful legacy of kings Manasseh and Amon. He depicted God's judgment on the coming Day of the Lord in terms of an invasion (Zeph. 1:1–18). That judgment, however, would be followed by the final restoration of the people of God (Zeph. 3:8–20).

These prophets who prophesied before the Exile pronounced God's judgment on his people's sins. They condemned the people's debasing the worship of the Lord by mixing it with or abandoning it for the worship of fertility gods like Ba'al. They condemned the immorality, self-indulgence, and oppression of the poor that accompanied false worship. They attacked the vain belief of some that the temple and religious rituals would protect God's people even though they lived in disregard for God's moral law.

However, Haggai, his younger contemporary Zechariah, and, subsequently, Malachi, faced a different situation. They addressed the disillusionment and discouragement of those who had returned to Jerusalem from the Exile. The return they experienced did not live up to the great visions of people like Isaiah and Ezekiel. Was this little city-state of Jerusalem all there was to it? Was the God of Israel really the true God? Was

> **Was this little city-state of Jerusalem all there was to it? Was the God of Israel really the true God? Was it worth separating themselves from their pagan neighbors?**

it worth separating themselves from their pagan neighbors? Due to resistance from surrounding peoples, these disheartened returnees had abandoned rebuilding the temple. In about 520 BC Haggai and Zechariah encouraged Zerubbabel, a descendant of David; Joshua, the high priest; and the people to resume the rebuilding. By reestablishing the temple and keeping the Mosaic law they would maintain their distinction as God's people.

Figure 8

HAGGAI

I. God calls the people to rebuild the temple. (Hag. 1:1–15)

II. God promises a hesitant people that he will glorify the temple. (Hag. 2:1–9)

III. God promises a defiled people that he will prosper them. (Hag. 2:10–19)

IV. God promises an obedient people victory. (Hag. 2:20–23)

ZECHARIAH

I. Visions of encouragement for the present. (Zech. 1:1–8:23)

II. Prophecies of the Messiah and God's coming kingdom for the future. (Zech. 9:1–14:21)

MALACHI

I. God confirms his love for his people. (Mal. 1:1–5)

II. God rebukes Israel's unfaithfulness. (Mal. 1:6–2:16)

III. God announces his own coming to purify and restore his people. (Mal. 2:17–4:16)

Malachi, the last Old Testament prophet, appears about 460 to 450 BC, some eighty years after the temple's rebuilding. Disillusionment has deepened. People are unconcerned about maintaining their distinction from the unbelieving world around them and lax in their religious practices. This book addresses these issues in the form of a debate between Malachi and the people of Judah. The last chapter of Malachi aptly concludes the Old Testament and anticipates the New with a description of God's coming to restore his people. God's coming will once again establish his people in obedient fellowship, in harmony with one another, and, ultimately, in the place of blessing.

II. THE MESSAGE OF THE PROPHETS

This brief survey has oriented us to the Prophet books. We have seen some of the particular situations they addressed. Now let's allow our eyes to sweep over the panorama of their message. Threat of judgment precedes promise of restoration.

A. The Prophetic Proclamation of Judgment: Breach of Covenant Leads to Exile from God's Presence in the Land

Indebted to God's Grace. The prophets insist that God's people should have been faithful out of deep gratitude for his gracious deliverances and blessings. Isaiah begins his book by publicly shaming them for their ingratitude: "Hear, O heavens, and give ear, O earth; for the LORD has spoken: 'I have nourished and brought up children, and they have rebelled against me'" (Isa. 1:2). The parable of the vineyard in Isaiah 5:1–7 shows the absurdity of their disobedience in light of God's great provision. In Ezekiel 16:1–19 God is the best of husbands who has done everything for his bride, that is, his people, but they have turned away in gross unfaithfulness. In Hosea 11:1–4 and Amos 2:9–11 God reminds his people of his delivering them from Egypt and subsequent care for their every need. Hosea describes God as a father loving, providing, and gently teaching

> The prophets continually expose the disgraceful nature of Israel's unfaithfulness by putting God's generous, undeserved provision before them.

his child to walk. The prophets continually expose the disgraceful nature of Israel's unfaithfulness by putting God's generous, undeserved provision before them.

Persistent in Disobedience. Despite God's grace, his people persistently broke his covenant. The Prophets specify their sins. The most fundamental violation, of course, was the abandoning of God for idolatry—a violation of the first commandments and the sin that began at Mount Sinai with the golden calf (Ex. 32:1–35). Hear the condemnation of Isaiah 2:6–8 (NRSV):

> For you have forsaken the ways of your people, O house of Jacob. Indeed they are full of diviners from the east and of soothsayers like the Philistines, and they clasp hands with foreigners. . . . Their land is filled with idols; they bow down to the work of their hands, to what their own fingers have made.

According to Jeremiah 3:6–10, God's people have pursued idols as passionately as a promiscuous woman pursues her lovers. They had chased after Ba'al and other gods whose disgusting and immoral worship was supposed to promote fertility of land, animals, and people. They

> Failure to render the loyalty to God required by the first four commandments results in the abuse of others forbidden by the last six . . . People imitate the character of their gods.

resorted to these practices because they would not trust the Lord to meet their needs. Sometimes they corrupted the worship of the Lord by worshipping him as if he were Ba'al. They relied on their performance of religious rituals while they lived in immorality and took advantage of others (Jer. 7:1–15; cf. Isa. 1:10–17; 66:3–4).

Idolatry inevitably leads to the worst immorality. Since, as Hosea 4:1–2 (NRSV) says, "there is no faithfulness or loyalty, and no knowledge of God in the land," then "swearing, lying, and murder, and stealing and adultery break out; bloodshed follows bloodshed." Isaiah accuses them of the worst lust and debauchery (Isa. 5:8–17; cf. 3:16–26). Idolatry leads to oppression, to the accumulation of wealth by a few at the expense of many, and to the abuse of the needy, such as the widow, the fatherless, and the stranger (Amos 2:6–8; Micah 2:8–10; 3:1–3, 9–10; 6:8; and Isa. 5:8–10, 23; 10:1–4; 58:2–12). Failure to render the loyalty to God required by the first four commandments results in the abuse of others forbidden by the last six commandments. People imitate the character of their gods.

As we saw in chapter 3, God delivered his people from Egypt, made covenant with them at Sinai, and brought them into the land in order to reestablish his plan for humanity: obedient fellowship with God, harmonious fellowship among the people of God, and responsible enjoyment of the place of fellowship with God. From the beginning the prophets consistently warned them that persistent breach of God's covenant through disobedience would mean expulsion from the land: exile.

B. The Prophetic Promise of Salvation: God's Undefeatable Grace Will Effect an Ultimate Restoration

Restoration through Repentance. The prophets begin announcing God's gracious offer of restoration through repentance. Isaiah 1:18 articulates that offer: "'Come now, and let us reason together,' says the LORD, 'Though your sins are like scarlet, they shall be as white as snow; though they are red like crimson, they shall be as wool.'" Listen also to Amos's cry:

> Seek good, and not evil, that you may live; so the LORD, the God of hosts, will be with you, as you have spoken. Hate evil, love good; establish justice in the gate. It may be that the LORD God of hosts will be gracious to the remnant of Joseph. (Amos 5:14–15)

The only hope for future salvation, then, rested in a gracious God rather than in an unrepentant people.

Some accepted God's offer of repentance. However, as the centuries passed, it became increasingly evident that the people as a whole were not going to repent, and therefore judgment became inevitable.

Restoration through a New Act of God's Grace. The only hope for future salvation, then, rested in a gracious God rather than in an unrepentant people. God had promised to redeem the world through Abraham's descendants. His promise would not be frustrated. The prophets begin this line of thought by looking for God to create a new beginning for his people. Thus Hosea speaks of God taking his people into the wilderness once more so that he can begin again with them. This time they will be his loyal spouse and he will fully bless them (Hos. 2:14–23). Through Isaiah, God promises that he will use Cyrus to bring his people back from exile and that he will rebuild Jerusalem (Isa. 44:24–28). As God once delivered his people from slavery in Egypt, so he will bring them back in a new exodus from captivity in Babylon (Jer. 16:14–15). Jeremiah announced this new beginning in the verse with which we began this chapter: "'For I know the plans I have for you,' declares the LORD, 'plans to prosper you and not to harm you, plans to give you hope and a future'" (Jer. 29:11 NIV).

However, the persistent, hardened, habitual nature of sin makes it clear that a mere second chance would not be enough. God must perform a new mighty act of salvation that delivers his people from their propensity to sin. As we saw in chapter 3, deliverance from slavery to Pharaoh typified this deeper deliverance. The Prophets promise that God is going to make this liberation from bondage to sin a reality. Jeremiah 31:31–34 and Ezekiel 36:24–28 are the classical expression of this prophetic hope:

"Behold, the days are coming, declares the LORD, when I will make a new covenant with the house of Israel and the house of Judah, not like the covenant that I made with their fathers when I took them by the hand to bring them out of the land of Egypt, my covenant that they broke, though I was their husband, declares the LORD. But this is the covenant that I will make with the house of Israel after those days, declares the LORD: I will put my law within them, and I will write it upon their hearts. And I will be their God, and they shall be my people. And no longer shall each one teach his neighbor and each his brother, saying, 'Know the LORD,' for they shall all know me, from the least of them to the greatest, declares the LORD. For I will forgive their iniquity, and I will remember their sin no more." (Jer. 31:31–34 ESV)

I will take you from the nations and gather you from all the countries and bring you into your own land. I will sprinkle clean water on you, and you shall be clean from all your uncleanness, and from all your idols I will cleanse you. And I will give you a new heart, and a new spirit I will put within you. And I will remove the heart of stone from your flesh and give you a heart of flesh. And I will put my Spirit within you, and cause you to walk in my statutes and be careful to obey my rules. You shall dwell in the land that I gave to your fathers, and you shall be my people, and I will be your God. (Ezek. 36:24–28 ESV)

These two prophecies complement and elucidate each other. In both of them God announces that he is going to make a radical break with his people's past by transforming their thinking and motivation so that they can live in obedient fellowship with him. The proclamation in Jeremiah is threefold: (1) forgiveness—God will remember their sins no longer; (2) transformation—God will write his laws on their hearts; (3) restored fellowship—he will be their God and they will be his people. God had instructed them long ago to keep his words in their hearts (Deut. 6:6–7). Now he promises that he will write his laws on their hearts: that is, he will give them hearts ready and willing to obey. A forgiven and transformed people will be able to live in his presence: he as their God, they as

> [God] will not only give them a new, sensitive heart (the heart of 'flesh') and a new spirit, but he will put his own Spirit within them.

his people, as God intended from the beginning (Ex. 6:7). Once fellowship with God is restored, the other aspects of God's plan follow.

Ezekiel reinforces the message of Jeremiah. God will "cleanse" them of their "uncleanness." He will not only give them a new, sensitive heart (the heart of "flesh") and a new spirit, but he will put his own Spirit within them. Ezekiel leaves nothing to the imagination. By putting his Spirit within his people God will cause them to "walk in" his "statutes" and to "obey" his "rules." The goal of the old covenant will be fulfilled in the new covenant, which it foreshadowed.

As the Davidic king was instituted in order to establish God's people in obedience, so God would use the coming Messiah whom David foreshadowed to establish this new order. The Prophets speak about this coming one in many ways. The most moving, already mentioned above, is the description of God's Servant in Isaiah 52:13–53:12 who suffers and dies for the iniquities of God's people in order that they might be healed.

The return from exile was indeed a mighty act of God. However, it was not yet the full deliverance promised by the prophets. The rebuilt temple was smaller and less ornate than Solomon's temple. Tiny Judah was but a shadow of the great restoration pictured by Isaiah (40:1–48:22) and Ezekiel (40:1–48:35). God's blessing did not yet extend to the nations. Even

> **The prophets who lived after the Exile . . . continued to promise a grand future restoration when God himself would come to his people (Hag. 2:6–9; Mal. 3:1; 4:5–6).**

his own people continued to have a problem with disobedience (Ezra 9:1–15; Neh. 13:1–31). Furthermore, the prophets who lived after the Exile realized these insufficiencies and continued to promise a grand future restoration when God himself would come to his people (Hag. 2:6–9; Mal. 3:1; 4:5–6).

We can now see clearly how integral the Prophets are to the grand story of the Bible. The Prophets addressed God's sinful people during the history recorded in Samuel through Nehemiah calling them back to the covenant inaugurated through Moses in the Pentateuch in order that they might fulfill God's promise to Abraham. The Prophets promise the coming of the Messiah and the final rule of God so longed for by the psalmists. The prophetic assurance that God's salvation will go beyond his judgment and reestablish his people in obedience through the Messiah finds its fulfillment in Christ as recorded in the New Testament. The result of the prophetic message will be the complete restoration of God's plan in the New Jerusalem (Rev. 21:1–22:21).

III. THE CONTINUING SIGNIFICANCE OF THE PROPHETIC MESSAGE OF JUDGMENT AND SALVATION

The way in which the message of the Prophets points to the ultimate universal fulfillment of God's covenant promise in Christ is of obvious continuing relevance. However, there are also a number of other ways in which the Prophets continue to shape the lives of the people of God. We will look first at the continuing impact of the prophetic message of judgment, then at their message of restoration and salvation.

A. The Continuing Relevance of the Prophetic Proclamation of Judgment

The Moral Imperative of the Law. The prophetic proclamation of judgment clarifies the moral imperative of God's law. God through the Prophets does not condemn the people because they failed to perform certain minute details of his law. He condemns them for their disloyalty expressed in their idolatry and disregard for the Sabbath. He condemns them for the way they have treated each other: for murder; marital unfaithfulness and lustful conduct; for theft; for lack of integrity; and for their greed. He condemns them for the way they have taken advantage of the weak, for their failure to care for the needy, such as orphans, widows, and strangers. He condemns them for injustice, such as the way they have devoured the property of the poor. The prophets condemn temple worship, offering sacrifices, and all religious observances as repulsive to God without such moral obedience. God takes no delight in either legalism or religiosity. The prophets emphasize the two Great Commandments and the Ten Commandments just as we have done in chapter 4.

Listen to Jeremiah's great "temple sermon":

"For if you thoroughly amend your ways and your doings, if you thoroughly execute judgment between a man and his neighbor, if you do not oppress the stranger, the fatherless, and the widow, and do not shed innocent blood in this place, or walk after other gods to your hurt, then I will cause you to dwell in this place, in the land that I gave to your fathers forever and ever.

"Behold, you trust in lying words that cannot profit. Will you steal, murder, commit adultery, swear falsely, burn incense to Baal, and walk after other gods whom you do not know, and then come and stand before Me in this house which is called by My name, and say, 'We are delivered to do all these abominations'? Has this house, which is called by My name, become a den of thieves in your eyes? Behold, I, even I, have seen it," says the Lord. (Jer. 7:5–11)

Jeremiah accused God's professed but disobedient people of using the temple like a robbers' hideout. They assumed that careful performance of temple worship would save them from God's judgment even though they were living in gross immorality. Isaiah 1:10–17 speaks for itself. Notice how God identifies both rulers and people with the wicked cities of Sodom and Gomorrah (Gen. 13:13; 18:20–21; 19:1–14).

Hear the word of the Lord, you rulers of Sodom; give ear to the law of our God, you people of Gomorrah: "To what purpose is the multitude of your sacrifices to Me?" says the Lord. "I have had enough of burnt offerings of rams and the fat of fed cattle. I do not delight in the blood of bulls, or of lambs or goats. "When you come to appear before Me, who has required this from your hand, to trample My courts? Bring no more futile sacrifices; incense is an abomination to Me. The New Moons, the Sabbaths, and the calling of assemblies—I cannot endure iniquity and the sacred meeting. Your New Moons and your appointed feasts My soul hates; they are a trouble to Me, I am weary of bearing them. When you spread out your hands, I will hide My eyes from you; even though you make many prayers, I will not hear. Your hands are full of blood. Wash yourselves, make yourselves clean; put away the evil of your doings from before My eyes. Cease to do evil, learn to do good; seek justice, rebuke the oppressor; defend the fatherless, plead for the widow.

The oft-quoted passage from Micah 6:6–8 sums up the Prophets' concern with the moral imperative of the law:

> With what shall I come before the LORD, and bow myself before the High God? Shall I come before Him with burnt offerings, with calves a year old? Will the LORD be pleased with thousands of rams, ten thousand rivers of oil? Shall I give my firstborn for my transgression, the fruit of my body for the sin of my soul? He has shown you, O man, what is good; and what does the LORD require of you but to do justly, to love mercy, and to walk humbly with your God?

The Social Nature of the Law. The Prophets reinforce what the rest of the Old Testament teaches: there is no such thing as private sin. Neglect of God and his commandments always leads to the abuse of my neighbor and to rupture in the harmony of the community. Such disharmony is the inherent effect of those sins against which the Prophets so passionately proclaimed the divine displeasure: violence, unfaithfulness, sexual impurity, deceit, theft, greed, oppression of the weak. On the one hand, a godly community is made up of godly people. On the other hand, however, godly people can enjoy the full blessing intended by God only within a godly community. It was because God's people as a community persistently refused to reflect his character that God expelled them from the place of fellowship with him.

> **The prophets are certain that the Lord God who delivered his people from Egypt is the Creator and the sovereign Lord of the Nations.**

The Universal Scope of the Law. The prophets are certain that the Lord God who delivered his people from Egypt is the Creator and the sovereign Lord of the nations. God gave his law to his people so that they would be a light to the peoples of the world. The prophetic oracles against the nations show clearly that God holds all people accountable, according to their knowledge, before his moral law. Thus Amos condemns Damascus (1:3), Gaza (1:6), Tyre (1:9), Edom (1:11), Ammon (1:13), and Moab (2:1) for their violence. Isaiah pronounces God's judgment on Babylon (13:1–14:23), Assyria (14:24–27), Philistia (14:28–32), Moab (15:1–16:13), Syria (17:1–3), Egypt (19:1–20:6), Arabia (21:13–17), Tyre (23:1–18), and many other nations (17:12–18:7). Ezekiel declares God's judgment on the nations for their violent mistreatment of Judah (25:1–32:32). Hear God's words in Isaiah 13:11: "I will punish the world for its evil, and the wicked for their iniquity; I will halt the arrogance of the proud, and will lay low the haughtiness of the terrible."

The Various Uses of the Law. By highlighting the moral imperative, community orientation, and universal scope of the law, the prophetic message of judgment facilitates all four uses of the law discussed in chapter 4.

The law's moral imperative and universal scope are fundamental to its religious use. Because the law condemns immorality, it drives us to God's grace for redemption. The apostle Paul is a good example. There is no evidence that he felt condemned because of failure to keep all of the regulations that had been added to the law in his time. His own testimony bears witness to the religious use of the law's moral imperative. He was convicted of sin because the law said, "you shall not covet" (Rom. 7:7). The moral law brought condemnation to his covetous heart that could be removed by nothing but the grace of God. Hear the law's call to repentance in Isaiah 1:16–17: "Wash yourselves, make yourselves clean; put away the evil of your doings from before My eyes. Cease to do evil, learn to do good; seek justice, rebuke the oppressor; defend the fatherless, plead for the widow."

The moral imperative and universality of the law underlie its civil use. At one level God has given his moral law to restrain the wickedness of all people; the prophets pronounced God's judgment on the nations. Thus God's people, within their countries and as they are able, seek to promote laws that restrain the wicked and promote the moral

Figure 9

Religious Use

The law shows us our need of Christ.

behavior enjoined by God's law. As we have seen above, the Pattern Principle is helpful here. The everyday laws help us understand how to apply God's moral law in the circumstances of modern life.

God's people are no longer a nation but a voluntary community among the nations. Any attempt to enforce religious practice by legal means is contrary to the nature of the gospel. Those who seek to live by Scripture, however, must remember that there is no neutral basis for the laws of nations. They are always based on some set of presuppositions, be they secular or God-honoring. Thus there is nothing that restrains those who believe the Bible from supporting laws that promote the fundamental moral principles taught by God's law. The book of Proverbs that we studied in chapter 7 teaches that God has built his moral law into the nature of the universe. Thus those who neglect his law do so at their peril. There is no other firm foundation upon which we can stand in opposition to violence, dishonesty, unfaithfulness, sexual impurity, greed, or exploitation of the poor and other forms of injustice.

Figure 10

Civil Use

The law restrains evil in society.

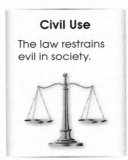

The way in which the Prophets highlight the moral imperative of God's law reinforces the continuing relevance of the moral use of the law. Those fundamental moral principles find support in the New Testament and continue to guide the conduct of the people of God. The prophetic emphasis on the law's moral imperative also underlies the evangelical use of the law. If God requires his people to live in conformity to these moral directives, then he will supply the grace necessary for obedience. Thus the evangelical use of the law leads directly to the significance of the prophetic promise of salvation and full restoration. The divine offer

Figure 11

Moral Use

The law is a continuing moral guide for life.

Evangelical Use

The law is God's promise of sanctifying grace.

of release from sin in Isaiah 1:18 is, through Christ, available for God's people in the present: "'Come now, and let us reason together,' says the Lord, 'Though your sins are as scarlet, they shall be as white as snow; though they are red like crimson, they shall be like wool.'"

B. The Continuing Relevance of the Prophetic Promise of Salvation

The prophetic message of judgment would lead to despair without the corresponding divine promise of salvation. God, through the Prophets, promises the full restoration of his plan. This promise assures us of the sufficiency of grace and the faithfulness of God. It also confirms and clarifies the Typological Principle explained in chapter 2.

The Prophetic Promise of Salvation Confirms the Typological Principle. The prophets know that the God who delivered his people in the past is the same God who will do even greater things for them in the future. They are convinced that his ways in the past provide a picture of the greater way in which he will yet deliver. If entering captivity is a return to

> The prophetic message of judgment would lead to despair without the corresponding divine promise of salvation.

Egypt (Hosea 7:16; 8:13; 9:3, 6, 17; 11:5), God's deliverance of his people from Babylonian exile is a greater exodus (Jeremiah 16:14–15; see also Isa. 43:16–19; 48:20–21; 51:9–11; 52:11–12) that produces a greater restoration. The Sinai covenant is a type of Jeremiah's "New Covenant" (Jer. 31:31–34). That first covenant was given in order to establish God's people in obedient fellowship with him and harmonious fellowship with each other. The "New Covenant" overcomes the stubborn rebellion of the human heart so that this fellowship with God and within the community of God's people can become a reality. The prophets look forward to a new and greater David (Isa. 9:7; 16:5) who, by the atonement he provides, will truly establish God's people in obedience. The new era of deliverance is pictured as an idealized Jerusalem (Mic. 4:1–5) and even as a new Eden (Ezek. 34:26–30). On the other hand, the flood has become a type or picture of God's judgment (compare Zeph. 1:2–3).

The Prophetic Promise of Salvation Affirms the Faithfulness of God and the Sufficiency of His Grace. The sinful history of God's people demonstrates the utter necessity of grace. Jeremiah 13:23 is the classic Old Testament statement of this need: the people of God cannot rid themselves of their propensity to go their own way in disobedience. God's promise of salvation through the Prophets, on the other hand, assures us that he will deliver the human heart from this bondage. He is both faithful to his promise of restoration and capable of bringing it to fulfillment. He has promised to put his Spirit within his people and to give them a new, obedient heart (Ezek. 36:24–28) appropriate for those who live under the new covenant (Jer. 31:31–34). Hebrews 10:15–18 claims that the provisions of this new covenant have become effective through the work of Christ.

He also promises a permanent homeland for the community of the people who have thus been freed for obedience. Many passages assure us that God is going to reestablish Jerusalem on a far grander scale as the center of a renewed community in fellowship with him. Even when Jerusalem is under siege, Jeremiah declares its future revival (Jer. 32:6–35). In Isaiah's and Ezekiel's prophesies of consolation (Isa. 40:1–55:13; Ezek. 33:1–48:35) this idealized restoration goes beyond literal fulfillment. The fact that the return from exile fell so far short of these prophetic visions only increased expectations as Haggai, Zechariah, and Malachi looked forward to God's ultimate salvation. This vision of the future finds its fulfillment in Christ, and, at his return, in the New Jerusalem, Heaven, and Earth of Revelation 21:1–22:21.

How appropriate it is, then, that the Old Testament ends with the Prophets. God's promise of salvation looks forward to the full restoration of God's plan that will be accomplished through the first and second comings of Christ. The last chapter of the Old Testament anticipates the coming of God. Malachi 3:1 says that, in the person of God's Son, our Savior, "The Lord, whom you seek, will suddenly come to His temple." The expectation of future restoration in 1 Chronicles through Esther and Job through the Song of Songs comes to full expression in the promises of the Prophets. See **Figure 12** and the full chart of which it is a part in Appendix 2. We will conclude our study in the next chapter with a brief overview of how this anticipated restoration comes to fruition in the New Testament.

Figure 12

NEW COVENANT YET TO COME

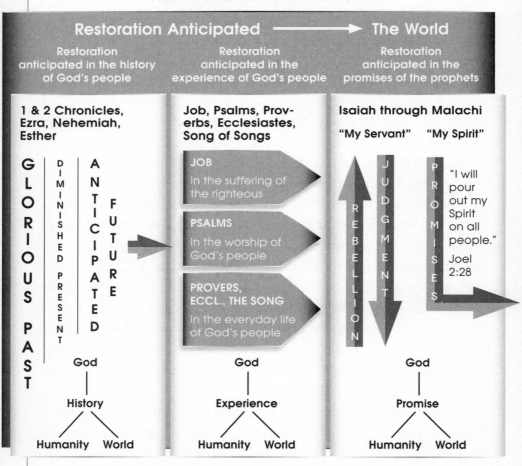

RESTORATION ACCOMPLISHED, EXPERIENCED, *and* CONSUMMATED

Christ Has Come in the Flesh;
Christ Is Present in His Church;
Christ Will Come in Glory

Matthew to the Revelation

Don't skip the genealogy in the first chapter of the New Testament (Matt. 1:1–17)! This account of Jesus' ancestors announces God's fulfillment of his plan for humanity. Note how carefully Matthew tells us that there were fourteen generations from Abraham to David "the king" (Matt. 1:6), fourteen generations from David to the Exile, and fourteen generations from the Exile to the Christ (Matt. 1:17). From Abraham to David "the king" to the Exile to Christ, who fulfills the promise of restoration that God made to Abraham in Genesis 12—in Christ all the families of the earth will be blessed. Christ fulfills this promise as the Messiah, the true descendant of David, the great King who saves his people from their sin and thus ends their exile from God.

Note further how four women are singled out from Christ's ancestry: Tamar, Rahab the harlot, Ruth the Moabite, and "the wife of Uriah" the Hittite (Matt. 1:3, 5–6). They represent people who were not physical descendants of Abraham. Matthew lists these women because he wants us to know that this restoration of God's plan is the good news of salvation for all the scattered nations of the world—scattered from God's presence through sin as described in Genesis 10–11.

The one who brings this fulfillment is unique: he is none other than the eternal Son of God who assumes our humanity through the womb of the Virgin Mary (Matt. 1:18–25). The prophet Malachi (3:1) declared that God would send his "messenger" to prepare the way for "the Lord" to come. Mark 1:2–3 affirms that John the Baptist was that messenger and that Jesus' coming was the coming of "the Lord" (cf. Isa. 40:3).

The rest of the New Testament agrees with Matt. 1:1–25: Christ fulfills God's Old Testament promise of restoration. In this final chapter we will conclude our study of Christian faith in the Old Testament with a brief overview of some of the ways in which the New Testament describes the fulfillment of this promise.

The New Testament account of restoration can be appropriately divided into three parts: the four Gospels;[20] Acts and the letters (both of Paul[21] and of other apostolic leaders[22]); and the Revelation. See **Figure 1**. According to the Gospels, Christ came in the flesh.[23] According to Acts

---

20. Matthew, Mark, Luke, and John

21. Romans, 1 and 2 Corinthians, Galatians, Ephesians, Philippians, Colossians, 1 and 2 Thessalonians, 1 and 2 Timothy, Titus, Philemon

22. Hebrews; James; 1 and 2 Peter; 1, 2, and 3 John; and Jude.

23. For us and for our salvation, he came down from heaven. He became incarnate from the Virgin Mary and was made man. (Nicene Creed)

and the letters, Christ is present in his church.[24] According to the Revelation, Christ will come in glory.[25]

Figure 1

GOD'S PLAN—ACCOMPLISHED, EXPERIENCED, CONSUMMATED

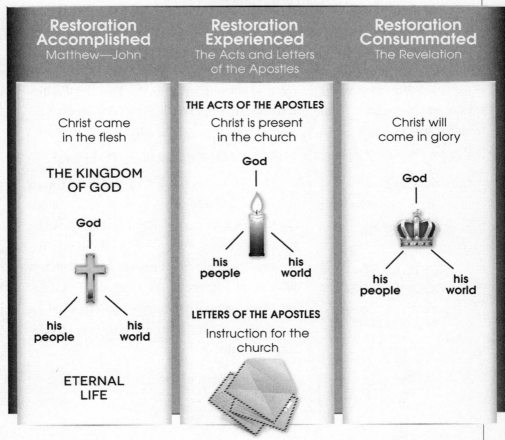

Restoration Accomplished Matthew—John	Restoration Experienced The Acts and Letters of the Apostles	Restoration Consummated The Revelation
Christ came in the flesh	**THE ACTS OF THE APOSTLES** Christ is present in the church	Christ will come in glory
THE KINGDOM OF GOD	God / his people \ his world	God / his people \ his world
God / his people \ his world	**LETTERS OF THE APOSTLES** Instruction for the church	
ETERNAL LIFE		

Each of these three sections makes a unique contribution to our understanding of the restoration brought by Jesus in fulfillment of the divine promise. The four Gospels focus on Christ's accomplishment of this

---

24. "Now you are the body of Christ and individually members of it" (1 Cor. 12:27 ESV).

25. "He will come again in glory to judge the living and the dead, and His kingdom will have no end." (Nicene Creed)

restoration at his first coming. Acts and the letters invite us to experience this restoration in the present. The Revelation directs our attention to the future consummation of restoration at Christ's return. Restoration: accomplished in the past; experienced in the present; consummated in the future. Thus we are encouraged to live by faith in the finished work of the incarnate Christ; in love through the power of the exalted, indwelling Christ; and in hope of the returning triumphant Christ. There is, of course, overlap that establishes a harmony between these various divisions of the New Testament. All parts of the New Testament speak of Christ's past accomplishment, present power, and coming in glory. And yet the distinctions we have made reflect the emphases or perspectives of each section.

I. RESTORATION ACCOMPLISHED: THE FOUR GOSPELS

Christ accomplished this restoration of God's plan for humanity through becoming a human being and giving himself up to death by crucifixion.

Figure 2

RESTORATION
ACCOMPLISHED
CHRIST HAS COME
IN THE FLESH.

That is why the cross has always been the most appropriate way of symbolizing his accomplishment. See **Figure 2** and the first column of **Figure 1**. We look first at how the three Synoptic Gospels present Christ's accomplishment. Then we will turn to the gospel of John.

A. The Kingdom of God in the Synoptic Gospels

Syn is derived from a Greek word that means "together." *Optic* comes from a word meaning "to see": think "optics" and "optician." The three "Synoptic" Gospels—Matthew, Mark, and Luke—each have special emphases. Yet to a large degree they see the life of Jesus together; they share a common timeline and perspective. One important commonality is their emphasis on the kingdom of God (equals "kingdom of heaven"). Jesus begins his ministry by proclaiming, "The time is fulfilled, and the kingdom of God is at hand. Repent, and believe in the gospel" (Mark 1:15).

The kingdom of God is the sovereign rule of God. Nothing has been right since Adam and Eve refused to trust God and deliberately rejected his rule in the Garden. As we saw in chapter 1, when they replaced God's rule with human rule—with self-rule—they shattered God's plan for humanity. They shut off the source of all joy by disrupting fellowship with God. Their self-justification fractured the love they had for each other. They no longer had free enjoyment of the world God had given them. The human race perpetuated their legacy as demonstrated by Cain's murder of his brother, Abel, by the violence and lust of Noah's day, and by the professed self-sufficiency of the builders of Babel. At Mount Sinai, God reestablished his rule over the people he had so graciously delivered from Egypt—yet they rebelled by worshiping the golden calf even before they left the mountain. We have seen how they rejected God's rule in Samuel's day by asking him to give them a "king like other nations." We have also seen how God used that request to institute David, a man after God's own heart, and his dynasty as an instrument for reestablishing God's rule. And yet the descendants of David fell ever further into disobedience, resulting in exile from the land of fellowship with God.

> **The great prophet Isaiah longed for the day when the cry would go out, 'your God reigns' . . . Jesus begins his ministry by announcing, 'The time is fulfilled . . .'**

The Old Testament points out the need for and anticipates the coming of God's sovereign rule. The great prophet Isaiah longed for the day when the cry would go out, "your God reigns," over Israel and over the nations of the world (Isa. 52:7). Jesus begins his ministry by announcing, "The time is fulfilled . . ."

The long history of rebellion has shown the depth of human bondage to sin and its destructive consequences. Rejection of God's legitimate rule has led to the tyranny of the self and to the dominion of Satan and all the evil powers associated with him. In order to establish the rule of God, Jesus must atone for sin and overthrow the power of evil. It is no surprise,

> [Jesus] would . . . show . . . the extent of his power by casting out a 'legion' of evil spirits—not in a holy place, but in an unclean, God-forsaken, gentile cemetery . . .

then, when Jesus begins his ministry in Mark's gospel by casting out an evil spirit in the Capernaum synagogue (Mark 1:21–28). He would soon show his disciples the extent of his power by casting out a "legion" of evil spirits—not in a holy place, but in an unclean, godforsaken, gentile cemetery (Mark 5:1–20). He exercised divine rule when he released the paralytic from his sin (Mark 2:1–12). Thus he claimed power to deliver from both sin and Satan.

As we learned in chapter 1, sickness and death are the direct result of rebellion against God. They are the marks of the kingdom of evil. When Jesus exercised the divine rule by healing the diseased and raising the dead, he claimed authority over Satan, sin, and all the consequences of sin—even death. He has delivered the people of God from a bondage that was deeper, more oppressive, and more destructive than "the land of Egypt . . . the house of bondage" (Ex. 20:2) from which they had been delivered long ago.

His parables and his teaching invited people to submit to the divine rule and to live even now as subjects of the kingdom of God. By its transforming power they would be a community of people who had an "appetite for God" (Matt. 5:6 MSG) whose righteousness came from inward transformation (Matt. 5:17–20) and thus exceeded that of those who emphasized outward conformity. Their relationship with God the King would be so intimate that they would call him "Father"—and they would experience his fatherly care and demonstrate a filial likeness.

Jesus' ministry culminated in his passion. He gave his life as "a ransom for many" (Mark 10:45). By his death and resurrection he atoned for sin, overcame the curse of death, and defeated the power of Satan. Thus he could say to his disciples, "All authority has been given to me in heaven and on earth" (Matt. 28:18). The incarnate Son of God has now taken his seat at the right hand of God on the throne of the universe (Heb. 10:11–14). He has accomplished all that is necessary for the defeat of evil and the establishment of God's rule. Yet that rule will not be made fully visible to the world until the return of Christ; only then will it be consummated in the new heaven and earth where the people of God will live free from sin in the fullest fellowship with him, in joyful harmony with one another, and in the complete enjoyment of the place God has prepared for them. Now is the time when Jesus invites us to freely submit to his rule.

Who is this Jesus who has accomplished all that is necessary for establishing the rule of God? Mark tells us that he is relating the gospel of "the Son of God" (Mark 1:1). No one who was not fully God and fully human could accomplish this deliverance from sin, death, and Satan. Only God can heal, as Jesus so often does, by merely speaking a word. The people in the synagogue marvel at the divine authority of his teaching (Mark 1:27). He exercises a divine prerogative when he forgives the paralytic's sin (Mark 2:1–12). When Jesus answers the inquiring rich man, he equates following him with the wholehearted love for God required by the Greatest Commandment (Mark 10:17–22; see Deut. 6:5). He affirms his unique relationship with God at the beginning of the last week of his life in the parable of the wicked tenants (Mark 12:1–12). God establishes his rule through this son of David because he is also the Son of God. Through his obedience unto death this Son of David fulfills the role of the Suffering Servant who was stricken "for the transgressions of my people" (Isa. 53:8).

B. Eternal Life in the Gospel of John

"The wages of sin is death" (Rom. 6:23 KJV). The apostle Paul made this statement in the first century AD, but its truth has been evident since Genesis 3. The options were clear. Adam and Eve enjoyed life in fellowship with God. If, however, they disobeyed, they would die: "but of the tree of the knowledge of good and evil you shall not eat, for in the day that you eat of it you shall surely die" (Gen. 2:17 ESV). Through their disobedience death became the common lot of their descendants. Restoration of obedient fellowship with the living God includes the restoration of life.

This fact is demonstrated in the Sinai covenant. Over and over again God promised his people life in the promised land if they would live in obedient fellowship with him. The price of disobedience was death: "See, I have set before you today life and good, death and evil" (Deut. 30:15). Moses warns God's people to love and obey God because he "is your life and the length of your days" (Deut. 30:20). This life included joy in God's presence, harmony among God's people, and enjoyment of the abundance of the land. It was offered not merely to individuals, but to the people of God. It was only as a community that they could live in harmony with one another. Thus, as we have seen in earlier chapters, exile from the land was death for the community of God's people. So restoration in Christ is their life.

As we saw in chapter 7, the teaching of Proverbs and the other Wisdom Literature reinforces this offer of life. The reward for pursuing wisdom "in the fear of the Lord" was life. Folly led only to death. On the surface both Sinai covenant and wisdom offer a good temporal life to those who live in obedient fellowship with God—"length of days" according to Deuteronomy 30:20 (ESV). And yet this joint offer of life clearly anticipates the theme of John's gospel: eternal life. Life that comes from fellowship with the eternal living God must be eternal life. As Jesus says, God "is not the God of the dead, but of the living" (Matt. 22:32). As the promised land was the prototype of the eternal new heaven and earth, so this promise of life in the land anticipated eternal life in God's presence.

This is God's promise to Abraham of blessing for the nations. Nothing less would be an adequate restoration of what was lost in Eden.

This is the theme of John's gospel: God sent his Son to bring the light of life into a hopeless, dark, and dying world (John 1:4–5). Those who "receive" (John 1:12) God's Son and "believe" in him (John 3:16) acquire this life. This belief is far more than intellectual assent. It is a total reliance upon Jesus that results in a life of obedience. Those who believe are "born" of God (John 1:12–13; 3:1–16) and can therefore be rightly called the "children of God." God puts his own life in them.

The irony of John's gospel is that those whom we would have expected to receive this gift of life—such as many of the Jewish leaders—vehemently rejected God's Son and put him to death (John 1:9–11). God, however, used their very opposition to make this life available. It was only by Jesus' death that life was offered to a dying world. It was by his giving his flesh "for the life of the world" (John 6:51), by the Good Shepherd's laying down his life for his sheep (John 10:10–11), by the "grain of wheat" falling "into the ground" (John 12:24) that he became the "resurrection and the life" (John 11:25) for all who would believe. He was the new covenant "Lamb of God" who gave them life by taking "away the sins of the world" (John 1:29, 36). The cross is always at the center of the gospel.

> When Jesus answers the inquiring rich man, he equates following him with the whole-hearted love for God required by the Greatest Commandment . . .

This crucified, risen, and exalted Son of God is the "bread of life" (John 6:35) who gives the water of life (John 4:7–14; 7:37–39). He continually sustains the life of his people and brings them the deepest satisfaction. They have their life in union with him just as the branch of a vine has its life in union with the vine (John 15:1–8). John makes the connection between obedient fellowship with God and life very clear.

This union with God leads to harmonious fellowship among the people of God. In his last conversation with his disciples before his death,

> **All were now to recognize the community of Jesus' disciples by the way they 'loved one another' as Jesus had loved them (John 13:34–35).**

Jesus made it very clear that they were to love one another "to the end" (John 13:1) as he loved them by washing their feet and by going to the cross (John 15:12–17). The nations of old were to see God's character reflected in the common life of his covenant-keeping people. All were now to recognize the community of Jesus' disciples by the way they "loved one another" as Jesus had loved them (John 13:34–35). The "Comforter," the Spirit of God, would make all of this a reality in their lives by applying the work of Christ, forming Christ within them, and helping them to understand the things of Christ (John 14:25–26; 16:12–15).

The third part of God's plan, a restored place of blessing and fellowship with God, remains a promise. It is a promise reaffirmed and certified by the work of Christ: "If I go and prepare a place for you, I will come again and will take you to myself, that where I am you may be also" (John 14:3 ESV). The entire New Testament awaits this glorious hope with renewed anticipation.

From the beginning, rebellion against God's rule and rejection of his kingdom brought death. The gospel narratives show us how Jesus came to accomplish what was necessary for the restoration of God's rule and the offer of life to a dying world. He provides what the Old Testament envisioned: abundant life in fellowship with God and in submission to his rule.

II. RESTORATION EXPERIENCED: ACTS AND THE NEW TESTAMENT LETTERS

As the people of God we enjoy the restoration that Christ has accomplished even as we await its consummation at his return. See column two of **Figure 1**. We live in a community that experiences the life of God through release from sin and power for faithful obedience. These benefits are made a reality in our lives through the presence and power of God's Spirit whom Christ has received from the Father and poured out on his people (Acts 2:33). Christ is being formed in each of us by the Spirit and is present in our community through the Spirit. He is at work among us through prayer, Scripture, sacraments, and our mutual care for one another in the body of Christ. Thus the candle representing the Holy Spirit, with the cross representing Christ, is an appropriate symbol for Christ's working through the Holy Spirit in his church as described in Acts (see **Figure 3**).

Acts is the story of the way in which Jesus continues to make the salvation that he has accomplished a reality in the lives of his people. The letters of the New Testament provide needed instruction for those who would live in this reality.

Figure 3

RESTORATION EXPERIENCED
CHRIST IS PRESENT IN HIS CHURCH

A. Acts: the Story of the Church Continues into the Present

The Acts of the Apostles continues the story of the Gospels. It begins with the instructions the risen Christ gave to his disciples before he went back to heaven (Acts 1:1–11). Jesus tells his followers to wait for the Holy Spirit whom the Father has promised to send. His words of commissioning in Acts 1:8 outline the rest of Acts: "But you will receive power when the Holy Spirit has come upon you, and you will be my witnesses in Jerusalem and in all Judea and Samaria, and to the end of the earth" (ESV). Acts 2:1–41 describes the anticipated coming of the Holy Spirit. Chapters 3–7 focus on the witness of Jesus' followers in Jerusalem. In chapters 8–12, their witness reaches Judea and Samaria. Chapters 13–28 narrate the spread of the gospel throughout the world.

Before we get to the world outreach begun in Acts 13, we read about the conversion of Paul (Acts 9:1–30) and the establishing of a predominately gentile church in Syrian Antioch (Acts 11:19–30). This mission-minded church would commission Paul and send him to preach the gospel throughout the world (Acts 13:1–4). Acts 13:1–14:28 describes the inflow of Gentiles on Paul's first missionary journey. The Jerusalem Council of Acts 15:1–41 makes it clear that these Gentiles need not be circumcised in order to be part of the people of God. Paul's subsequent missionary journeys take him to Greece (Acts 16:1–18:21), Asia Minor (Acts 18:22–21:14), and Rome (Acts 21:15–28:31). God's words to Ananias on

> The Holy Spirit purifies . . . directs . . . and empowers the church. The Holy Spirit is both the architect and the energy for the worldwide expansion of the church.

the occasion of Paul's conversion are fulfilled (Acts 9:15–16): Paul bears witness before Gentiles (Acts 13:44–52; 17:22–31), "kings" (Acts 24:10–21; 26:1–32), and the "children of Israel" (Acts 22:1–21; 28:23–29).

The coming of the Holy Spirit is the central event of Acts. His presence is the distinguishing mark of the New Testament people of God. The Holy Spirit purifies the church, directs the church, and empowers the church. The Holy Spirit is both the architect and the energy for the worldwide expansion of the church. His coming is the culmination of Christ's work as recorded in the Gospels, the fulfillment of the Father's promise found in the Old Testament, and the means by which we as the people of God are incorporated into the work of Christ.

First, the Holy Spirit's coming is the culmination of Christ's work as recorded in the Gospels. Some have suggested that Acts could be called the "Acts of the Holy Spirit" as well as the "Acts of the Apostles." It could also be called the "Acts of Jesus." Luke introduces this book as the continuation of "all that Jesus began to do and teach" in the gospel of Luke (Acts 1:1). It is the risen Christ who receives the Holy Spirit from the Father and pours him out upon his church (Acts 2:33). Christ is present in his church through the Holy Spirit. Thus it is through the presence of the Holy Spirit that Christ's work is applied to our hearts (Acts 15:6). It is through the presence of the Holy Spirit that we are incorporated into Christ and made members of the people of God. Look again at **Figure 3**.

Second, the coming of the Holy Spirit through the work of Christ is a grand fulfillment of God's Old Testament promise and the means by which we experience the restoration of God's plan accomplished by Christ. As we have seen, the first and most fundamental part of God's plan for humanity is that we would live in obedient fellowship with him. God's people can now experience that fellowship in a deeper way than ever before. God does not dwell among them in a tent or temple. He dwells in them individually and collectively. The community of the faithful is the temple of God. Through the work of Christ, the Holy Spirit purifies them from the sin that separated them from God. The Holy Spirit empowers them for victorious living and directs their lives. Long ago Moses had wished that the Lord would "put his Spirit" upon his people (Num. 11:29). Isaiah (44:3), Ezekiel (36:25–27), and Joel (2:28–29) had prophesied a time when God's people would have a purified and thus much richer fellowship with him because they would share in his Spirit. Through Christ the desire of Moses and the vision of the prophets has become a reality. The coming of the Holy Spirit is the "promise of the Father" (Luke 24:49; Acts 1:4–5) through which we have the most intimate fellowship with him.

The indwelling Holy Spirit also brings the second aspect of God's plan to fuller fruition. The opening chapters of Acts reveal a community united in joyful, harmonious fellowship (Acts 2:43–47). The followers of Jesus willingly gave of their property to meet the needs of their brothers and sisters (Acts 4:32–37). They dealt with conflict by generously addressing the concerns of others. For instance, when the Greek-speaking widows complained of neglect, the church established a committee of Spirit-filled Greek speakers to address the problem (Acts 6:1–6). When the people of

> **The people of God . . . still wait . . . for the restoration of the third part of God's plan. They will not fully enter the place of fellowship with God . . . until the return of Christ.**

God live in contention they reject the harmony that the Spirit brings.

The people of God in Acts still wait with expectation for the restoration of the third part of God's plan. They will not fully enter the place of fellowship with God and the fullness of all blessings until the return of Christ. However, the privilege of fellowship with God that they now enjoy through the Holy Spirit is the pledge of that final blessing. The followers of Jesus throughout the ages are part of the church started in Acts. The privileges that his earliest followers enjoyed through the Spirit poured out by the risen Christ are available for the people of God today.

B. The Letters of the Apostles: Continuing Instruction for the Church

It was the summer of 1969. I had just met the woman who would become my wife. She was living in Ann Arbor, Michigan; I was far away in Richmond, Virginia. There was no Facebook in those days! I got my mail through a mail slot in the front door. My eyes often looked at the floor below that slot to see if I had a letter with an Ann Arbor return address in her beautiful handwriting! How wonderful it is to see that envelope (or that e-mail) from one we love. How happy we are to receive a letter with good news. Throughout the centuries letters have been life lived at a distance. The letters of the New Testament reach across two millennia and connect God's people today with the life of the early church and its apostolic leaders. The New Testament letters address the people of God after Christ's coming as the Old Testament prophets did before. The prophets called God's people of old to live in obedience to the Sinai covenant. The letters instruct God's people today about life in union with Christ through the power and presence of God's Spirit.

The instruction these apostolic leaders gave the earliest churches is of vital importance for all who are indwelt by Christ through the Spirit of God. The wealth of these letters is in the diversity of the ways in which they describe various aspects of the restoration brought by Christ and in the variety of the life situations they address. Through diligently studying them we gain deeper insight into the work of Christ that "surpasses understanding." By heeding their instruction we find guidance amid the many and varied circumstances of our lives. Those who wrote these letters have packed much truth into a small space. Thus it would take many pages to provide an adequate summary of the way these letters describe the restoration brought by Christ and its implications for daily living. Hopefully the following comments will whet your appetite for life-long reading and study of the precious truth God has given us in the New Testament letters.

C. The Letters of Paul: Apostle and Missionary

The first thirteen New Testament letters are attributed to the pen of the apostle Paul.[26] Acts showed us Paul in action spreading the gospel, making disciples, building the church. The letters reveal Paul's mind and heart, his deep understanding of the work of Christ, his passionate concern for the perseverance of his converts, and his God-given insight into the ways of godly living. The Old Testament has made the depravity and persistent sinfulness of humanity abundantly clear. In Romans, Paul presents the death of Christ validated by his resurrection as atonement for this sin. God's people are brought into right relationship with him through the forgiveness provided by Christ (Rom. 5:1–21). They are also

---

26. Romans, 1 & 2 Corinthians, Galatians, Ephesians, Philippians, Colossians, 1 & 2 Thessalonians, 1 & 2 Timothy, Titus, and Philemon

delivered from bondage to sin and empowered for holy living through Christ (Rom. 6:1–23; 8:1–17). Thus they are called to surrender themselves to God as they walk in the Spirit, awaiting the redemption of all things at Christ's return (Rom. 12:1–2). In 1 Corinthians, Paul addresses a variety of typical problems faced by the Corinthian church—from pride and divisiveness to sexual immorality and idolatry. Second Corinthians focuses on the nature of Paul's suffering and ministry as an ambassador for Christ. In Galatians, Paul argues that faith in Christ and the coming of the Holy Spirit fulfill God's promise to bless the nations through Abraham. Ephesians and Colossians affirm the unity of all believers— both Jew and non-Jew—in Christ, his triumph over all powers, and his sovereignty over the universe. Philippians and the two letters to the Thessalonians are filled with joy at God's work and the recipients' faithfulness. Paul thanks, encourages, and instructs these faithful churches as he seeks to lead them to maturity in Christ. The Thessalonian letters also address concerns about the return of Christ. Titus and the two letters to Timothy instruct church leaders in faithful doctrine and practice. According to Paul, God's people are his temple filled by his Spirit and thus in closest fellowship with God (1 Cor. 3:16–17; 2 Cor. 6:16–18; Eph. 2:19–22). They are empowered by the Spirit to live in harmony as the body of Christ while they await the consummation of redemption at Christ's return.

D. The Letters of Other Apostolic Leaders: Truth in Diversity

Eight letters by various apostolic leaders follow the letters of Paul.[27] Hebrews is the first and most prominent of these. We might call Hebrews the mystery letter because we do not know the identity of its author. However, the author of this book was a person of passionate concern for the perseverance of his hearers, of deep insight into the all-sufficiency of Christ, and of discernment concerning Christ's fulfillment of the Old Testament. Through obediently offering himself, Christ, our Great High

---

27. Hebrews; James; 1 & 2 Peter; 1, 2, and 3 John; and Jude.

Priest, provides cleansing from sin and access into God's presence (Heb. 8:1–10:18). By atoning for sin he has established the new covenant of heart obedience prophesied by Jeremiah (Heb. 10:15–18). We, as God's people, must continue to live in the certainty of God's promise for the future and in the reality of Christ's sufficiency for the present until we enter the eternal city at Christ's return (compare Heb. 10:39). James is full of practical wisdom for Christian living today. The two letters of Peter encourage believers amid suffering, assure them of judgment on those who live in immorality denying Christ, and urge them not to lose heart because Christ has not yet returned. The three letters of John remind us that those who truly trust Christ as the divine/human Son of God will live in love with one another out of obedience to the one who loved them so much that he went to the cross. Jude concludes these letters by assuring his hearers that God will judge false teachers and all immoral people who reject Christ.

Thus the New Testament letters provide a rich tapestry that uses many images to describe the way in which the work of Christ enables God's Spirit-filled people to do the following: live in obedient fellowship with God and in harmony with one another as they await entrance into God's promised place of blessing at Christ's return.

III. RESTORATION CONSUMMATED: THE REVELATION

Do you ever skip to the end of a novel and read the last chapter to see how it all turns out? There are, of course, many references to the return of Christ in the Gospels and letters. Christ promised his return (John 14:1–3). Paul corrected both the Corinthians and Thessalonians because they had misconceptions of this event. However, the last book in the New Testament focuses on the return of Christ and the final restoration of all things. The third part of God's plan—enjoyment of the world as the place of fellowship with God—will then reach fulfillment. And with this restoration of the universe the first two parts of the divine plan take their final, glorious form.

Christians differ in their understanding of the Revelation. Some think that the book gives us an outline of history from Jesus' first to his second comings. Others believe it provides a detailed sequence of end-time events. Despite these differences, some things are clear. Jesus gave the visions of the Revelation to the apostle John (Rev. 1:1–2) in order to encourage the suffering people of God. Throughout history the people of God must endure the opposition of Satan and of the unbelieving world that he controls. This opposition will only intensify before the return of Christ. Through his henchmen Satan demands the total worldwide loyalty that belongs to Christ alone (Rev. 13:1–18). Believers, however, have every reason to persevere to the end. Through his death and resurrection Christ has won the victory over Satan and all of his forces once and for all. The very intensity of Satan's opposition is an indication that he knows he has been defeated and that his time of resistance is short. As the Lamb who was slain, the Christ who alone is worthy to open the seals holds the destiny of the world in his hands (Rev. 5:1–14). History is also the story of repeated divine judgment on the rebellious. This judgment anticipates the final judgment and thus serves as a warning to the disobedient and an invitation to repentance.

Figure 4

RESTORATION
CONSUMMATED
CHRIST WILL
COME IN GLORY

The victory won by Christ on the cross, though now hidden from worldly eyes, will be fully manifested and realized at his return. All will then know that he is "King of kings and Lord of lords" (Rev. 19:16). Thus the crown is a fitting symbol for the victorious Christ who reestablishes universal divine rule (see **Figure 4** and column 3 of **Figure 1**). Human civilization in rebellion against God, represented by the city of Babylon (Rev. 17:1–18:24), will be overthrown and replaced by the city of God: the New Jerusalem, the new heaven and earth, the eternal dwelling place of the people of God (Rev. 21:1–22:5). This city in its entirety is the Most Holy Place where God's people will live in his presence. This city represents a new God-centered community in which God's people will live in perfect harmony, free from anything ungodly or evil. This city is the place where God's people as a renewed humanity will have a restored relationship with and enjoyment of God's renewed creation. Thus, the Bible that began with the destruction of God's plan for humanity ends with its glorious restoration in Christ. Genesis 3–11 tells us the beginning of the story: sinful humanity was expelled from Eden and established the God-excluding city of Babel. The Revelation discloses the end: God's final judgment upon that human city of Babylon and his establishing of his people as a renewed humanity in the eternal city of God. This city includes but far surpasses all that was lost when Adam and Eve were banished from the Garden.

CONCLUSION

All the New Testament writers agree with Paul: "In Jesus we hear a resounding 'yes' to all of God's many promises. This is the reason we say 'Amen' to and through Jesus when giving glory to God" (2 Cor. 1:20 The Voice). God's promise of restoration is fulfilled in Jesus Christ. We have looked at many of the ways in which the Old Testament has prepared the people of God for this fulfillment. We have seen how God's acts of salvation, the persons he used to deliver his people, and the institutions he set up to sustain them in obedience foreshadowed what he has done in Christ. We have noted how the persistent disobedience of his Old Testament people pointed to the need of the deeper deliverance from sin brought by Christ. We have observed the way in which Old Testament persons provide us with examples of obedience and disobedience to emulate or shun. We have discussed how the Old Testament law continues to inform the life of the people of God since the coming of Christ. Because the apostles and other early Christian leaders were certain that all God's promises had been fulfilled in Christ, they did not hesitate to speak of

Christian Faith in the Old Testament. In Christ, God offers life to a dying world through reestablishing his sovereign rule over a world that has been in rebellion since divine rule was rejected in Eden.

We have shown how God's revelation of old has found fulfillment in his "Son" (Heb. 1:2) in order that "your spiritual experience become richer as you see more and more fully God's great secret, Christ himself! For it is in him, and in him alone, that [we] will find all the treasures of wisdom and knowledge" (Col. 2:2b-3 PHILLIPS).

> To the One who sits on the throne and to the Lamb
> Be blessing and honor and glory and power
> Throughout the ages. (Rev. 5:13b The Voice)

Amen.

APPENDIX I

INTRODUCTION: THE BOOKS IN JESUS' BIBLE

I must have been about twelve or thirteen. I was standing on the side porch of our church with my best church buddy. Someone had mentioned the discovery of the gospel of Thomas. My friend Jimmy asked, "Will they put it in the Bible?" Instinctively I answered, "No." As you can guess, he responded with "Why not?" I couldn't answer his question. Now I know that there are many reasons why the gospel of Thomas is not in our New Testament. One of the most important is that it was not written until the end of the second century.[28]

Jimmy was talking about including the gospel of Thomas in the New Testament. However, the related question as to which books should be in the Old Testament is also important. Why do the thirty-nine books, and only these thirty-nine books, make up our Old Testament? There are several things that it is helpful to observe before we address this question. First of all, as we have shown throughout this book, the books of the Old Testament form a coherent whole. They all pertain to the story of God's redeeming rebellious humanity through Abraham and his descendants. We have demonstrated the intimate relationship between the Pentateuch, the historical books, and the Prophets. The Psalms and Proverbs are also linked to this drama of redemption. Even the Song of Songs is related to this story through its association with Solomon.

---

28. See Craig A. Evans, *Fabricating Jesus: How Modern Scholars Distort the Gospels* (Downers Grove: IVP, 2008) 52–77, for a helpful discussion of the gospel of Thomas.

Second, there is an implicit and sometimes explicit claim to authority that runs through the books of the Old Testament: the five Books of the Law with which the Old Testament begins affirm the unique authority of God's revelation through Moses (Num. 12:6–8; Deut. 31:24–29). The later Old Testament writings, such as Chronicles, Ezra, and Nehemiah (compare Ps. 119) confirm the authority of the Books of the Law. The writers of the Prophets were conscious of God's unique activity through them (Jer. 1:1–3; Hosea 1:1–2; Joel 1:1). The attribution of Psalms and Proverbs to David and Solomon respectively is a claim to authority that associates these books with the books of Moses.

However, the crucial point for those who follow Jesus is that he and the apostles accepted these books—and apparently only these books—as Scripture.[29] According to the New Testament, Jesus and the apostles believed that he fulfilled the drama of redemption contained in these writings. We will argue that there was a generally recognized fixed list of "Old Testament" books acknowledged by the Jews of Jesus' day which he and the New Testament writers also accepted.[30]

I. THE TESTIMONY OF JEROME AND THE TALMUD (FROM THE FOURTH AND FIFTH CENTURIES AD)

Let's begin with Jerome's clear testimony from the fourth century AD. Jerome studied Hebrew under Jewish scholars and was the greatest Christian biblical scholar of his day. He reported that the Jewish Bible contained twenty-two books in three divisions: the Law, the Prophets, and the Holy

---

29. The New Testament, of course, had not yet been written. The earliest Christians appear to have accepted the Gospels and other New Testament writings as on a par with the Old Testament almost from the beginning.

30. Roger Beckwith, *The Old Testament Canon of the New Testament Church* (Grand Rapids: Eerdmans, 1985), provides comprehensive and convincing evidence for this position. He believes that the Jewish canon originated with Judas Maccabeus in 164 BC. At that time when Judas restored the temple he also replaced the holy books that had been kept there and divided the non-Torah books between the Prophets and the Writings. Whether or not the evidence he offers is sufficient to establish Judas as the one who fixed the number and order of the canonical books, it is sufficient to establish the existence of an accepted closed canon of sacred books in Jesus' time.

Writings. According to his report the Law contained five books: Genesis, Exodus, Leviticus, Numbers, and Deuteronomy. The Prophets consisted of eight books: Joshua, Judges (including Ruth), Samuel, Kings, Isaiah, Jeremiah (including Lamentations), Ezekiel, and the Book of the Twelve Prophets. In this list 1 and 2 Samuel and 1 and 2 Kings are each one book. The Book of the Twelve contains the twelve Minor Prophets of our Bible. Jerome lists nine Holy Writings in the following order: Job, Psalms, Proverbs, Ecclesiastes, Song of Songs, Daniel, Chronicles, Ezra-Nehemiah, and Esther. As in the case of Samuel and Kings, 1 and 2 Chronicles form one book. Jerome also said that some Jews separated Ruth from Judges and Lamentations from Jeremiah, placing both of these books among the Holy Writings and counting the books as twenty-four.[31] When we divide Samuel, Kings, Chronicles, and Ezra-Nehemiah into two books each and separate the Book of the Twelve into the twelve Minor Prophets, these twenty-four books become the thirty-nine books of our Old Testament.

The tractate *Baba Bathra 14b* in the Babylonian Talmud also divides the sacred books among the Law, the Prophets, and the "Writings."[32] It contains the same books as those reported by Jerome but includes Ruth and Lamentations as part of the Writings, thus implying that the number of the books was twenty-four. Also the order of the books in the Writings differs from Jerome's: Ruth, Psalms, Job, Proverbs, Ecclesiastes, Song of Songs, Lamentations, Daniel, Esther, Ezra-Nehemiah and Chronicles. Although this tractate comes from at least a century later than Jerome, it professes to report earlier tradition, which may go back to the third if not the second century.[33]

Both of these sources divide the canonical books into three sections: the Law, the Prophets, and the (Holy) Writings. Both indicate that the

---

31. Beckwith, *The Old Testament Canon*, 119–21.

32. The five books of the Law are assumed rather than enumerated. For a translation of this tractate see Jack N. Lightstone, "The Rabbis' Bible: The Canon of the Hebrew Bible and the Early Rabbinic Guild" in *The Canon Debate*, ed. Lee Martin McDonald and James A. Sanders (Grand Rapids: Baker Academic (Grand Rapids: Baker Academic, 2001), 178–179.

33. On the dating of this tradition see Lightstone, "The Rabbis' Bible," 178; Beckwith, *The Old Testament Canon*, 122.

number of books is twenty-two/twenty-four. Both contain the books currently in the Jewish Bible and the Protestant Old Testament.

II. THE TESTIMONY OF ECCLESIASTICUS TO THREEFOLD BIBLE (FROM THE SECOND CENTURY BC)

The division of the Old Testament into three parts—the Law, the Prophets, and a third section later called the Writings—is ancient and invites us to investigate the origin of the Old Testament by looking at each of these parts. It is tempting to find a reference to this threefold division in Jesus' words recorded in Luke 24:44: "the Law of Moses and the Prophets and the Psalms."[34] There is a clear reference to this division in the preface added to the Greek translation of Ecclesiasticus in the last part of the second century BC:[35] "Many great teachings have been given to us through the Law and the Prophets and the other books that followed them."

A. The Law

By the "Law" the ancient translator of Ecclesiasticus is referring to the Pentateuch, the five books of Moses—Genesis, Exodus, Leviticus, Numbers, and Deuteronomy—which were recognized as a distinct closed group and as Scripture long before the time of Jesus, at least by the time of Ezra. Their recognition is supported by their translation into Greek in the third century BC, by the fact that the Jewish philosopher Philo (born ca. 25 BC) wrote commentaries on them, and by their use in the Dead Sea Scrolls. To this consensus the New Testament also bears witness,

---

34. Scholars debate whether "Psalms" represents the "writings" as the main book in that group. Perhaps our problem is that we are asking this text a question it isn't intending to answer. Jesus is talking about how what has been said about him is fulfilled. He probably mentions "Psalms" because there was so much in that book that pointed to him.

35. Ecclesiasticus, sometimes called the Wisdom of Jesus, Son of Sirach, or just "ben Sirach" ("ben" being the Hebrew for "son") was written in Hebrew sometime before 180 BC by Jesus son of Sirach and translated into Greek by his grandson shortly after 132 BC. The quotation above comes from the preface added to the Greek translation by the grandson. The original Hebrew text no longer survives. Ecclesiasticus consists mostly of proverbs reminiscent of the canonical Proverbs.

citing the Law many times and quoting all of these books as authoritative Scripture.

B. The Prophets

There is no doubt that the Law was the foundation of the rest of the Old Testament. As we saw in chapter 8, the Prophets called people back to their covenant relationship with God, which was narrated in and founded upon the five books of the Law. In chapter 7 we saw that the Psalms were divided into five books, perhaps in imitation of the Law, and were to be prayed and sung by people whose "delight" was "in the law of the Lord" (Ps. 1:2). According to the first-century Jewish historian Josephus (*Against Apion* 1.29; 37–42), Jews believed these books derived their inspiration from God's Spirit, a belief rooted in many Old Testament passages and confirmed by the New.

The Prophets were also a recognized group of scriptural writings along with the Law well before the time of Christ. The writer of Ecclesiasticus (49:10), Josephus, and the people who wrote the Dead Sea Scrolls all recognized the twelve Minor Prophets as one book, usually called the Book of the Twelve. Philo, Josephus, the authors of the Dead Sea Scrolls, and other Jewish writers recognized the prophetic books enumerated by Jerome as Scripture.[36] Often Scripture was referred to as "The Law and the Prophets," though the whole could also be referred to simply as "The Law."

C. The Writings

But what about the section that the Babylonian Talmud called the "Writings" and Jerome referred to as "Holy Writings"? Did that part of the Jewish Bible contain a defined list of books in Jesus' time, or was it still somewhat undefined and fluid? After all, our earliest witness to this third section, Ecclesiasticus, refers definitely to "the Law and the Prophets," but somewhat generally to "the other books that followed them."

---

36. Jerome's list included Joshua, Judges, Samuel, and Kings among the prophetic books as well as Isaiah, Jeremiah, Ezekiel, and the Book of the Twelve (our twelve minor prophets).

Common usage and references in the above sources and the New Testament make it clear that Psalms, Job, and Proverbs were recognized as Scripture. But what about the other books in the Writings? And what about other now "apocryphal" or "pseudepigraphal" books?[37] Were they included by some in this group?

III. THE TESTIMONY OF JOSEPHUS AND OF THE DEAD SEA SCROLLS (FROM THE FIRST CENTURY AD)

The key to answering these questions is the Jewish historian Josephus who lived from the mid-to-late first century AD. In *Against Apion* Josephus presents the Jewish faith to a gentile audience. This presentation includes a discussion of the books that made up the Jewish Bible of his day (*Against Apion* 1.29; 37–42). Josephus presents the accepted books in an order that would be understandable to his audience rather than using the threefold division of Ecclesiasticus. He does, however, affirm that the Jews accepted only twenty-two books[38]: "so among us [the Jews] there are not myriads of discordant and competing volumes, but only twenty-two volumes containing the record of all time, which are rightly trusted" (1.38).[39] He says that there were five books of Moses "which comprise both the laws and the tradition from human origins until his [Moses'] passing" (1.39). Furthermore, "from Moses' passing until Artaxerxes who was king of the Persians after Xerxes, the prophets after Moses wrote up what happened in their time in thirteen volumes" (1.40). Finally, "The remaining four

---

37. "Apocryphal" literally means "hidden" and is used to designate those books included in the Old Testament by the Roman Catholic, Orthodox, or Oriental Orthodox Churches in addition to the books of the Jewish Bible. Here is the list of additional books included in the Roman Catholic Old Testament: Tobit, Judith, Greek Additions to Esther, Wisdom of Solomon, Ecclesiasticus (Sirach), Baruch, Epistle of Jeremiah, Prayer of Azariah, Susanna, Bel and the Dragon, 1 Maccabees, 2 Maccabees, 1 Esdras, 2 Esdras, and the Prayer of Manasseh. "Pseudepigraphal" means "false writings." This term is often used in reference to other Jewish writings from the third century BC to the first century AD that were not accepted in any canon of the Old Testament.

38. 4 Ezra 14:45–46, from the end of the first century AD, and the Greek translation of the Book of Jubilees, probably from the first century BC, bear witness to a twenty-four book Old Testament canon.

39. These quotations from Josephus are taken from Steve Mason, "Josephus and His Twenty-Two Book Canon" in *The Canon Debate*, 113.

(volumes) comprise hymns toward God and advice for living in human community" (1.40). Josephus argues that no further books have been included since the time of Artaxerxes because "the exact succession of the prophets failed" (1.41). Josephus wrote to convince his non-Jewish readers of the antiquity and veracity of the Jewish writings.

Josephus's insistence that there were twenty-two and only twenty-two books affirmed that the list of books in the Jewish Bible was fixed. These books could be identified. From Josephus's use of biblical material elsewhere, it is very likely that this list contained the following books: in the Mosaic law—Genesis, Exodus, Leviticus, Numbers, and Deuteronomy; in the thirteen books of the Prophets—Job, Joshua, Judges (possibly including Ruth), Samuel, Kings, Isaiah, Jeremiah (possibly with Lamentations), Ezekiel, the Twelve Prophets, Daniel, Chronicles, Ezra-Nehemiah, and Esther; and in the four "hymns" and "advice"—Psalms (perhaps with Ruth), Proverbs, Ecclesiastes, and the Song of Songs.[40]

Josephus asserted that all Jews recognized these books as Scripture, that none of them dared add to them or subtract from them, and that many Jews had died rather than speak a word against them (1.42, 43). Josephus would hardly have asserted the unique authority and universal acceptance of these twenty-two books if it were not true, since his non-Jewish audience could easily have checked the accuracy of his statements by going to the local synagogue. If they had found Josephus's claim to be false, it would have invalidated the antiquity and authority of the Jewish Scriptures that Josephus was defending and thus would have detracted from the respect for the Jewish faith that he sought to engender.[41]

Evidence from other Jewish sources such as the Dead Sea Scrolls and the books of the New Testament confirm the evidence from Josephus. Manuscripts of all the books in the Jewish Bible except Esther have been

---

40. Beckwith, *The Old Testament Canon*, 119. See also Mason, "Josephus and His Twenty-Two Book Canon," 121–24.

41. Mason, "Josephus and His Twenty-Two Book Canon," 125–26.

found among the Dead Sea Scrolls.[42] The people who wrote these scrolls gave special place to the five Books of the Law. There are many copies of these books among the Dead Sea Scrolls. Some manuscripts of each of these books are in old-Hebrew script instead of the script that was used for most of the other scrolls.[43] The Scrolls also include commentaries on the five Books of the Law. There are also many copies of the Prophets among the Dead Sea Scrolls, along with commentaries on some of the prophetic books. It is true that the biblical books among the Dead Sea Scrolls sometimes have minor differences in wording. This diversity, however, is no argument that the people who wrote the Dead Sea Scrolls rejected these books as Scripture. Such variations in wording were common in all branches of Judaism, as witnessed by Josephus and the New Testament writers.[44] There is no clear evidence that the people who wrote the Dead Sea Scrolls used books that were not listed by Josephus as Scripture.[45]

---

42. Josephus's affirmation that the accepted books covered history until the time of Artaxerxes shows that Esther was included.

43. VanderKam too easily dismisses this fact by noting that four other fragments are written in the same script—one from Job, one from Joshua, and two unidentified. See James C. VanderKam, "Questions of Canon Viewed through the Dead Sea Scrolls," in *The Canon Debate*, 94. Job was probably thought to have lived in the time of Moses, and Joshua was Moses' attendant and successor. The five books of Law in the Pentateuch are the only books written in the old-Hebrew script apart from these fragments. Surely these fragments are the exception that proves the rule.

44. VanderKam, "Questions of Canon Viewed through the Dead Sea Scrolls," 94–96.

45. There are manuscripts or fragments of manuscript among the Dead Sea Scrolls from three different writings that were free reworkings of the first five books of the Bible. These reworkings contained rearrangements, paraphrases, harmonizations, and interpretations of the five books of the Law. These writings are referred to as *Reworked Pentateuch*, the *Temple Scroll*, and *Jubilees*. James VanderKam has argued that the people who wrote the Dead Sea Scrolls considered these books Scripture on a par with the five books of the Law of Moses (VanderKam, "Questions of Canon Viewed through the Dead Sea Scrolls," 96–107). He suggests that, just as the five books of the Law were supposedly rewritings of earlier traditions, so these books were rewritings of the books of the Law. His arguments, however, are contradicted by the care shown for the Pentateuch evinced in the text above. If Genesis, Exodus, Leviticus, Numbers, and Deuteronomy were a reworking of earlier traditions, those traditions have disappeared. By contrast, these five books have not been replaced by others for they are still honored as Scripture. VanderKam also neglects the fact that Josephus reworked the Pentateuch in his *Antiquities* just as thoroughly as these writings in the Dead Sea Scrolls reworked it. There can be no doubt that Josephus affirmed the scriptural nature of the Pentateuch and denied such authority to his own writings (Mason, "Josephus and His Twenty-Two Book Canon, 126). If the writers of the Dead

IV. THE TESTIMONY OF THE NEW TESTAMENT

We must pay attention to two important facts if we want to understand the way in which the New Testament attests the list of books given by Josephus and approved as Scripture by contemporary Judaism. First, with the possible exception of Jude,[46] the New Testament quotes only books found in Josephus's list with scriptural authority.[47] That is, it only cites books in the thirty-nine-book Old Testament as Scripture.[48] Second, the New Testament writers were familiar with many apocryphal and pseudepigraphical books, but they never quoted them as Scripture. There may be as many as 150 allusions to these books in the New Testament.[49] New Testament writers drew on the resources of their day, just as preachers and writers do today. The reason they did not cite these books

---

Sea Scrolls attributed scriptural authority to any of these other books, it was probably a deviation due to their sectarian character.

46. Jude cites *1 Enoch*, possibly as Scripture, and alludes to the *Apocalypse of Moses*. We would suggest that this exception only underscores the rule. While we would not want to exclude Jude from the canon, we should note that its inclusion was long disputed, partly because of its citation of *1 Enoch* and that, if, as some scholars believe, 2 Peter 2 is a reworking of Jude, these references to *1 Enoch* and the *Apocalypse of Moses* have been omitted.

47. If we remember that 1 and 2 Samuel, 1 and 2 Kings, and 1 and 2 Chronicles were each counted as one book, and that the Twelve Minor Prophets were one book, then Craig Evans's evidence would indicate that Jesus quoted or alluded to all of the Old Testament books but Song of Songs, Ruth, Lamentations, Ecclesiastes, Esther, and Ezra-Nehemiah (Craig A. Evans, "The Scripture of Jesus and His Earliest Followers" in *The Canon Debate*, 185–95. The evidence presented by Martin Hengel shows that the New Testament writers directly cite all the Old Testament books as Scripture with the exception of Judges, Ruth, Chronicles, Ezra-Nehemiah, Esther, Song of Songs, Lamentations, and Ecclesiastes: Martin Hengel, *The Septuagint as Christian History: Its Pre-history and the Problem of its Canon* (Grand Rapids: Baker Academic, 2002), 107. Hengel's list is identical with Evans's except that it also includes Judges. No one would dispute Judges' place in the prophetic books at the time of Jesus. Furthermore, the omission of Ruth and Lamentations is probably not significant. Both books were small and were often combined, in the case of Ruth, with either Judges or Psalms, and in the case of Lamentations, with Jeremiah.

48. Again, with the possible exception of Jude. See note 46.

49. Lee McDonald has amassed considerable evidence that the New Testament alludes to apocryphal books in a number of places. See Lee M. McDonald, *The Formation of the Christian Biblical Canon* (Peabody, MA: Hendrickson, 1995), 259–67. The important thing, however, is that neither Jesus nor the New Testament writers ever come near to citing this material as Scripture. As Daniel Harrington has shown, this material is better understood as background to understanding the New Testament than as direct citation. See Daniel J. Harrington, S.J., "The Old Testament Apocrypha in the Early Church and Today" in, *The Canon Debate*, 196–210.

as Scripture was not because they were unfamiliar with them. They knew and used them, but nowhere did they cite them as Scripture. Thus it appears that the writers of the New Testament made a clear distinction between those books in the Jewish Bible that they were free to cite as Scripture and other literature that they could use but had no scriptural authority. The pattern of scriptural quotation in the New Testament is, then, in full agreement with Josephus's list of scriptural books accepted by contemporary Judaism.[50] The sometimes free way in which New Testament writers cite the Old Testament does not differ from the way in which Josephus, the Dead Sea Scrolls, and other contemporary literature cited Scripture. Such free citation is, then, no argument against the scriptural authority of the books cited.[51] The New Testament's citation of the Old substantiates our contention that Jesus and the apostles assumed the validity of the list of books accepted by their contemporaries as Scripture and preserved in our thirty-nine-book Old Testament.[52]

V. THE TESTIMONY OF THE CHURCH FATHERS

If Jesus and the apostles followed the list of books in the Jewish Bible, why did the church fathers begin to quote from the apocryphal books now

---

50. Thus when McDonald asks if those books in the Jewish canon not cited in the New Testament should be excluded from the canon, he completely misses the point. See footnote 48 above. We are not arguing that we should accept the Old Testament books because the New Testament cites all of them. We are arguing that the New Testament bears witness to (and thus agrees with) the list of Old Testament books commonly accepted by contemporary Judaism as Scripture.

51. McDonald, *Formation*, 103–5, fails to take this comparative Old Testament use into account and thus his reading of the evidence is askew. Later rabbinic disputes about Ezekiel, Proverbs, Ecclesiastes, Song of Songs, and Esther do not belie this consensus. Doubt about these books probably arose from various and sometimes different reasons. For instance, Ezekiel was seen as not being in harmony with the Books of the Law. These discussions were about books already accepted in the canon.

52. Ellis is a bit more cautious: "To summarize briefly, one may say with some confidence that the Bible received and used by our Lord was, with the possible exception of Esther, the Old Testament received today as sacred Scripture by Jews and Protestants": E. Earl Ellis, *The Old Testament in Early Christianity: Canon and Interpretation in the Light of Modern Research* (Grand Rapids: Baker, 1992), 126.

included in the Old Testament by some branches of the church? Why do some early copies of the Bible in Greek include some of these books?

First, it is important to note that the earliest church fathers did not make many references to these apocryphal books. For instance, *1 Clement* alludes to Judith and twice quotes the Wisdom of Solomon. The writer does not, however, introduce these quotations in a way that clearly establishes their scriptural authority.[53] Indeed, some of the church fathers' earliest quotations are from extracanonical books not in the Apocrypha, such as Tertulian's quotation from *1 Enoch*. He justifies his usage on the basis of Jude's reference to *1 Enoch* and because *1 Enoch* seemed to refer to Christ (*On Female Fashion*, 1.3.1–3).

The thirty-nine books of the Jewish Old Testament were written in Hebrew or in Aramaic, a language closely related to Hebrew. Most of the other books that some branches of the church include in the Old Testament or that were cited by the church fathers were originally written or widely circulated in Greek. With the possible exception of Luke and the author of Hebrews, all the New Testament writers probably spoke Aramaic as their mother tongue and had some knowledge of Hebrew. It would be easy, after ties with Judaism were broken, for the apostolic fathers and their successors, who could no longer read the Bible in Hebrew, to find Christ prefigured in other popular Jewish literature in the Greek language. As noted above, this is the reason why Tertulian quoted *1 Enoch*.[54] The fathers quoted this literature in order to convince others that Christ was the fulfillment of God's plan of restoration. Nevertheless, people like Origen in the second century and Jerome in the fourth, who could read the Old Testament in Hebrew, still believed that the list of books in the Old Testament should be the same as those in the Jewish Bible—the Bible used by Jesus and the apostles.

---

53. Donald Hagner, *The Use of the Old Testament in Clement of Rome* (Leiden: Brill, 1973), 68.

54. Tertullian, however, was aware that *1 Enoch* was rejected by some because it was not in the Jewish Bible (*On Female Fashion*, 1.3.1). Thus indirectly his testimony confirms the importance of the Jewish Bible for determining the books that should be in the Christian Old Testament.

CONCLUSION

Josephus's testimony confirms the fact that the list of accepted Old Testament books attested by Jerome in the fourth century was already accepted by first-century Judaism. This list is identical to the thirty-nine books that all branches of Christianity continue to include in the Old Testament, though some branches would add additional writings. The way in which these books were used by first-century Jewish literature substantiates their acceptance as Scripture. The New Testament confirms the general acceptance of these books as Scripture. New Testament writers (with the possible exception of Jude) cite only books from this list as the word of God. It appears that Jesus and the New Testament writers never addressed the question of which books were Scripture because they accepted the common contemporary Jewish list of approved books. As those who follow Jesus, we acknowledge the authority of the books that he and his first followers accepted as Scripture. It is the story and promise of these books that he came to fulfill.

APPENDIX II

GOD'S PLAN FOR THE WORLD

THE OLD COVENANT

CREATION

Humanity in God's Image

JUDGMENT — PURGE — BRING — EMBLEM — BLESSINGS — LET — NOT

The World
God's Plan—Established And Lost
(Gen. 1–11)

A Family
Restoration Promised
(Gen. 12–50)

A Nation
Restoration Institutionalized at Zion
(Judges–2 Kings)

Restoration Inaugurated at Sinai
(Exodus–Joshua)

ADAM

Creator

The three parts of God's plan

1. Obedient fellowship with God.
2. Harmonious fellowship with the people of God.
3. Responsible enjoyment of God's world.

Innocence/ Disobedience

God
|
Humanity — World

ABRAHAM

Restoration of God's plan promised to Abraham.

1. "The Lord said to Abraham." (Gen. 12:1)
2. "I will make you into a great nation." (Gen. 12:2)
3. "To your offspring I will give this land." (Gen. 12:7)

"All peoples on the earth shall be blessed through you." (Gen. 12:3)

God
|
Promise
|
Humanity — World

MOSES

Exodus through Deuteronomy

1. **Our God—the Exodus.** "I am the Lord your God who brought you out of Egypt, out of the land of slavery. (Ex. 10:1)
2. **My People—Mount Sinai.** "I will take you as my own people, and I will be your God" (Ex. 6:7)
3. **My Land—Canaan.** "For the Lord your God is bringing you into a good land." (Deut. 8:7)

Joshua

God
|
My Law
|
Humanity — World

they forsook the Lord God of their fathers . . . (so) he sold them to their enemies all around." (Judg. 2:12)

DAVID

"My King"

God chose David and his descendants to lead His people so that they would "walk in his ways and keep his decrees as written in the law of Moses (1 Kings 1:3). Thus they would continue to be . . . .

1. In fellowship with God.
2. As the people of God.
3. In their God-given land.

"My City"

Jerusalem with the temple on Mount Zion became . . . .

1. The focal point of Israel's fellowship with God.
2. The symbol of his presence that made them his people.
3. The assurance of his presence with them in the land.

God
|
Promise
|
Humanity — World

The Lord said, "I will also remove Judah from My sight . . . and will cast off this city, Jerusalem . . . and the house of which I said, 'My name shall be there.'" (2 Kings 23:27)

CHRISTIAN FAITH IN THE OLD TESTAMENT—PART TWO

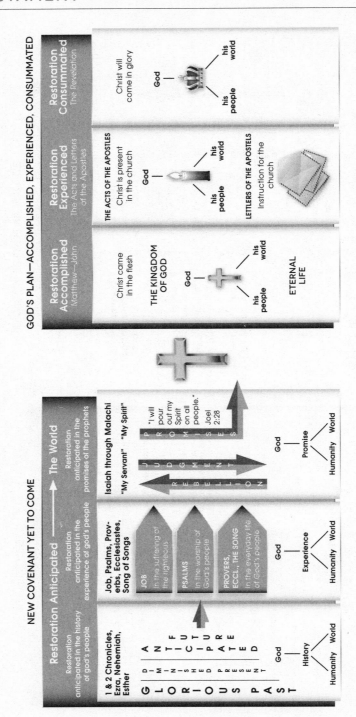